THE SCEPTICAL OCCULTIST

Terry White was born in London in 1952. After reading zoology at Unviersity College Wales, Aberystwyth, and clinical immunology at Brimingham Medical School, he embarked on a career in the immunology and pathology of parasitic and tropical infections. He held several research posts in Britain and Australia, followed by a lectureship at London University.

His books have included *The Making of the World's Elite Forces*, *Swords of Lightning*, and *The Fighting Techniques of the Special Forces*. He has contributed chapters to several other works and has written numerous articles for national newspapers, magazines and professional journals.

Terry White lives in Oxfordshire with his wife Kathleen, another escapee from professional science, and their son.

THE SCEPTICAL OCCULTIST

Terry White

ARROW

For my wife Kathleen and our wonderful son, Christopher

This edition published by Arrow Books Limited 1995

1 3 5 7 9 10 8 6 4 2

Copyright © 1994 Terry White

All rights reserved

The right of Tery White to be identified as the author of this work has been asserted by him in accordance with the Copyright, Designs and Patents Act, 1988

This book is sold subject to the condition that it shall not, by way of trade or otherwise, be lent, resold, hired out, or otherwise circulated without the publisher's prior consent in any form of binding or cover other than that in which it is published and without a similar condition including this condition being imposed on the subsequent purchaser

First published in the United Kingdom in 1994 by Century Random House UK Ltd, 20 Vauxhall Bridge Road, London SW1V 2SA

Arrow Books Ltd
Random House UK Ltd,
20 Vauxhall Bridge Road, London SW1V 2SA

Random House Australia (Pty) Limited
20 Alfred Street, Milsons Point, Sydney,
New South Wales 2061, Australia

Random House New Zealand Limited
18 Poland Road, Glenfield
Auckland 10, New Zealand

Random House South Africa (Pty) Limited
PO Box 337, Bergvlei, South Africa

Random House UK Limited Reg No 954009

A CIP catalogue record for this book is available from the British Library

Papers used by Random House UK Limited are natural, recyclable products made from wood grown in sustainable forests. The manufacturing processes conform to the environmental regulations of the country of origin.

ISBN 0 09 930248 9

Filmset by SX Composing Ltd, Rayleigh, Essex
Printed and bound in the United Kingdom by
Cox & Wyman Ltd, Reading, Berks

CONTENTS

	Acknowledgements	vii
	Foreword	xi
1	Of Philosophers and the Evidence for Miracles	1
2	Telepathy	27
3	Psychokinesis and Poltergeists	50
4	Ghosts	79
5	Hauntings	128
6	The Marian Apparitions	146
7	Miraculous Cures	183
8	Returning from the Abyss? Reincarnation	200
9	Demonic Possession	230
10	Explaining the Inexplicable	264

Appendix – Useful Contact Addresses   282
Chapter Sources   284
Selected Bibliography   298

Acknowledgements

But for three people this book would not have been written. Few writers could wish for a better literary agent than Juri Gabriel. It was Juri's tireless work which got the project out of the planning stage. Mark Booth of Century turned an idea into reality and enthusiastically shepherded the manuscript through the many stages from inception to publication. My wife Kathleen cheerfully assumed the tedious chore of editing and rewriting my stilted prose. No amount of editorial 'weed-killer' can eliminate every mistake and those which remain are the responsibility of the author.

This book has numerous authors. I would like to thank the British Society for Psychical Research for allowing me to quote from their cases and publications. It could not have been written without the co-operation of the British Society for Psychical Research. The Society's Secretary, Eleanor O'Keeffe, was a constant source of encouragement and advice and provided the vital introductions to members and investigators. Nick Clark-Lowes, the Society's Librarian, kept me supplied with books and suggested research material I was not even aware existed.

John Stiles, the SPR's Honorary Spontaneous Cases Officer, provided me with an illuminating glimpse of the field cases investigated by the Society. That any of my own cases ever reached the report stage, was due entirely to the efforts of my co-investigator, Theresa Ross. Theresa's ability to ferret out historical material and locate witnesses would be the envy of many journalists and historians.

Other research material for this book came from specialised sources not always on the shelves of the local library. The staff at the Bicester Library enthusiastically dealt with the flood of requests for books and papers. Few university librarians would have shouldered this burden with the same professionalism and kindness.

Psychologists, philosophers, physicists and scientists of all descriptions with experience of 'paranormal' phenomena, patiently listened to my enquiries, providing advice and expert opinion. I would especially like to thank the following for their contributions: Dr John Beloff, the well-known philosopher/parapsychologist and contemporary of Dr Jan Ehrenwald, for our discussion on the significance of Ehrenwald's hypothesis of the mother-child relationship as the 'cradle of ESP'. Dr Beloff kindly gave permission for me to quote passages from his book *The Relentless Question: Reflections on the Paranormal*; Hilary Evans, an acknowledged expert on hallucinations and apparitions, as well as an engaging author and speaker. I much appreciated our discussions and I am very grateful to Hilary for sharing with me two modern cases of collective apparitions, one of which appears in Chapter Four; Professor David Fontana, who directed me to his papers on the Cardiff poltergeist and provided some illuminating insights into the importance of belief-systems; Dr Murray Laver, D.Sc., for his papers and for a very helpful discussion on dowsing and clairvoyance; Dr Charles McCreery, for a most enjoyable discussion on hallucinations and apparitions and for allowing me to read parts of his doctoral thesis. My thanks also to his colleague, Dr Celia Green, the Director of the Institute of Psychophysical Research, for her paper on waking dreams; Professor Ian Stevenson, who patiently answered all of my enquiries about his research into reincarnation-type cases and enabled me to obtain copies of his department's publications; the Exhibits Section of the Imperial War Museum for their identification of Allied aircraft involved in operations against the railways in northern Burma during World War Two; and Dr Barrie Colvin, founding member of the Poltergeist Research Institute, who kindly described his own paranormal investigations and provided me with his notes relating to the 'Eric' case.

The religious aspects of parapsychology were a foreign country and without willing, helpful guides, the chapter on

Acknowledgements

possession could not have been written. Many in this field work as priests or scientists. A few wear both hats. Everyone I contacted was more than helpful in providing me with information and publications, expert opinion, personal experiences and introductions to colleagues. Certain priests and ministers spoke 'off the record' and confidentiality prevents me from crediting them with particular contributions. I would like to thank Monsignor Louis McCrae, Father Aldo Tapparo, Reverend Dr David Gill, Reverend Mr Howell-Everson, Reverend Giles Harcourt, the Reverend Professor Leslie J. Francis, Canon Dominic Walker, O.G.S., Reverend Basil DeMal, Reverend Martin Israel, Reverend Dr Frazer Watts, the Venerable Michael Perry and Professor Newton Maloney Ph.D. A very special thanks must go to the Churches' Council for Health and Healing who unfailingly fielded all of my enquiries.

The Royal College of Psychiatry in London searched through their extensive computerised data-base to provide me with references on the psychiatrists' view of possession and kindly introduced me to members who specialised in this area. I owe a similar debt of gratitude to the Royal College of Pathologists and the Royal Society of Medicine, both of which provided me with essential information relating to congenital circumcision.

Ralph Allison M.D., described in detail his own experiences with multiple personality disorder patients and alter-personalities which claim to be spirits. Dr Allison very kindly gave me permission to quote his conversation with 'Dennis' which came from his own book *Mind in Many Pieces*. My thanks also go to the Reverend Robert Solomon for sharing with me the fruits of his Master's thesis on mental illness and possession.

Parapsychology began with the efforts of a handful of intrepid Victorian investigators and, with the contraction of university-based science, the societies of psychical research continue to run with the torch. The future lies with those young investigators clever enough to cope with modern instrumentation, determined enough to spend months, even years, researching a case and committed enough to fund their own investigations. My thanks to members of the Cheltenham Psychical Research group who often provided the much needed expertise in investigations and who opened their case files to me.

Foreword

> The Scientific Age threw the baby out with the bathwater. Disapproving of the supernatural on principle, the scientists denied not only the supernatural cause, but the experiences themselves. Visions, telepathic communications, precognition – anything that could not be put under the microscope and dissected – were either signs of derangement or the impositions of charlatans ... If the scientists were confronted with someone of obvious sobriety, intelligence and integrity, who nevertheless insisted that he had seen an apparition or had had a prophetic dream, the situation was embarrassing. Precognition could be written off as coincidence. The apparition might be a dream, or imagination, or hallucination or indigestion. Miraculous healings: coincidence, faulty diagnosis, imagination. Poltergeist manifestations: lies, faking, or good old faithful coincidence.
>
> From Victoria Branden's *Understanding Ghosts*.

I have never had more than a passing interest in the paranormal, so I had never felt it necessary to scorn the work of parapsychologists. I had always believed that science was an activity; an immensely successful activity, but certainly not a religion. My training in the life sciences had nothing to say about ghosts, telepathy or the movement of objects by will power.

I had had no experiences which I would have described as 'paranormal'. Once, while engaged in a long walk across Dartmoor, three companions and I were confronted by a ball of white-blue light. It was 2 a.m. and we had watched a 'spotlight' approach for more than five minutes, believing it to be a vehicle. Finally, a bluish-white sphere stopped within fifteen

The Sceptical Occultist

metres of us and we stood and watched it for nearly ten minutes. It was approximately nine to twelve feet off the ground, twice the size of a football and perfectly motionless. Finally, it moved off at right angles to its original path, descended to ground level and contoured the tussocks until it crossed the ridge just west of King's Tor. While we were watching the light, there was a desultory discussion as to its nature. The weather had been appalling, even for Dartmoor (the 1987 hurricane was hours away) and somebody suggested that we had encountered 'ball lightning': the sort of electrical phenomenon responsible for the spheres of light which are sometimes seen attached to the wings of commercial aircraft. It was as good a rationalisation as any and that ended the discussion.

Three days later, the walk finally came to an end. Very tired and wet, we had to help compile a report on the week's activity, stating where we had been and what we had been doing. All went well until we came to the early hours of Thursday morning and the ball of light. I was the group leader for that day and I watched the faces of the other people in the room as I related the story. Concern for my mental health soon turned to embarrassment when the other three team members verified my account. Finally, when it seemed we would never get beyond the light, I suggested our rationalisation of ball lightning. The sense of relief in the room was palpable; a scientific explanation was comforting and 'ball lightning' looked good in the report.

This single instance left me with an enduring curiosity, not for the paranormal but for the way that even educated people respond to the anomalous experiences of others.

During my research, I discovered, with some surprise, that similar balls of light had been reported during a religious revival in Wales in the 1930s and had long been associated with religious visions. I was also fortunate to hear the well-known psychoanalyst, Peter Eastham, deliver a paper at the 16th International Conference of the Society for Psychical Research. Eastham related that, during therapy, one of his patients claimed regularly to have watched similar phenomena on the hills outside the town. He attempted to rationalise this in terms of archetypal experiences but the woman was

Foreword

adamant, she *saw* balls of light. Peter Eastham is blessed with an open mind and, like all good investigators, he decided to apply logic to the situation. He suggested that the next time his patient went to look for the lights, he would accompany her. Several days later, Eastham and his patient went into the countryside together and, to his very great surprise, he too saw the lights. While we may want to put different interpretations on these experiences, the fact remains that the experiences themselves are real. The American parapsychologist, Gaither Pratt, called these anomalous experiences the 'gems of fact'.

During the long process of researching and writing this book, I turned to John L. Casti's *Paradigms Lost* for recreational reading. Casti, a fine mathematician and an engaging author, provided contact with the world of science and commonsense as, with a deep sense of foreboding, I prepared to research the chapters on the Marian apparitions, reincarnation and possession. I was experiencing a culture-shock. I could believe in the possibility of telepathy and even psychokinesis but I drew the line at visions of saints, reincarnation and demonic possession. Like Casti, I had constructed my book around a sort of trial, with the author presenting the evidence for the defence and prosecution by way of expert testimony. Who was I to insult the reader's intelligence with yet another book of 'ghost stories'? Unfortunately, this device was of little help as I found it difficult to relate material to the reader, which I myself could not believe.

During Casti's appraisal of quantum mechanics, I was amused to find that he could not resist taking a pop at parapsychology. Modelling an example of one of J. B. Rhine's early experiments, Casti demonstrated the ease with which two cunning frauds, 'Alexandra' and 'Anastasia', could manipulate the experiment seemingly to demonstrate telepathy.

I had a similar problem, only my 'cunning frauds' were three profoundly mentally retarded children. The three papers on my desk suggested the children enjoyed telepathic communication with their mothers. The papers were supported by eye-witness testimony from psychiatrists and psychologists, who claimed to have witnessed telepathy in their own children and in patients undergoing therapy. One of the psychiatrists, Jan Ehrenwald, had brought these observations together with his hypothesis that the mother-child relationship was the 'cradle of ESP'. My problem was that I had never experienced a single instance of telepathy with my eighteen-month-old son, nor had I known other parents who reported such things. The papers were finally discarded and very quickly became buried in a 'snow-drift' of incoming material. I moved on to examine the lab experiments with the psychic, Paval Stepanek.

Shortly, I was to have an experience which forced me to reassess the work of these psychiatrists. I will recount it in sufficient detail for the reader to understand the psychological impact it had on the author.

In the middle of June 1993, on a rather cold dismal day, I collected my son, Christopher, from his childminder. My son lived in a world bounded by teddy bears and Thomas the Tank Engine and it was our normal routine to wave at the trains at the local station. Every evening the driver would respond by sounding the horn and my delighted son would remind me that it was just like the peep, peep, Thomas made when he passed other engines. We would then spend the next thirty minutes at the local park. This day was to be different.

As we walked back to the car, a large grey balloon, which appeared to loom menacingly over the roof-tops, caught his eye. I explained that it was the balloon used by the Royal Air Force to train parachutists. He knew all about 'balloons' and insisted on seeing it. As the alternative was standing around swings and slides in the cold wind, I was happy to oblige.

When we reached the airfield, I found a warm nook out of the wind and, placing Christopher on the top of a gate, we soaked in the weak sunshine. There was quite a show going on. While the novice parachutists waited for their turn to jump from the balloon, an aircraft was dropping teams of freefallers high above us. Vehicles came and went and soon Christopher was relating the movements on the airfield with all the excitement and banality of a racing commentator. Subconsciously perhaps, I sought an escape. Then far to the east, a line of trees caught my eye, igniting a series of memories which had lain buried for more than twenty years.

Foreword

In 1969 some months after my parachute course, I had been sitting in the mess with a friend, K.M. We had trained together and were inseparable. That night, the sergeant-major put in an appearance looking for volunteers. They wanted people to help train American pilots on mock-operational drops, he told us, promising that it would be 'very exciting'. He was not knocked over by the rush of volunteers. I was bored, however, and worked hard at overcoming K.'s reservations. We discussed it for some time and then walked down the hall to add our names to the flight manifest.

At last light on the next evening, the aircraft took off and headed out over the North Sea. There were only eight of us on board. The seemingly endless hours were occasionally punctuated by luke-warm coffee and the sound of men retching into sick-bags. After what seemed an eternity, we were given the first action order. Gratefully, we left the aircraft, approximately half a mile from where Chris and I were now lounging in the sunshine.

There was no moon that night. The ground was an inky black, bordered by darker silhouettes of blackthorn hedges and tree-lines. I looked around in amazement. It was farmland. We were not over the dropping-zone! It was clear to me that the pilot had drifted off his approach path and turned on the green light too early. I lost sight of the other parachutists in the darkness and passed over the top of a tree with only feet to spare. I decided that I had to try and land in the next field. I started to 'spill' air from the canopy.

As I pulled on the lift-webs and the parachute swung round, I was faced with an even bigger disaster. There in the darkness, I could just make out the shape of a little semicircular building of the type frequently used as shelters for free-range pigs. I was seemingly faced with a close encounter in the darkness with frightened animals. Stunned by the impact of the landing, I must have lain on the ground for several minutes.

When I came to my senses, the little field was silent. There was no grunting or scuffling of animals. After rolling up the parachute, I walked over to the building. Inside, in the darkness, I felt a coil of wire and what appeared to be farm machinery. There were no pigs or animals of any description. The farmer appeared to be using the building to store farm equipment. After slowly working my way through several blackthorn hedges, I was finally reunited with K. and the others. We sat down behind a hedge and lit cigarettes. I told him about the 'pigs' and we both laughed. In my mind's eye, I was able to conjure K.'s smiling face as I had seen it that night in the flare from my cigarette lighter.

While I played with these memories, Chris had continued his frightful running commentary on the comings and goings on the airfield. Suddenly, I became aware that he had stopped. After a brief pause, he started grunting. I thought to myself, 'that sounds like a pig grunting. No!' I quickly countered, 'that was crazy, a classic example of delusional thinking.' I asked him why he was making the noise. He gave no answer but fell silent. Then he returned to his commentary and I remarked that it was time to go home. As always, we negotiated and I agreed that we would stay just long enough to watch the balloon drop another stick of parachutists. We watched the first man leave the cage, his parachute developing gracefully. Just in case Chris chose to forget our agreement, I reminded him again. He made no answer but suddenly I felt his body go tense. He pointed at the parachutist and, with a wild, menacing tone of voice, turned to me and shouted *'These men must be careful or the pigs will get them.'*

I was speechless. If I had not immediately recounted these events to my wife on returning home, I would suspect my memory was playing tricks. I spent the morning of the next day walking around the airfield to rationalise Chris's remark. There are no animals anywhere near the dropping-zone. To the east, the farm in which I had landed is given over entirely to crops. To the west, a second farm bordering the airfield has crops but they also keep a herd of dairy cattle. Christopher would have needed telescopic vision to even notice the farm house and the animals are kept in sheds behind the building. My son understood little of what he had seen on the airfield. Under questioning, he told me that the 'men went up into the sky on a balloon' and when asked how they descended, he replied, 'on another balloon'. When I asked about the 'pigs' he looked blank.

Foreword

I would not want to offer this event as an instance of 'telepathy' but it is representative of the class of experiences described by Ehrenwald and others. The psychiatrist, Berthold Schwartz, recorded more than ninety-one instances of telepathy involving his daughter, Lisa. He believed that they occurred at the intersection of the child's and parent's emotional needs. Schwartz would have argued that I had wanted so desperately to experience an instance of telepathy and my child had unconsciously provided that instance.

This book, then, is about such experiences. Each case is presented through the words of the witnesses and investigators. In more than 150 years of scientific study of the occult, this is some of the best evidence we are ever likely to be given. I leave the reader to decide the relative merits of each case and to ask if perhaps, we have discarded the baby with the bathwater.

1

Of Philosophers and the evidence for Miracles

This first chapter is by way of pre-trial hearing. The prosecution's case here is as simple as it appears damning: parapsychology is the study of miracles, spectacular and insignificant; but these so-called miracles are little more than the product of human stupidity, gullibility and superstition. Miracles offend wisdom and run counter to the laws of nature; they simply cannot happen.

> A miracle is a violation of the laws of nature; and as a firm and unalterable experience has established these laws, the proof against a miracle, from the very nature of the fact, is as entire as any argument from experience can possibly be imagined ... There must, therefore, be a uniform experience against every miraculous event, otherwise the event would not merit that appellation. And as a uniform experience amounts to a proof, there is here a direct and full *proof*, from the nature of the fact, against the existence of any miracle; nor can such a proof be destroyed, or any miracle rendered credible, but by an opposite proof, which is superior ... The smallest spark may here kindle into the greatest flame because the materials are always prepared for it. The *avidum genus auricularum*, the gazing populace, receive greedily, without examination, whatever soothes superstition and promotes wonder.

This is the sceptic's first line of attack and these words come to us from the pen of a philosopher. David Hume was an intellectual giant, a sceptic's sceptic and the rock against which claims of miracles always seem to founder whenever parapsychologists and philosophers come together to discuss the paranormal.

After his death, two of his great essays, *A Treatise of Human Nature* and *Philosophical Essays concerning Human Understanding* (later retitled *An Enquiry concerning Human Understanding*) would ultimately ensure his recognition as one of the greatest philosophers in the British Empiricist tradition. However, amongst his contemporaries, Hume achieved notoriety for another essay. In *Of Miracles* Hume proposed an argument which he said would serve as a constant and timeless refutation to all miracles. Hume urges us on the balance of probabilities to reject the greater miracle, that a paranormal or supernatural event has actually occurred, in favour of the lesser miracle that the report is wrong or seeks to deceive. For testimony to establish a miracle beyond any doubt, it should be more miraculous that the account is wrong than the event it seeks to establish.

> Nothing is so convenient as a decisive argument of this kind, which must at least silence the most arrogant bigotry and superstition, and free us from their impertinent solicitations. I flatter myself, that I have discovered an argument of like nature, which, if just, will, with the wise and learned, be an everlasting check to all kinds of superstitious delusion.... That no testimony is sufficient to establish a miracle, unless the testimony be of such a kind, that its falsehood would be more miraculous, than the fact, which it endeavours to establish.... When anyone tells me, that he saw a dead man restored to life, I immediately consider with myself, whether it be more probable, that this person should either deceive or be deceived, or that the fact, that he relates should really have happened. I weigh the one miracle against the other; and according to the superiority, which I discover, I pronounce my decision, and always reject the greater miracle.[1]

Interpreted simply, Hume's argument warns us that when we see something that appears to be out-of-step with everyday reality, we have a tendency to ascribe it to the supernatural. For every 'miracle' there will be commonsense explanations, which will insistently clamour against the more uncommon interpretation of the evidence. Sometimes the more rational explanation may not immediately be apparent. Our intuitive grasp of the way probability works tends to be poor and we fall prey to illusions of randomness, pattern and connection which are interpreted as 'meaningful coincidences' or events directed by a higher intelligence.[2] The old example, beloved of statisticians, is that there only needs to be twenty-three

Of Philosophers and the evidence for Miracles

people present at a party to provide an even chance that two of the guests will share the same birthday. It may seem extraordinary that a person should enjoy two very large lottery wins in a short time interval but, when all the possible lotteries that person might have entered are taken into account, their good fortune can be shown to fall within the bounds of probability.

Oxford Professor Antony Flew endows Hume's argument with a more terrible importance.[3] This distinguished philosopher has warned parapsychologists that they seem blissfully unaware that Hume's argument represents an epistemological barrier, 'It is directed not at the question of whether miracles occur but at the question of whether – and if so how – we could know that they do, and when and where they have.'

Flew's interpretation derives from the special status which philosophers give to knowledge. While researching this book, I interviewed an American who had made Qabalah magic his life's work. During a discussion on what might count as evidence for reincarnation, he grew increasingly angry at my scepticism, finally retorting, 'You are a scientist, you have to look for evidence but I know there is a reality beyond this world, I know we come back, I know the body is just a spacesuit!' This is the siren's call of the mystic, the person who believes himself to be the one-eyed man in the kingdom of the blind. Epistemology, or the theory of knowledge, seeks to test such claims and asks under what conditions we can know things, as opposed to merely believing them to be true.

When faced with delineating knowledge from belief, D. W. Hamlyn, Professor of Philosophy at the University of London, presented his students with a paranormal example drawn from D. H. Lawrence's fictional short story, *The Rocking-Horse Winner*.[4] The hero of Lawrence's tale is Paul, the young son of parents whose expensive tastes far exceed the family income. There is never enough money. Their fortunes seem set to change, however, when the little boy, astride his rocking-horse and in a wild trance, consistently cries out the names of winning race horses. Bets are laid and the horses gallop home to win – Paul is never wrong. Surely, in this example, the child can be said to *know* that a certain horse will win in the forthcoming races?

No!, says Hamlyn emphatically, no amount of true belief ever equals knowledge. Knowledge has a very special status. To be in a position to claim to *know* something, he argues, one must be able to certify or give one's authority to its truth. Of course, we could still be simply wrong or self-deluded. Philosophy warns us that absolute certainty is a scarce commodity, and is not to be found outside the operations of logic and mathematics.

Epistemology, then, points out how much of the information about the world, which comes to us second-hand and which often passes for knowledge, dissolves, upon analysis, into mere belief. By the philosopher's stringent criteria, no amount of testimony, which we cannot certify as true, will ever serve to prove the existence of miracles – and worse – Hume urges us always to accept the lesser miracle that all such testimony is untrue or simply fraudulent.

Hume's argument will echo throughout the pages of this book. In a later chapter, the reader will be asked to consider probably the greatest and most completely documented miracle of the twentieth century.[5] In 1965, John Connolly Fagan, an easy-going, middle-aged, Glasgow docker was diagnosed as suffering from an aggressive form of stomach cancer. During surgery it was discovered that the tumour had spread to the colon and local lymph nodes. Faced with widespread disease, the doctors could only excise the great white growth in the stomach wall and perform the necessary corrective surgery to keep the digestive tract functioning. Pathological investigations strongly indicated that much of the tumour still remained.

The prognosis was grim and represented a death sentence for John Fagan who was anticipated to live a year at most. As predicted, he gradually declined in health. Finally, in what appeared to be the last hours of life, with what was left of his stomach almost totally destroyed by cancerous ulcers and with what appeared to be part of the stomach wall in the sick-bucket beside his bed, he made a spontaneous recovery. So complete was his recovery, that the next morning he was able to sit up in bed and eat two boiled eggs, his first meal in many weeks. After an exhaustive and often hostile examination of the case by more than seven doctors, his cure was ascribed, by the Vatican, to the intercession of a Scottish martyr.

There is another, clinical, explanation for these events. Although it offers a complete account of what happened to John Fagan, it is weak, perhaps even wildly improbable, but it is the 'lesser miracle' and the reader may find that it casts doubt upon, if not destroys, one of the most stunning and complete accounts of a 'miracle' that we are ever likely to be given.

Experiencing a miracle at first-hand puts us in no better position. The experience is subjective and there are always more common, plausible explanations. Hauntings and apparitions may be merely hallucinations; extra-sensory perception just meaningful coincidences; the movement of objects by will-power explained by fraud or simple physics; reincarnation simply childish fantasy mixed with repressed memories; and spirit possession may really be a manifestation of multiple personality disorder.

Long before parapsychology moved into the laboratory, dedicated investigators from the British and American Societies for Psychical Research were attempting to study objectively the 'minor' miracles of clairvoyance and telepathy in carefully constructed, well-controlled experiments. However, even when these experiments seemed to demonstrate the existence of paranormal phenomena beyond any reasonable doubt, some investigators, plagued by uncertainty, later repudiated the results. Scepticism and doubt have become such a stumbling block for the new science that the eminent philosopher/parapsychologist, John Beloff, has investigated some of these cases at length to discover what exactly made the researchers disown their results.

Stephan Ossowiecki,[6] a Polish engineer, appeared to possess the most extraordinary powers of clairvoyance. He not only appeared able to read the contents of sealed letters but to provide personal details about the writer which did not appear in the text. One example of his legendary feats was provided by Professor Charles Richet, when he was invited to Warsaw to test the clairvoyant in May 1921. Richet presented him with two personal letters, sealed in identical envelopes. One was selected at random by Ossowiecki but the medium seemed to have difficulty concentrating and asked for the test to be repeated on another day. As powers of clairvoyance may be affected by many factors outside the medium's control, this did not seem to be an unreasonable request, although it did reinforce the investigator's suspicions that Ossowiecki might have been using fraud or super-sensory clues obtained from the package or the experimenters themselves. Now here is the rub: Richet had to leave Warsaw and he left the envelope with his co-experimenter, Geley, whom he trusted implicitly. Geley, unaware of the letter's contents, handed the envelope to the medium at a sitting some days later. Ossowiecki rubbed the outside and began to provide an analysis as Geley recorded the monologue,

> Someone is talking about a lady called Berger. A man of fifty wrote this letter, which is a reply to a letter from Professor Richet. This letter does not come from Paris; it comes from a place near the sea. It is about various matters. It is an invitation. There is something about this lady called Berger. She is thirty-three years old. She is married. I cannot read it. It is written very fast, not in any order, a muddle. It is a musical man who wrote it!

The letter was a badly written and incoherent invitation for Richet to lecture to various societies. It contained the words 'You will be Mme Berger's guest of honour' and mentions it was written 'in great haste'. Ossowiecki made a single error: the letter was from Berlin and not 'from a place by the sea'. The rest is correct, including the details about the author and Mme Berger.

Now Charles Richet was not present at the experiment but he trusted his colleague. When investigators from the British Society for Psychical Research performed their own experiments, the same situation was actually written into the experimental design. The aim was to test for clairvoyance, ruling out telepathy or the possibility that Ossowiecki might gain his information from reading the experimenter's mind. More importantly, the protocol also excluded the possibility that Ossowiecki's information might be gained from facial expressions and body-language unconsciously provided by the experimenter as the medium fished for correct information.

To this end, an experiment was designed. A crude drawing was prepared in London, before being elaborately secured in bulky wrappings in such a way as to leave no clue as to the contents. To guard against the package being secretly opened, the investigator also used some private seals known only to himself. The package was taken to Warsaw and handed to a co-experimenter. The investigator then returned to London, ensuring that Ossowiecki had no contact with the man who prepared the drawing. Within hours, the clairvoyant was allowed to handle the package and under constant observation he attempted to reproduce the drawing still sealed inside the package. Ossowiecki's sketch and the package, still unopened, were returned to the SPR headquarters for evaluation.

Both parapsychologists were notable scholars and hardened investigators well-versed in the fraud and subterfuge which often passed for psychic ability. In this 1924 experiment, Dr Eric Dingwall conducted the investigation with co-experimenter Dr von Schrenck-Notzing, a well-known German parapsychologist. Nine years later, the experiment was repeated by Dr Theodore Besterman and co-worker Lord Charles Hope. On both occasions Ossowiecki managed to make an almost perfect reproduction of the drawing. Both teams published their results, claiming to have been satisfied that experimental protocols had not been breached and that Ossowiecki's ability to make the drawings defied normal explanations. Later both Dingwall and Besterman disowned their results. Why?

Asked by John Beloff[7] to explain his retraction, Dr Eric Dingwall explained that for a few hours the package had been in the hands of his co-experimenter, Dr Schrenck-Notzing, and, as Dingwall had now lost confidence in his co-worker, he could no longer vouch for the experiment. This evasive and somewhat disingenuous attempt to discredit Schrenck-Notzing failed to satisfy Beloff who wrote to Dingwall again, asking him to be more specific,

> I inquired, in particular, whether he was suggesting that Schrenck-Notzing had conspired with Ossowiecki to fool him, or whether he thought that Ossowiecki had somehow outwitted

Schrenck-Notzing. I asked how, on either hypothesis, he proposed to explain his own published statements to the effect that the day after the critical session the target-package was returned to him intact, with all its seals and private codemarks undisturbed. To this Dr Dingwall replied that it was obvious that, like many parapsychologists, I adhered to what he called 'the magical way of looking at the world' and, this being so, it would be a mere waste of his time to answer any more of my silly questions. So that was that.

Dr Besterman's reasons appeared even more obscure. He told John Beloff that he had developed reservations about the experiment but that these did not in any way reflect upon his co-experimenter, Lord Charles Hope. Beloff concluded that neither of these scholars seemed to have any particular reason to doubt the conclusions of their own research. The scepticism arose from the irresistible force of the 'lesser miracle',

> You may say that this only goes to prove what unreasonable people skeptics really are. This may be so; certainly skeptics are just as capable of being irrational as believers. Yet, can we blame them? The point is that, when he perished in the Warsaw uprising of 1944, Ossowiecki, arguably the greatest sensitive on record, left behind him no successors. The law of cognitive dissonance suffices to explain the sequel; in the fullness of time every miracle, no matter how incontrovertible it may have once appeared, will lose its lustre.

We may have to accept that parapsychology will never be able to provide the same burden of proof as the conventional sciences. The reader, sitting as a juror, will have to decide each case on a balance of probabilities, using his or her own experiences; in fact, very much the same skills and shortcomings as those required of juries sitting in a court of law. However, we can ask with the hindsight of nearly 250 years, of which more than 100 years have been spent in the scientific study of the paranormal, whether all of the arguments Hume used to support his case would still carry the same weight today.

Miracles are born of superstition, Hume tells his readers, which is why they are never endorsed by men of learning and good sense,

> For first, there is not to be found, in all history, any miracle

Of Philosophers and the evidence for Miracles

attested by a sufficient number of men, of such unquestioned good sense, education and learning, as to secure us against all delusion in themselves; of such undoubted integrity, as to place them beyond all suspicion of any design to deceive others; of such credit and reputation in the eyes of mankind, as to have a great deal to lose in case of their being detected in any falsehood.

This book deals almost exclusively with cases attested by men of 'good sense, education and learning' but here let us play the Devil's Advocate. After the Reverend George Campbell had published his *Dissertation on Miracles* in 1762, arguing forcibly against Hume's essay, Hume wrote to Campbell, hoping to console him with the story of the essay's beginnings. In what appears to be a cynical attempt to profit from religious intolerance, the letter reveals that *Of Miracles* was directed not at the Protestant Church but at the Roman Catholics and, in particular, Hume's intellectual adversaries, those Catholic storm-troopers of the Counter-Reformation: the Jesuits.[8]

Superficially it has always appeared that Roman Catholicism has been more credulous of miracles than the reformed churches.[9] While researching the Marian apparitions (visions of the Virgin Mary) for this book, I was surprised to discover that nearly every single well-documented case has provoked the unconcealed hostility of Mother Church. In fact, it was the Inquisition, and not enlightenment and reason, which broke the tradition of Marian apparitions in Catholic countries between the sixteenth and nineteenth centuries. Today, the Catholic Church, forced to work within a world shaped by science, is even more wary of religious miracles. The articles of Catholic faith do not include the many and various Marian apparitions, alleged cases of demonic possession or apparent instances of miraculous cures. While the Vatican may choose to lend its authority to certain miracles and apparitions, this does not bind the faithful, who are left to decide the matter for themselves.

While discussing such matters, a Catholic spiritual adviser, and exorcist to a large Midlands' diocese, explained his scepticism resulting from many years of investigating cases of possession, adding, 'I would have to accept the possibility of such things happening but I would want to dispute each and every case.' Miracles are seen as a dangerous intrusion into the spiritual life of the parish, and a priest faced with an apparition of the Virgin Mary or a miraculous healing which is not accepted by the church authorities can find himself caught in the cross-fire between the beliefs of his congregation and the directives of his superiors. Let us now ask if we can find an instance of a modern religious miracle of the type that so offended Hume and which was witnessed by a few good men of sense, education and learning.

Father Herbert Thurston S.J. was a Jesuit teacher and an accomplished writer whose hard-headed approach to religious miracles earned him the respect of fellow scholars. Much of his work avoided the type of miracle which had so incensed Hume but he broke this rule to provide an eye-witness account of what could be described as an 'impossible impossibility'. Thurston started his account by relating how, during Victor Emmanuel's invasion of the Papal States in September 1870, a statue of St Dominic, exposed for veneration during a mass at Soriano in Calabria, was seen to move! It stepped off its pedestal and slid across the floor, apparently tracing the outline of a cross. A few brave individuals caught hold of the statue and were dragged along with it. After an extensive search, no evidence of machines or trickery was discovered.

Here we seem to be entering the world of nonsense. Here we have the type of miracle from which most parapsychologists would turn away. Indeed, Thurston assures his readers that he would not have insulted their intelligence by recounting such a story, were it not for the fact that a similar incident had occurred within living memory on the island of Malta.[10]

In November 1893, two priests and two lay brothers teaching at an English Jesuit boys' school took a class of boarders to the village of Mellieha for a picnic. Close by was a shrine with a very dignified statue of the Virgin Mary holding the Infant Child. Carved from a single piece of rock, the life-sized effigy stood in a grotto close to the sea. A local legend claimed that whenever the statue had been removed to the little church facing the cavern, it would, overnight, return to the cave under its own volition. More surprisingly, there had also been

Of Philosophers and the evidence for Miracles

numerous claims that one of the Virgin's hands would move. None of the priests gave any credence to these fables but both Jesuits and boys were curious to see the statue which had inspired such stories.

They arrived after lunch and the boys were conducted into the cave in groups. While a crowd of boys, accompanied by two fathers, was inspecting the statue in the dim light of the grotto, Father John McHale S.J. asked some of the boys what part of the statue was reported to move;

> They told me it was the right hand, and I turned my eyes to look at it. It was perfectly still. But almost immediately I was startled by seeing the little finger move gently backwards. This was followed by the next two fingers, then by the forefinger, and last of all by the thumb. When the fingers had assumed a very graceful position, the whole hand moved gently upwards some ten or twelve inches, came slowly down again and ended by forming a beautiful cross. The fingers then resumed their original hook-like position, and after a pause of a few minutes the gesture was again repeated.

This was seen by the two priests, some of the borders and a few local boys who had joined them, but the last thing that the Jesuits believed was that the statue was actually moving. They reasoned that it had to be their own heads that were in motion. One father pressed his head against the wall, while the second squeezed his head between two railings. Still the Virgin's hand moved, while one of the hands of the Christ Child also appeared to bless the onlookers, its face transfigured into that of a 'little child crying for joy'.

The Jesuits, well versed in theology and science, thought that they might have discovered the 'secret' of the shrine: simple mass delusion. Was it, the fathers asked, only seen by the catholics in the group? No, a protestant boy replied that he saw the Christ Child's hand moving, while the infant's head seemed to sway from side to side. Perhaps then, the priests reasoned, once they left the grotto the 'spell' would be broken and the illusion would come to an end. Consequently, as one priest continued to watch, the second went outside to fetch the lay brothers and the rest of the children. The spell was not broken and all who could fit into the cave apparently continued to watch the statue move for more than thirty minutes.

The Sceptical Occultist

This account came to Thurston from John McHale S.J. who died in 1911. Thurston remembered him as 'a man of acute perceptions and shrewd in all practical affairs of life', while his companion, Father John Gordon S.J., was a sceptical Scot with a particular hatred of 'deceit and shams'. Thurston also wrote to some of the boys who had witnessed the event and obtained convincing affidavits, albeit some thirty years after the event.

This, then, is the stuff of miracles. Illusion, hallucination or mass delusion they may be, but the testimony alone seems to elevate this subject above the charge of superstition and nonsense. Hume is wrong when he says, '*It is strange*, a judicious reader is apt to say, upon perusal of these wonderful historians, *that such prodigious events never happen in our days*.' Miracles, religious and secular, magnificent and humble, are with us still. Psychical researchers bear witness to the abundance of haunting and poltergeist cases which are brought to their attention every year; while icons and statues, religious and profane, are watched and even photographed, moving, weeping and bleeding.

There are even annual miracles.[11] Machine-guns and shells ruthlessly scythed down men and trees during the terrible battle at Delville Wood on 9–13 July, 1916. When the fighting was over, 150-odd survivors of a 3,000 strong South African brigade cut down a blasted tree and fashioned the wood into a simple cross. This poignant memorial to their fallen comrades still stands in a garden of remembrance at Pietermaritzburg, the capital of Natal Province. Every year on the anniversary of the battle, the cross is reputed to 'weep'; a resinous substance being exuded from the cross-beams to form a continuous stream of liquid which accumulates at the foot of the cross. Every year after the date of the battle, the old dead wood is cleaned by local volunteers and on each new anniversary the resin starts to flow again.

Twice yearly in Naples, Italy, a similar miracle takes place in front of thousands of spectators. Two phials of blood, said to be that of the fourth-century martyr, St Januarius, are venerated during ceremonies in the saint's honour. During these proceedings the blood liquefies, often bubbling and foaming

Of Philosophers and the evidence for Miracles

in the process. The phials have been sealed by age and are said to be impossible to open without breaking the glass. Consequently, samples have never been available for chemical analysis. However, in 1902, scientists at the University of Naples were allowed to pass a beam of light through one of the containers to obtain a spectroscopic analysis of the contents. The investigation is said to have revealed the presence of blood, plus other foreign substances. But even if we assume the relics are fraudulent (we have every reason to do so as the phials do not appear until the end of the fourteenth century), and we reject the testimony describing the bubbling and foaming liquefaction, we are still faced with the curious observation that Italian scientists were able to obtain a peak on an absorption spectrum consistent with intact haemoglobin – the oxygen carrying protein inside red blood cells – after more than 600 years! This illustrates a puzzling aspect of some miracles. We might expect, on the basis of Hume's argument, an easy refutation and a simple scientific explanation. What the scientific investigator often encounters is a series of complexities which, like a nest of Russian dolls, appears to confront him at every level.

If the *experiences* are real, rather than the product of superstition and delusion, we might expect to see discrete patterns which cut across both culture and time. And, indeed, such patterns do appear to be present in the results of surveys conducted by parapsychologists.

Do you believe in ghosts? In 1894, those intrepid early investigators in the British Society for Psychical Research published responses from the public to the question, *'Have you ever, when believing yourself to be completely awake, had a vivid impression of seeing or being touched by a living being or inanimate object, or of hearing a voice; which impression, so far as you could discover, was not due to any external physical cause?'*[12]

Some 17,000 members of the public replied to the questionnaire and the results were published as the now famous *Report on the Census of Hallucinations*. Approximately one in ten respondents answered 'Yes'.

Any idea that most of these experiences, or indeed any, resulted from an encounter with a ghost or the soul of a dead person was never really a consideration. Many people who had previously related their experiences to the SPR had reported seeing apparitions of people who were still *alive*. Other people have reported seeing apparitions of buildings, animals, vehicles and even brick walls. Many of the apparitions also seem to lack any way of interacting with the physical world. And while apparitions have been seen to open doors, draw curtains and remove objects from tables, when the experience was over, the doors were still closed and the objects were still in place.

While some of us will want to hold that human beings, and perhaps even animals, possess souls which survive death, what are we to make of apparitions of buildings, gardens, ships and trains? Apparitions can be complicated, containing both 'living' and inanimate objects. People have seen ghostly horses and carts driven by phantoms. The observer will report the sound of the hooves on the road and even feel the rush of cold air as the ghostly entourage passes within a few feet. On the basis of our religious belief we might feel able to account for the survival of the man, perhaps even the horse, but what of the cart and the rest of the regalia?

Not surprisingly, it was reasoned that many of these experiences were hallucinations originating in the person's own subconscious. More interestingly, other experiences hinted at the possibility of a direct correspondence between two minds. Telepathy seemed an attractive hypothesis to explain those instances where, say, an apparition of a living person was seen by two people in a room, while a third saw nothing; or cases where the vision was found to coincide with the death of the person recognised in the apparition.[13]

To be experienced out there in the 'real world', both telepathic impressions and internal hallucinations would be processed by the brain and projected out on to the person's visual field. Consequently, they would often appear to be indistinguishable from objects such as tables and chairs. Ghosts – if there are such things – would, lacking a body, also have to avail themselves of telepathy. The problem remains that these different types of experiences would be qualitatively identical.

How much evidence was there for telepathy? The early investigators reasoned that these experiences could only be

Of Philosophers and the evidence for Miracles

analysed for evidence of telepathy by reference to some external event. A sizable sub-group of apparitions appeared to cluster around the death of a recognised friend or relative and seemed to provide an accessible reference point. Were these apparitions a last message, a sort of telepathic SOS, or were they just mere coincidence?

The Society's Literary Committee used a case submitted by a member of the public, in order to calculate the probability of an apparition being recognised at around the time of that person's death. Let us consider, they said, one particular case, where a man left his bedroom and, while on the landing, saw an apparition of an old lady in a black bonnet and shawl, dressed very much like his mother. The figure left a room and descended the stairs and the man's wife, coming up the stairs, appeared to brush past the apparition but reported later that she had seen and felt nothing. The apparition disappeared and, shortly after, the man received news that, precisely at the same time, his mother, dressed in a bonnet and shawl, had died in another town.

For argument's sake, they assumed that the observer in this case had only thirty years of intelligent life, during which time he slept for nine hours each day. He was awake for fifteen hours and consequently enjoyed $15 \times 365 \times 30 = 164{,}250$ hours of waking, intelligent life. Now assuming, again for the sake of argument, that he saw the apparition within a quarter of an hour of the moment of his mother's death, then if the apparition was no more than a random hallucination, it might have been seen in any one of the 657,000 quarter-hours of life during those thirty years. So the probability of the coincidence, of it being experienced at the same time as the mother's death is 1:657,000. But not all random hallucinations are of old ladies dressed in black. Let us assume, they said, that the man did not see his mother but rather a class of hallucinations that vaguely resembled an old lady in a black bonnet and shawl and this represented ten per cent of all apparitions (which is outrageously high). Now the probability of the apparition occurring in the right quarter-hour is more than 6.5 million to one. For this one case to be explained simply on the basis of chance-coincidence, it would have required some 6.5 million English adults, living at the time of

15

the Census, to have experienced a marked visual hallucination at some point in their lives.

But this case did not stand alone. A relatively small, but significant, number of people had reported to the SPR that they had seen apparitions of friends and loved-ones at around the time of their deaths. The members of the Literary Committee reasoned that if only another nine similar cases were considered, it would increase the probability tenfold and would have required some 65 million English adults (more than the population of England at that time) to have experienced a distinct hallucination, to make it probable that these ten cases had occurred by chance. It was clear that this was not the case, as, of those 17,000 members of the public who answered the Census Question, the majority (15,316 people or ninety per cent of those polled) answered 'No'.

But still SPR investigators agonised over the possibility of fraud.[14] What if a large number of respondents had simply played a practical joke on the Society? The psychical investigator G. N. M. Tyrrell takes up the story in his classic masterpiece, *Apparitions*,

> It was, of course, suggested at the time that the collectors might have been hoaxed. [Edmund] Gurney points out with regard to this suggestion, that a hoax in answering the Census Question would not have been a particularly exhilarating joke, since the reply had only to be Yes or No. Would the hoaxer have said that he had had an experience when he had not, or the other way about? It seems more probable that he would have said Yes when he should have said No. But that would have had the effect of increasing the number of Yeses, and therefore increasing the probability that the coincidences were due to chance. The effect of hoaxing, if it ever occurred, must have been negligible.

Here then, is the argument for telepathy, drawn from spontaneous cases of apparitions. While these statistics fall far short of proof, these are not the sort of patterns that one might expect if all experiences of apparitions were just hallucinations – or for that matter sophistry and illusion.

The *Report on the Census of Hallucinations* is supported by more recent surveys. In 1979 the parapsychologist, J. Palmer, put the same question to residents and students in Charlottesville, Virginia.[15] Of the 622 persons responding to the Census Question, Palmer found that 7.5 per cent answered in the affirmative, just slightly less than the original survey. The respondents appeared to fall into two distinct sub-groups: those who professed many psychic experiences and those who reported none. The major difference between the two studies was that the Americans reported experiences in which they felt themselves being touched or heard a voice, while the British study reported mainly visual hallucinations.

However, this type of survey gives us little information on what it is like to actually *experience* an apparition. This information was provided by Celia Green and Charles McCreery when they published the results of a survey undertaken between 1968 and 1974 by the Institute of Psychophysical Research in Oxford.[16] Appeals in the press and on radio for first-hand accounts of experiences of perceiving apparitions elicited 1,800 replies from the public. More than half of those who responded claimed to have had more than one experience. Seven people in ten realised at some point during the experience that they were seeing an apparition and most apparitions were perceived as being close to the participant (one in eight occurred at twelve feet or less). The majority were seen (84 per cent), while some were heard (37 per cent) or felt (15 per cent) and were therefore different from hallucinations of the insane which are predominantly auditory. Most apparitions were of human figures but only exceptionally were they recognised. Of those that were recognised, a third represented people who were still living, and they were quite unlike everyday experiences in being restricted to one sense; usually sight (61 per cent). More realistic apparitions were rarer, employing two (25 per cent), three (9 per cent) or all four senses of sight, sound, touch and smell (5 per cent).

Still the evidence suggests that many 'ghosts', upon investigation, may be hallucinations. But why should such a high proportion of the population experience this sort of hallucination at all?

One sub-group of people commonly experiences apparitions and, at some point in time, most of us will fall into this group. At that juncture, one in two of us are likely to experience apparitions over a long period of time. When Dewi Rees knocked on doors in Mid-Wales, the startling information that he was given, in the privacy of kitchens and livingrooms, provided one answer as to why apparitions are so common and why, under certain circumstances, they can prevent us from going mad.[17]

The data Rees published in 1971 was drawn from healthy patients in a large, friendly medical group-practice in Llanidloes.[18] Introduced by the local doctor and assured of confidentiality, sixty-six widowers and 227 widows told Rees of experiences that most had never even dared to share with relatives and close friends. One in three regularly admitted to seeing, hearing or touching their dead spouse. But even this was an under-estimate as Rees rejected as 'dreams' all experiences which occurred after the person retired to bed. The Oxford study demonstrated that one quarter of all their cases occurred just after waking up in the middle of the night. Other people reported a sense of the presence of the deceased. In total, nearly half of those interviewed admitted to continuing to have some contact with their deceased spouses.

What, in fact, these people were experiencing were postbereavement apparitions or the 'hallucinations of widowhood'. Rees discovered that they were most common during the first ten years of widowhood; they often lasted for years and were strongly associated with a happy marriage and parenthood. The proportion of men and women reporting apparitions was about equal and the sorts of people most likely to see phantasms of the deceased partner were those with professional or managerial jobs in the over-40 agegroup. The idea that many bereaved men and women continue to 'live' with their dead spouse may seem fantastic but Rees's results confirmed other studies of bereaved individuals in south-east London and Tokyo.

What is the point of nearly one in two bereaved people experiencing some sort of apparition of their departed lovedones? One explanation is that at times of crisis, such as bereavement, the subconscious conjures these phantoms to

Of Philosophers and the evidence for Miracles

help heal the feelings of loss and assist the individual in coping with loneliness, ultimately preparing him for renewed independence. The power of this healing mechanism is underscored by a case reported by psychologists Robert Masters and Jean Houston.[19]

Their subject, S., was widowed while still in her early fifties and after a long and loving marriage to a very dominant and assertive husband. The psychologists' notes described S. as a 'willing and very happy satellite of a strong, aggressive male figure who made all of her decisions, gave her abundant affection and provided for all of her material needs and most of her wishes'. When her husband died suddenly, S. understandably found herself unable to cope with her loss. She even denied that he was dead, leaving his clothes in the wardrobe and his toiletries in the bathroom. Finally, she broke down and started drinking to ease the pain of an anxious depression. As the drinking increased, her behaviour became unstable and violent and friends, who might have been able to offer the much-needed emotional support, began to avoid her. In a world distorted by depression and alcohol, S. found herself very much alone and drifting towards disaster.

Carefully monitored by her psychologists, and under the influence of 200 micrograms of the drug LSD (d-lysergic acid diethylamide), S. was able to conjure a powerful sense of her dead husband's presence. The apparition listened attentively as she told him how much she missed him and poured out the dreadful catalogue of misfortunes which had befallen her since his death. Her 'husband' offered sympathy but managed to convey the impression that he 'didn't really approve' of her behaviour. Finally, he gave her a long loving smile conveying 'whole worlds of encouragement and strength', then slowly turned and walked away.

'At long last', S. told her psychologists, her husband was, '... Gone ... Dead. Really dead. He has made me understand that and I have got to accept it. That's what he would want me to do. That is the meaning of what I just went through.' Although under no illusion that she had actually conjured her husband's spirit, S. stopped drinking and began to live a richer and happier life.

We have arrived at a possible answer to age-old phenomena. Our question now turns on whether some experiences are more than hallucinations and if, and when, we will ever be able to say where hallucinations end and ghosts begin.

Psi is a term used by parapsychologists to denote the unknown factor in psychic experiences. People may acquire information which seems to have come to them from outside the range of their normal senses. A person develops the feeling that a close relative is in danger, or dreams of a tragedy or, like Paul in *The Rocking-Horse Winner*, appears to be able to predict specific events far into the future.

If the information is of the sort that could not possibly have existed in another person's mind it is termed *clairvoyance*. In the laboratory, at least, the term *telepathy* is used when the information only exists in someone's mind. In actuality, it is often difficult to separate clairvoyance from telepathy and parapsychologists may use the umbrella term *general extrasensory perception* (GESP) when it is impossible to divorce one from the other. *Precognition* specifies telepathic or clairvoyant awareness of information which does not exist. The last psi phenomenon is *psychokinesis* (PK) used to denote those situations in life or in laboratory experiments where a person seems to affect a physical event or situation by will-power or mind control.

Like apparitions, psi phenomena appear to cut across time and culture. Surveys have shown them to be prevalent in Great Britain, the United States, the Netherlands, Denmark, Switzerland, Finland, Austria, the former Soviet Union and India. One in three school children in India, and approximately the same number of adults in Russia, reported experiencing at least one inexplicable event. Half of these strange events occur in dreams, the remainder being intuitive or taking the form of an hallucination. In a 1990 Gallup Poll in the United States, nearly three in ten adult Americans reported instances of telepathy and one in ten described seeing at least one apparition.

Of course many factors complicate these sorts of surveys. The inexplicable event might just have been a powerful coincidence or the person might really have known the information all along. Many of us possess knowledge which is not readily called to mind. Some people recall telephone numbers or credit card PIN numbers only as they write them down or actually type them into the relevant machine. Some information is inhibited and is only recalled in connection with some other event or under hypnosis or in psychotherapy. Thus information may actually have been accessible but this was not consciously realised at the time. Alternatively, the memories of the event may have been exaggerated or falsified or indeed the whole story may have been an exciting 'ghost story' which finally acquires the status of a memory as it is recounted over and over again.

There are three ways of cutting through the uncertainty to arrive at a deeper analysis. The first is to use statistics to analyse the data but, while the biological and human sciences employ the same techniques to analyse their results, this way is simply not strong enough to counter the force of the 'lesser miracle'. The second method involves using psychological tests to construct a picture of the respondents, their beliefs and their physical and mental capabilities, which are used to judge their experiences; but this approach falls on the same sword as the first. The third way is to ask whether the results of a survey seem to provide a missing 'jigsaw piece' which fits into a puzzle created by other work or even another science.

In 1963, the Freiburg Institute in Germany published the results of a survey on spontaneous phenomena.[20] The responses were rigorously screened and half the cases dismissed. Of those which survived this selection process, 500 respondents reported 1,000 paranormal events. The majority were women, which came as no surprise to the investigators as many previous studies had shown a preponderance of women reporting psychic experiences. Precognitive experiences occurred more frequently in dreams, while telepathic experiences seemed able to operate in both the waking state and altered states of consciousness – dreams. Most experiences referred to unpleasant or sad events (85 per cent), just under half referring to deaths. The women's reference persons were drawn from the close family circle (husband, parents, children, and siblings). While the reference figure was often male, the respondent's mother also featured strongly in these experiences. The investigators explained these findings in terms of the sociological role of women, 'The woman, who always feels herself a connecting link between ancestors and descendants, preserving and passing on the traditions, remains more intensively attached to the family.' In contrast, men, the investigators decided, were more egocentric, seemingly concerned with themselves or their mothers or reference figures outside the family circle. Let us note here that a central finding of this study centres around the woman, the mother, the wife.

One of the problems in assessing research such as the Freiburg study is that there are very few theories or models in parapsychology. Sigmund Freud in 1933, wrote that telepathy might be 'the original archaic method by which individuals understand one another, and which has been pushed into the background in the course of phylogenetic development'. But if telepathy is a vestigial relic of our past, like the appendix, might it not still be common in Stone Age societies? Indeed, there is evidence of extra-sensory perception in tribal cultures. Anthropologists without a shred of interest in the paranormal have witnessed apparent incidents of telepathic communication amongst Australian Aborigines. Russ Hausfeld, an Australian anthropologist who worked amongst the tribes in the Northern Territory, can recall one instance of a man suddenly standing up at the camp-fire and announcing that his father was very sick. He then turned and walked out into the night, beginning a long journey to a remote encampment in the tribal trust lands. The news of his father's illness, travelling by more conventional means, arrived many days later.[21] Extra-sensory perception in tribal societies has also been documented by parapsychologists but this hypothesis does not explain why telepathy is seemingly prevalent in developed societies which enjoy unlimited access to telephones, fax machines, the numerous other types of instant electronic communication and high-speed travel.

There is another theory; one which does account for the prevalence of psi in developed societies and its apparently constant renewal with each generation. Most importantly, it also appears to dovetail neatly with other research such as the

Freiburg study. Jan Ehrenwald was a psychiatrist whose work occasionally seemed to bring him face to face with the inexplicable. After a number of encounters with schizophrenic patients who seemed to be able to read his thoughts, he finally wrote a paper on schizophrenia and telepathy. This was sent to a British psychology journal but the manuscript, written during the Second World War, was lost in an air-raid. Ehrenwald rewrote it in 1958 and submitted it to an American journal but, on reflection, he withdraw it. It was finally published sixteen years later.[22] Since the 1930s, psychiatrists and psychoanalysts had begun to report instances of telepathy which centred around mothers and their children. Now, doctors who discussed their experiences in terms of telepathy and ESP were no longer thought unsound or shunned by their colleagues; and their papers, published in the academic press, seemed to provide missing pieces of a 'jigsaw' that Ehrenwald had been attempting to assemble in his mind for many years. His theory was simple: ESP was produced by the most dependent, intimate and emotionally charged relationship that most human beings ever experience – the special bond between mother and child.

In Ehrenwald's hypothesis, telepathy, in the form of distress calls and messages of comfort, endearment and reassurance, provides a means of communication between the mother and her helpless baby. As the child becomes independent and learns to speak, these external telepathic influences become progressively screened out and, in fact, Ehrenwald argues that a failure to develop that mental insulation ultimately leads to breakdown and madness.

At first sight, this theory appears to lead to another dead-end as it seems difficult to test the reality of telepathic communication between mother and infant. In fact, like all good scientific theories, Ehrenwald's thesis has a number of testable consequences.

In the cut and thrust of daily living, we might fail to recognise instances of telepathy between ourselves and our children. Might these be more obvious to a trained observer who is open to this possibility? Dr Louisa Rhine, one of the pioneers of university-based parapsychology, collected numerous anecdotes of this type.[23] The examples often appear trivial but, on reflection, are striking: 'A woman was pondering the name of a man whose telephone number she was reluctant to call. At that very moment her two-year-old daughter said his name: *Arno Kraus*.'

Psychoanalyst Dorothy Burlingham has also described telepathic events in children. In one instance, her ten-year-old son seemed to recount an unusual story about gold coins, which was very similar to an account just related to her by one of her patients undergoing psychotherapy. In another instance, a mother had just decided to give her child a bicycle for Christmas, when the youngster in another room cried out 'I know what you are going to give me for Christmas: a bicycle.' Psychiatrist, Berthold Schwarz, also recorded more than ninety-one observations of apparent telepathy, involving his daughter, Lisa, when she was between one and three and a half years of age. He concluded that several predisposing factors seemed to be necessary for these events to occur. Firstly, he cites the symbiotic nature of the parent-child relationship. Secondly, there seemed to be a tendency for the little girl to want to provide evidence for her father's 'emotionally charged' expectations regarding the validity of ESP. Lastly, Schwarz believed that the child's prevailing mood, degree of contentment and psychological needs played a role, noting that these episodes occurred most frequently 'at the intersection of the parents' and child's emotional needs'.

Anecdotes are still anecdotes but there is harder evidence to be had for Ehrenwald's hypothesis. For example, might we not expect occasionally to see evidence of telepathy in situations where a handicapped child continues to depend on his mother? Or perhaps where an adult is unable to maintain that mental insulation, something that has been postulated to occur in schizophrenia. During long-term psychotherapy, the therapist and his patient often find themselves in a surrogate parent-child relationship. Might we not expect to find evidence of telepathy here also?

In fact, psychologists and psychiatrists working in all of these areas have reported apparent instances of telepathic

Of Philosophers and the evidence for Miracles

communication.[24] A child with Spastic Diplegia and congenital cataracts in both eyes came to the attention of investigators when he startled an ophthalmologist by suddenly 'reading' the visual acuity charts when his mother was in the room. In a similar case, a Latvian girl with a severe reading disorder was examined by Ferdinand von Neureiter, a Professor of Forensic Pathology. The child appeared only to be able to read printed material when her mother was looking at the same text. But, incredibly, the child's ability to read continued when her mother was reading the book while sitting behind a curtain or even in another room! We will discuss these and other cases in the next chapter when we come to hear the evidence for telepathy. It remains here to convince the reader that there is a case to answer; that much of the evidence discussed in this chapter raises the subject above the level of superstition, falsehood and fable, and invites further investigation.

Philosophers of science hold that a good scientific theory must provide testable consequences and stand up to testing but will often be capable of encompassing other competing theories and explanations. Let us briefly return to the Australian Aboriginals and the prehistoric man hypothesis for ESP. In August 1949, psychologists Ronald and Lyndon Rose conducted a series of ESP experiments at Woodenbong Aboriginal Settlement on the north coast of New South Wales.[25] While one psychologist monitored the agent, who was trying to 'send' information on target cards telepathically, the other experimenter sat with the subject and recorded the calls. Twenty-three subjects performed a total of 296 experimental runs, producing results well above what might have been expected on the basis of chance-coincidence.

Further analysis of the results revealed that most of the statistical significance resulted from the correct guesses produced by one subject. Lizzie Williams was a half-caste Aboriginal who was crippled and suffered from diabetes. During the experiments, she was caring for her very active two-year-old great-grandson, who was playing on the ground around her feet. The little boy was more than a handful for the crippled old lady and Lizzie frequently had to divide her attention between the child and the requirements of the experiement. The puzzled psychologists noted in their report that her best scores occurred when Lizzie was forced to divert her attention to the child.

Was it just a highly unusual coincidence that Lizzie Williams could guess the target cards correctly when the little boy clamoured for her attention? Or did her concern for her great-grandson re-open an extra-sensory pathway, which, inadvertently, also allowed her access to the target information? If we plump for coincidence, we also accept that this is just one in a whole series of coincidences which seem to support Ehrenwald's hypothesis. We must also ask ourselves at what point the idea of a coincidence ceases to have any real meaning and just becomes an excuse for our unwillingness to accept the greater miracle.

2

Telepathy

Prosecution's claim is that telepathy simply cannot happen. Alleged instances of telepathy arise from 'meaningful coincidences' and self-delusion. In the laboratory, results which appear to show telepathy are simply obtained by sensory cues or fraud.

Most of us know at least one person who believes that they have been graced with a paranormal experience. Many such experiences can be interpreted as telepathy or mind-to-mind contact between two people who share a close emotional bond. This contact may take the form of a vague impression of the person in question or it may appear in a dream. Sometimes the impression is dramatised in a visual form. Mrs Y., a woman who was born in Dublin but spent most of her life in London, was washing dishes when she seemed to 'see' the form of an old friend, N., who had never before travelled outside Ireland. Several days previously, and completely unbeknown to the woman, N. had arrived in London and was staying with his sister.

> I had just washed up at the sink. As I was drying my hands, I looked up at the wall. The flat was old and there were terrible damp marks covering the wall. I could suddenly, in my mind's eye, see them [N. and his sister] coming down my road. I can't explain it any better. It wasn't a vision, it was in my mind's eye. I dried my hands and was putting my coat on, when a knock came to the door and in they walked. It was very strange as they had been the last people in my thoughts. I had never experienced the sixth sense before that day.[1]

In its most highly dramatised form, this sort of 'information' is presented as a ghostly figure or apparition. Such 'phantasms of the living' manifestly cannot be the soul or 'astral body' of the person identified in the apparition, as they remain blissfully unaware of their ghostly double.

Many other cases seem to occur at a time of crisis and it is this conjunction which argues against the obvious explanation of coincidence. The following events were described to Edmund Gurney by a lady who had been on holiday with her husband on the shores of Lake Coniston,[2]

> I woke up with a start, feeling I had had a hard blow on my mouth, and with a distinct sense that I had been cut, and was bleeding under my upper lip, and seized my pocket-handkerchief, and held it (in a little pushing lump) to the part, as I sat up in bed, and held a few seconds, when I removed it. I was astonished not to see any blood, and only then realised that it was impossible anything could have struck me there as I lay fast asleep in bed, and so I thought it was only a dream! – but I looked at my watch, and saw it was seven, and finding Arthur (my husband) was not in the room, I concluded (rightly) that he must have gone out for an early sail, and [as] it was so fine.
>
> I then fell asleep. At breakfast (half-past nine), Arthur came in rather late, and I noticed he rather purposely sat further away from me than usual, and every now and then put his pocket-handkerchief furtively up to his lip, in the very way I had done. I said, 'Arthur, why are you doing that?' and added a little anxiously, 'I know you have hurt yourself! but I'll tell you why afterwards.' He said, 'Well, when I was sailing, a sudden squall came, throwing the tiller suddenly around, and it struck me a bad blow in the mouth, under the upper lip, and it has been bleeding a good deal and won't stop.' I then said, 'Have you any idea what o'clock it was when it happened?' and he answered, 'It must have been about seven.' I then told what had happened to me, much to his surprise, and all who were with us at breakfast.

Crisis cases can be experienced as apparitions ('crisis apparitions') but again there is no reason to invoke ghosts or spirits. There have been cases where the individual seen in the apparition survived the crisis and others where the person died but the apparition was seen weeks or even months before their death. Many of these experiences hint at telepathy and yet, after decades of laboratory-based research, there is still a

Telepathy

fierce controversy over whether telepathy has been adequately demonstrated.

Attempts to establish telepathy scientifically have been dogged with problems. There must be physical barriers between the 'psychic' and the target information. Some barriers are more apparent than real. Alternatively, if the 'psychic' is really an accomplished fraud or stage magician, he may have many means at his disposal to breach quite elaborate barriers; or the experimenters may unconsciously aid the subject in providing sensory cues, such as body language and changes in the tone and inflection of the voice. Some 'mediums' routinely use such cues when they fish for information from clients. Even in well-controlled experiments with seemingly genuine psychics, the performance may rely on the degree of empathy of the psychics with the experimenters and whether they believe the experimenters are sceptical of their abilities. Some experimenters routinely get good results, while others have never been able to obtain results above chance-coincidence. All of this provides a fertile ground for the sceptics and critics of parapsychology. Even when impressive results are obtained in seemingly well-controlled experiments, the sceptic has the old standby objections of experimenter incompetence or fraudulent collusion with the 'psychic'.

These difficulties are really not surprising if telepathy depends upon an emotional link, and that link in turn depends on the emotional states of two people. But would the evidence be more convincing if the 'psychic' was a mentally and physically retarded child and the experimenters were sceptical doctors and psychologists; not parapsychologists?

One morning in the autumn of 1937, Raleigh M. Drake, Professor of Psychology at the Wesleyan College in Macon, Georgia, was sitting at his desk. In front of him was a letter from an old student asking for his help.

> In the Fall of 1937, I received a letter from a former student who asked if I might be able to help a boy who was having unusual difficulty in school, especially in reading. It was also timidly mentioned, no doubt, because the student knew of my scepticism regarding the topic, that the boy possessed the 'ability to read minds, having on numerous occasions been able to tell other people exactly what they were thinking, or what

they saw the day before . . . The child cannot read unless someone is at his side looking on his book. He reads well then but when left alone, he cannot read.' I expressed my willingness to examine the boy as to the cause of the reading disability and the cause of the supposed mind-reading ability, which I fully expected to be due to some minimal sensory cue.[3]

The child was called 'Bo' and he was eleven years old. During his delivery a forceps injury had caused extensive brain damage, resulting in profound mental and physical retardation. Even at eleven, Bo was unable to cope with first or second year school work. He could not copy simple drawings, repeat three sentences or a five-digit series of numbers. On two different IQ tests he scored 55 and 53 respectively. The injury had also left him partially crippled. Bo was unable to join in the games of other children. He could not run, roller-skate or ride a bicycle and negotiated stairs with difficulty. He suffered from muscular spasms and was hyperactive, with an extremely short concentration span. He was emotionally blunted and showed no distress on being parted from his mother during some of the experiments and was never seen to express joy or sorrow or to have any memory of such events.

Hoping to identify an unusual talent which might have formed the basis of a special educational programme, or at least explain the alleged instances of telepathy, Drake subjected Bo to a series of tests. These showed below average mechanical, mathematical and artistic abilities, a poor memory and normal sight and hearing.

The first ESP tests with Bo were not encouraging and simply exemplified the problems of performing any task with a hyperactive, sub-normal child. Instead of the mind-reading reported by Drake's former student, there was a lot of guessing at numbers and words as the mother encouraged her child with 'what's the next letter?', 'what's this word?' or 'what's the next number, Bo?' The first hint that there might be a telepathic link came when Drake pulled a textbook of psychology from the bookcase and placed it in front of Bo's mother. Astonishingly, the child repeated words from the pages of the open book, while he glanced distractedly around the room. Suppressing his excitement, Drake moved closer to the woman, whose eyes were firmly fixed on the unfamiliar words.

Telepathy

As he watched her face, he was convinced that there was not even a perceptible movement of her lips or the merest hint of a whisper.

On 12 October, 1937, Drake saw Bo and his mother a second time. Most of the period was spent administering tests and discussing Bo's education. The mother had withdrawn Bo from school in a desperate attempt to teach him herself. The child was demanding her total concentration but, with much coaxing and numerous threats, she was finding that he could be made to focus on the task in hand. At the end of the session, Drake quickly wrote down twelve numbers on a sheet of paper and handed it to the mother. Then, with a piece of paper held in front of his eyes, Bo was asked to guess the numbers one at a time. Bo only made three errors in the twelve numbers he called.

Trial number	Numbers on which the mother concentrated	Numbers called by the child
11.	12	9, 2, 3, 5, 12
12.	3	4, 6, 3
13.	5	1, 0, 2, 9, 2, 4, 5
14.	6	6
15.	7	7
16.	10	10
17.	5	11, 12, 12, 14, 9, 4, 5
18.	3	3

Drake was intent on moving to more formal, controlled experiments, which would produce the sort of results likely to be taken seriously by his scientific colleagues. On 5 January, 1938, the experiment was repeated with a series of eighteen numbers, of which Bo got six right at the first call. An illuminating event took place at the thirteenth number, five, which Bo only arrived at after seven attempts. Losing her temper, his mother told him that he was not concentrating and threatened to beat him if he did not do better. After Bo called 'four' which was wrong, his mother took a small stick and hit him hard enough to frighten him. He immediately called 'five' which was correct and thereafter produced four correct calls on the first attempt.

Professor Drake began to use ESP or 'Zener' cards on 5 January, 1938. The Zener deck was developed at Duke University by J. B. Rhine, the father of experimental parapsychology. The pictures on the cards represent universal symbols (star, square, circle, cross and wavy lines) which were considered to be more friendly and accessible than a long series of confusing letters or numbers. Each of the five suits contains five cards giving a total of 25 cards in a deck. At each call, the subject has a 1 in 25 chance of guessing the correct card. On the basis of chance, a subject should manage five correct guesses in a run of twenty-five cards.

While researching this chapter, I decided to familiarise myself with ESP cards and their use. On a wet Saturday afternoon, my wife acted as a sender, while I sat in another room recording my guesses. After a number of trials (25-card runs), my average score was just below five. The highest score attained on any of the runs was seven. All of which conformed to the iron laws of probability theory.

With Dr Bruce from the university mathematics department assisting, Drake embarked on a trial run before Bo had seen any of the pictures on the cards. The first card pulled by the mother was a star and Bo immediately called 'star'. The second card was a cross and after much hesitation the child asked 'What card mother?' Finally, the mother asked him to spell the word for the picture and with much coaxing Bo managed 'c-r-o-s'.

It became clear to the experimenters that a lot of time would need to be spent familiarising Bo with the symbols on the cards. To this end, the child spent a weekend with the Drake household. During these two days, Drake's wife and two children attempted to act as 'sender' but were unsuccessful. Most of the time the child rode around the house on his tricycle, shooting imaginary robbers. When it was occasionally suggested that he should try to guess the cards, he told them to 'shut up'. He did, however, become conversant with the symbols, giving them his own names. Drake's hard work was about to pay dividends.

Telepathy

On 30 January between much 'crying, fussing, rebelling, fidgeting and counter-talk', ninety calls were successfully completed. With his mother acting as 'sender', Bo correctly identified sixty-six cards, or an average of eighteen in a 25-card run. On 1 February, Drake conducted another experiment in the child's home. Using 'bribery, threats or just catching him in the right mood', they managed to get 595 calls of which 373 were correct. On average, Bo had correctly identified sixteen cards in a 25-card run.

Drake decided that the time had come to tighten the experimental conditions to exclude the possibility of the mother consciously or unconsciously providing verbal cues to the cards or, indeed, the unlikely possibility that mother and son were using a subtle code.

From 13 February, Bo was blindfolded and placed across the room with his back to his mother. Various signals were tried to indicate the next card but Bo's score fell back to that expected by chance. It was clear that the child required the verbal cue from his mother. With warning, Bo's mother was confronted with four words which were to be used to signal the card. These were 'ready', 'and', 'go' and 'all right'. One of these would be used in each run and would form the only cue provided by the mother. In addition, the child was no longer told if he was right or wrong in his calls and he was to be given only one chance to identify the card.

The two experimenters now felt that they were testing Bo's ability under conditions which would exclude any possibility other than telepathy. With one experimenter watching the child and the mother and the other recording the cards pulled and the child's calls, the experiment began. The silence in the room was broken only by the signal 'ready' and the child's calls.

Out of the twenty-seven runs, each of twenty-five cards, there were 373 correct calls or an average of fourteen correct calls per run. On 6 March, 1938, Professor Drake happily parted with the dollar bill which he had promised Bo for the first run of twenty-five which was perfect. Out of a total of 675 cards, the child had called 567 correctly giving an average of twenty-one correct cards per run.

In late March the experiments were modified to exclude any verbal contact between mother and child. The ready signal was provided by a toy cricket. Despite the lack of verbal contact, and the 'lack of attention-getting value in the cricket', Bo continued to obtain average scores of ten correct calls per run.

In the laboratory, the abilities of 'psychics' tend to peak and then decline. Bo was no exception and by May his score had fallen to that expected by chance. Sceptics point to this decline and argue that, as the experimental conditions are tightened, so the subject's 'powers' decline; the inference being that the subjects receive their information through the normal avenues of the senses or by fraud. But Bo's scores declined long after he had been tested under the most stringent conditions. Drake admitted that it was conceivable that the mother was employing a secret code, using different inflections on words to indicate different cards. But as there were four ready words and five suits of cards, the code would have required at least twenty covert signals. In discussing the results Drake drew attention to the weakness in this argument,

> When it is recalled that the percipient cannot even do first and second grade work in school, that he cannot spell words more complex than 'boy', 'car', or 'house', that he has an I.Q. of about 55, that he has no special memorial or other mental or skilled ability, or that he can only with difficulty draw simple figures as squares or crosses, it will be seen how gratuitous it is to impute him with the ability to learn numerous sets of five auditory inflections with the corresponding ESP symbol for each.

The story of Bo might have remained a curiosity were it not for reports of a very similar case which were reaching the scientific community. In 1935 a small book had been published in Latvia by Professor F. von Neureiter, the well-known Director of the Institute of Forensic Medicine at Riga University. The book, written in German and bearing the rather starched title *Immediate Knowledge of Alien Thought Contents Acquired In An Unknown Manner*, detailed von Neureiter's work with a ten-year-old Latvian peasant girl, Ilga K.

Telepathy

Like Professor Drake, the pathologist had been contacted by a third party, a medical practitioner, Dr F. Kleinberger, who was convinced that Ilga could 'read minds'.[4]

At eleven years of age, Ilga had the mental age of a four-year-old. She had difficulty reading and writing and even the most basic arithmetic was beyond her comprehension. Like Bo, the initial consultations were disappointing; Ilga cried bitterly and seemed afraid of the members of staff who crowded into the professor's room hoping to see a miracle. It took many sessions, some at Ilga's home village, to gain the child's confidence but by then von Neureiter and his colleagues were in no doubt that they were dealing with telepathy. What happened subsequently was reported in the investigator's published notes.

In Test 9, one of the investigators, Professor Bruckmann, handed Ilga's mother this calculation on a sheet of paper:

$$4.4 + 5.5$$

After glancing at the paper for several seconds, the woman turned to von Neureiter and complained that she did not understand the task. The professor was explaining that the dots were multiplication signs ($4\times4 + 5\times5 = 41$), when the child suddenly exclaimed 'Forty-one'. The experimenters concluded that the mother was just considering the results of the calculation when the 'transmission' took place.

In another test, the mother was seated behind a curtain while her child played on the floor around the professor's desk. Professor Amsler handed the woman a list of words and figures:

$$\begin{array}{ccc} \text{ger} & \text{til} & \text{tli} \\ 123, & 213, & 312 \end{array}$$

Without being asked to do so, and without interrupting her play, the child reproduced the entire list without a single mistake.

In Test 38, von Neureiter took the mother's place and attempted to 'send' to Ilga the figures '9' and '2' and then the first line of a poem *Mate gaja uz kleti* taken from a Lithuanian school book. The child was in an adjoining room.

I concentrate with exertion upon my task, sharply accentuating every syllable in thought . . . yet in spite of all my efforts the percipient remains silent. I am just about to close the book discontentedly and to break up the experiment when my look [attention] is caught by the word *Brute* (bride) in the context of the Lithuanian poem, the first words of which I was trying in vain to transmit. And at that very moment the child, situated in an adjoining room, uttered the word. Thus this was the way by which the reception happened to work perfectly – or better because – I refrained from volitional sending.

When von Neureiter saw the word *Brute* he began to wonder why this obsolete word of German extraction had been used in a modern Lithuanian children's book, 'I did not in any case, think any longer of my original task.' The investigators concluded that the mother was the best sender but not the only person who could seemingly pass information to Ilga. Her brother Victor also proved a good agent in experiments. The best results were obtained when both the child and the agent were relaxed and content.

Another experiment seemed to indicate that Ilga had no powers of clairvoyance. While Ilga and her mother were in an adjoining room, Dr Kleinberger hid his watch under one of the cushions. The mother was then brought into the room and informed of the task. Immediately Ilga burst into the room shouting 'The watch is under the cushion!' However, Ilga was unable to say which cushion the watch was under and the child only found it after a lot of searching. The most striking of Ilga's 'talents' was her ability to read any book in any language provided that it was seen simultaneously by her mother.

> She managed to read any test offered to her mother, be it in Lithuanian, German, French, English or Latin. The mistakes she committed corresponded in every respect with those appropriate to her mother's degree of education. For instance, she spelled numbers she came across in the French context in Lithuanian language, she pronounced French words phonetically in the Lithuanian way.

Ilga had an IQ of 42 and a mental age of three to four. Left to her own devices, she was totally incapable of learning to read more than a few meaningless letters.

Telepathy

Reports of Ilga's abilities soon spread throughout the Baltic Republics and Germany where they caused a sensation. Most of the public and scientific response was favourable to the idea of telepathy. One professional sceptic and stage magician, who devoted his time to debunking the paranormal, wrote to Professor Hans Bender, 'Here we have proofs as they ought to be given.' But very soon all of this was to change. The Latvian Ministry of Education established a committee to investigate the purported telepathic transmissions. The investigators were all established authorities in the fields of psychological medicine, physics and phonetics. On 5 June, 1937, they published a report which concluded that Ilga's ability to receive information was not based on telepathy but on acoustical and visual signals provided by her mother. What had gone so wrong that two teams of highly esteemed experts could draw such very different conclusions?

Two factors complicated the issue. Professor von Neureiter had omitted from his report all the problems associated with working with a mentally handicapped child. Ilga expected little presents as rewards for her part in the experiments and could become very moody if the routine was suddenly changed. In fact, von Neureiter had all the problems described by Drake in his work with Bo but had decided that such banalities had no place in a scientific report. He was also very credulous and was happy to label what he saw as 'telepathy' without exploring the 'super-normal' explanations.

The other factor was one which nearly always complicates parapsychological investigations, namely that, despite all scientific controls and reliable instrumentation, the object of study is a human being. Professor Drake had experienced enormous difficulties in preventing Bo's mother from encouraging her child and in Ilga's case the problem was magnified as her mother was rather excitable and could not be prevented from mouthing and even uttering the words she was trying to transmit.

A third investigation was conducted in July 1936, by a team from the Psychological Institute of Bonn University, which included the now famous German parapsychologist, Professor Hans Bender. Their aim was to study the nature of the sensory cues and determine whether all the results could be ascribed to acoustic aids.

The Germans' initial experiments centred on Ilga's performance in a soundproof booth at the Riga broadcasting station. When isolated from her mother, Ilga became very anxious and no telepathic transmissions took place. Reasoning that the mother's encouragement might be necessary for the child to demonstrate telepathy, the psychologists rigged a loudspeaker system between Ilga and her mother and the experimenters outside the booth. The recordings from these experiments tended to confirm the Latvian commission's observations that Ilga's mother was providing more than encouragement and would often pronounce the first syllable of the target word. For example, when asked to transmit the word 'kupite' the mother was heard to say 'Nu saki (now say) nu'*k*.' Sometimes the mother would also silently pronounce the target word as if willing her child to repeat it. The psychologists then devised a most ingenious ploy. A loudspeaker system connecting the mother with her child in the soundproof booth allowed the usual encouragement but, at the very moment the mother was allowed to see the target word, the link was disconnected and a recorded female voice or 'artificial mother' continued giving encouragement. The ploy fooled Ilga but no telepathic transmission was observed.

There was no doubt that on some, perhaps many, occasions, the mother was providing auditory clues but this left the problem that on other occasions these cues were not in evidence. This was demonstrated by a particularly revealing experiment conducted in Ilga's home. With mother and daughter sitting back to back at a distance of approximately nine feet, the mother attempted to 'send' a series of target words under three types of conditions. Hans Bender provided the transcript of one attempt. The target word was 'Dumi'.

All the trials in this series of experiments had the same outcome. The child simply did not respond to just audible whisperings and word-transmission was never obtained in this way.

Controls on Mother	**Ilga's utterances**
1. Mother's lips tightly closed and closely watched by experimenter.	'I can't hear at all what mother's thinking.'
2. Mother just audibly and repeatedly whispers target word.	'You hoot like an owl. [Prompted by experimenter] No I can hear but I can't understand the word.'
3. Mother only offers usual encouragement (Now say it, think it over, etc.).	'du-bi ... du-bit ... du-mi'.

Another observation which prevented the Germans from totally excluding telepathy was Ilga's use of synonyms. When her mother was presented with a picture showing a dog with puppies, the child said 'kucens' (puppy) but the mother maintained that she was trying to send 'Suns' (dog). When the target was 'bumbina zala' (a green marble), the child repeated 'lo-ti-da', the Latvian synonym for marble. In other experiments it seemed impossible that the child could have even heard her mother's encouragement.

In an experiment made from one room into the other the child made such a noise with a pail (which unfortunately had been given to her as a reward) that the governess could hardly understand the encouragements of the mother. Nevertheless the number 333, which repeated as usual with 'tris-tris-tris' was successfully transmitted.

The German team recorded an open verdict on Ilga's ability to receive telepathic transmissions from her mother.

Hans Bender also made a careful perusal of the Latvian commission's report in order to obtain more conclusive evidence. Some of the experiments were designed by an expert in phonetics and the Director of a Deaf-and-Dumb Institute. The mother was placed in the soundproof chamber at the

Riga radio station. Although he could not hear her, as the mother began to 'transmit' her target words, the dumb-mute expert was able to read from her lips every word which was to be transmitted. But as Bender rightly argued, many of the commission's experiments were designed to avoid visual signals or lip-reading – if indeed, the child could lip-read!

In other instances, Ilga appeared to repeat correctly very complex sentences with minimal help from her mother. At the end of the series of experiments, which were recorded on disk, the phonetic expert concluded

> . . . after every word of encouragement there follows on the part of the mother the opening sound of the next syllable for example t'd, t'm, etc. The fact that the girl repeats not a whole word but separate sounds or syllables of the word proves the girl listens attentively.

And yet, as Bender demonstrated, this vitally important evidence was *not* present on the transcripts made from the recordings. All that appeared on the transcripts was the mother's usual encouragements.

Some of Ilga's remarkable ability could be ascribed to auditory clues provided by her mother, but Bender concluded that the commission had erred on the side of the scientific explanation to much the same degree that Professor von Neureiter had been prepared to invoke telepathy,

> This underestimation of these important cases seems to me to be the result of a tendency towards a rationalization and generalization, which, seeking to satisfy the requirements of a full explanation *according to one principle*, naturally sees only one side of a complex phenomenon.

To emphasise this point, Bender referred to those experiments where the Latvian commission had used an 'artificial mother'. Dr Kleinberger, who had initially brought Ilga to the attention of von Neureiter, was present at these experiments and was now convinced that he was seeing a purely scientific phenomenon based on auditory cues provided by the mother. The woman was asked to 'send' a long series of words during which her voice was recorded on disks. What happened next was related by Dr Kleinberger in a letter,

Telepathy

> ... when these were played it became positively evident that the opening sound expected by all of us could *not* be heard. And now Ilga was placed in front of these records and told she would now hear her mother from a loudspeaker. It was then that the most amazing thing happened.

With the mother attempting to send the series of words, the child could only hear her mother's recorded encouragements.

> Ilga now, actually reproduced quite a number of words or only syllables in a striking way and did this in places on the record at which *absolutely* nothing could be heard besides the encouragements of the mother; so there was no opening sounds.

After the experiments, the physician had the records amplified and played back. The mother's voice was so loud as to be distorted and still the first syllables of the target words could not be heard.

> Now *this* was actually the situation which impressed me most of all, namely that Ilga – if all this is correct – is capable of 'hearing' something which I with my normal sound auditory sense could *not* hear even with the highest degree of amplification.

Dr Kleinberger and many other members of the commission decided that instances such as the above were due to auditory clues which could not be heard by the normal ear. But if the cues which the mother was said to provide could not be detected, is it possible, Bender enquired, to exclude telepathy totally?

While the experts continued to debate the case of Ilga K, a far more impressive case was emerging in England. This child's performance would overcome many of the objections raised in the case of Ilga and seemingly allay any lingering doubts about Drake's experiments with Bo by apparently demonstrating telepathy over seven miles of telephone cable. And if fraud or some verbal code were to be invoked, it can only be said that an almost blind, mentally and physically retarded boy was able not only to outwit some of the best scientific minds in Britain but to fool totally members of the Magic Circle.

For reasons of confidentiality, even today the child is still referred to as the 'Cambridge Boy'.[5] For convenience we shall call him 'John'. John was born in 1938, blind, with a poorly co-ordinated body and mental retardation. The medical diagnosis was Spastic Diplegia with congenital cataracts. When the boy was nine months old, the consultant ophthalmologist, Dr E. G. Recordon, operated on his eyes and was able to restore part of the vision in his right eye. With tremendous support from his doctors, John learned to walk with callipers and his speech improved, but much of the success was due to the efforts of his mother. In their paper, the investigators remarked, 'In every respect the mother was emotionally involved in trying to help her backward son. There was no relation of this kind with the father; it was the mother who always practised with her son.'

It was during a later consultation with John and his mother that Dr Recordon noticed something rather odd. John's sight was still extremely poor and he still had great difficulty in reading the letters on the visual acuity charts and yet occasionally he appeared to be able to 'guess' the letters with uncanny accuracy. It soon became clear to Recordon that the boy could only read the charts when his mother was in the room. It gradually began to dawn on the ophthalmologist that he might be witnessing telepathy and he brought this to the attention of Sir Rudolph Peters and his colleagues, Professor F. J. M. Stratton and Sir Bryan Matthews, at Cambridge University.

The initial tests in the boy's home were very encouraging. John and his mother were separated by a screen, although it was clear from the way the boy moved his head, that he could not see well. Nevertheless, John's ability to 'guess' numbers and letters exceeded anything which might have occurred by chance.

The last seven experiments were conducted over the telephone with his mother's voice and John's replies recorded on tape. On 18 December, 1957, during one of these sessions, the mother sat with investigators at the Animal Research Centre Institute at Babraham, Cambridge and telephoned her son at home, a distance of some seven miles. John's mother

Telepathy

responded to the boy's calls with 'right' or 'no' and John was allowed to call until he had guessed the correct letter or number. This breach of the usual protocols for telepathy experiments was a concession to John's ability to cope with the task and reflected the way his mother had taught him letters and figures.

The first trial used a group of twenty-five letters, followed by sixty numbers and a second group of twenty-five letters. Both letters and figures were compiled at random and pasted on to the backs of cards which were shuffled and presented to the mother in reverse order. The numbers were drawn from 1 to 10 and at each call there was a 1 in 10 probability of guessing the number by chance. The probability of guessing a correct letter drawn from the alphabet was 1 in 26. For brevity, only the results of the second group of letters are presented here.

Given	Guessed	Given	Guessed	Given	Guessed
A	O,A	T	T	B	B
H	A,H	U	G,U	J	G,U,J
W	C,W	N	N	D	G,U,H,J,S,G,D
O	O	W	T,B,W	B	B
Discarded		X	E,N,X	R	I,R
C	C	Discarded		D	G,U,C,K,Q,B,D
A	A	Discarded		I	I
Z	T,G,U,Z	H	I,H		
R	O,I,R	N	N		

John responded quickly and the entire experiment lasted only seventeen minutes. When the results were analysed it was found that he had correctly identified almost a quarter of the target information on his first attempt. On his second and third attempts, he correctly identified 26.7 per cent and 20.0 per cent respectively. Separated from his mother and the target information by seven miles, John on his first three guesses correctly identified the targets with an accuracy of 84.5 per cent. This wildly exceeded anything which should have occurred by chance. Furthermore, the boy's score was remarkably consistent over the seven experiments conducted by telephone. The investigators believed that they were faced with only two possibilities: either they had witnessed a genuine case of telepathy or the boy and his mother had used some kind of verbal code.

One of the constant criticisms raised by sceptics against these sorts of experiments is that the subject can employ a code so subtle that it can only be detected by an accomplished magician. With this possibility in mind, the tapes from the experiments were passed to Dr Ian Fletcher, an accomplished stage magician and a member of the Magic Circle. Fletcher's analysis of the tapes later formed the basis of a short report,

> Having listened, very carefully, to some tape recordings made by this boy and his mother, during telepathic tests arranged by Sir Rudolph Peters *et al*. I have not been able to detect any code. Two fellow members of the Magic Circle also listened to one of the tapes with me and we felt reasonably convinced that no auditory code was being used. ... He gives a very quick call in response to the cue to make his guess and a considerable amount of mental training would be necessary to give an immediate 'guess' by using an auditory code. Without giving away known stage methods some indication of the target could be conveyed by the agent by voice inflection and pauses etc. We listened for all of this and failed to discover its use.

Children like John, Bo and Ilga, although uncommon, may not be as rare as we might at first expect. There is another case on record. In 1894, a group of French physicians headed by Dr Quintard described a seven-year-old boy who could solve complex sums but only when they were calculated by his mother. Like the other three cases, the French child only came to the attention of science because a physician or psychologist not only spotted the child's unusual behaviour but was sufficiently open-minded to consider telepathy. Although Ehrenwald himself admitted that deaf and dumb and blind children had not provided the expected 'bonanza' for parapsychology, it is not clear how many experiments have been conducted with severely handicapped children and their mothers.

Telepathy

In disadvantaged children, telepathy can be rationalised as a form of compensation for their handicaps. What role might it play in normal child development? The child psychiatrist, Joan FitzHerbert, argued that it might act as an additional form of communication between mother and child. Dependent, helpless and without language, the infant is nevertheless connected into the very core of his mother, sharing thoughts and memories, which are experienced in a non-verbal way.

FitzHerbert believed that the telepathy hypothesis solved a number of puzzling problems in child psychiatry. She saw adopted children, whom she was convinced could not have known of their adoption by normal means, who began to express hostility as part of their rejection of their adoptive mothers. They seemed to 'know' that their adoptive parents were not their real parents. She treated many children from orphanages who appeared to have innate knowledge of sexuality and reproductive organs and who had fantasies of watching sexual intercourse. Today, such accounts would automatically trigger accusations of child abuse but FitzHerbert believed that in some cases these 'memories' were acquired telepathically from a mother-figure on the institution's staff.

Patients in therapy have related memories which took place before their birth or even conception. Some have even thought themselves to be their own mothers and described their birth not in terms of the child but from the perspective of the mother in labour. Then, there are the frank instances of 'telepathy' which have been reported between patient and therapist. Of course, very different explanations can be found for all of these experiences but, within the context of Ehrenwald's hypothesis, they all appear to provide missing pieces of the jigsaw.

All the psychiatrists and psychoanalysts who shared Ehrenwald's ideas agreed on one point. In adult life, a constant stream of information from another mind would be lethal. Ehrenwald cited the well-known illustration of the 'embarrassment of a deer' which had to rely on ESP to detect the presence of a tiger,

> It would be unable to decide whether this danger referred to

a tiger in the vicinity now, to one a hundred and fifty miles away, to one that would be there tomorrow. And to this we have to add that if it were a deer conversant with the subtleties of Freudian symbolism it could not even be sure whether the animal was a tiger at all and not the veiled intimation of sexual aggression.

Ehrenwald believed that a 'screen' develops to filter out telepathic impressions as the child becomes independent of his mother. After that, all that we experience is 'telepathic leakage', most of which is repressed. Joan FitzHerbert argued that this is why we have difficulty in remembering our earliest memories of infancy. Without so-called 'infantile amnesia' we would not be able to sort out which memories were our own and which were derived from our mother. This, she believed, would lead to confusion and psychological disturbance. Those unfortunates who suffered from that enigmatic disorder, schizophrenia, were thought by Ehrenwald to have been unable to construct the screen and he recorded a number of seemingly telepathic encounters with his schizophrenic patients.

These ideas also provide an explanation for the numerous reported instances of 'telepathy of the dying' and crisis apparitions. Close to death, or in mortal fear, the unconscious, no longer repressed, might send out a 'telepathic SOS'. How this is received depends on the state of the recipient's mind. In many individuals who are bound by an emotional link to the person in crisis, the telepathic telegram is simply repressed. They feel, hear and see nothing. In others, the information is repressed but they encounter it later in their dreams or by way of a vague feeling that something has happened to that person. In contrast, if the recipient is in a relaxed state of mind or other factors are satisfied, the message is organised in such a way that it cannot be ignored and is projected into the mind's eye as a vision or appears out there in the 'real world' as a ghostly figure or apparition. It is worth noting that the woman, the mother and the wife feature strongly in these reported experiences.

Much of the success of scientists' attempts to establish the reality of mind-to-mind correspondence seems to depend on this 'telepathic leakage'. Some of the best results have been obtained while the subject was in an altered state of consciousness which might by-pass the screen or allow access to repressed information.

Telepathy has been reported in dreams, both spontaneously and in the laboratory. It has allegedly been demonstrated in subjects under hypnosis or under conditions of sensory deprivation, such as those employed in the Ganzfeld procedure where the eyes are covered by half table-tennis balls and the subject is exposed to white noise. The psychologists, R. E. L. Masters and Jean Houston, although highly sceptical of parapsychology, obtained some striking results when subjects were asked to describe target pictures while under the influence of the drug LSD (d-lysergic acid diethylamide). Gifted subjects in normal states of consciousness have seemingly demonstrated telepathy or precognition over long periods of time. Paval Stepanek delighted parapsychologists for more than ten years by identifying hidden test materials with a frequency well above that which might be obtained by chance.

Nevertheless, all of the experimental situations have been flawed by problems with reproducibility and the difficulties in designing experiments which take account of the human factors, while excluding *every* possibility of the subject learning of the target information by normal means. However, it might also be argued that, if laboratory experiments do depend on 'telepathic leakage', it is not surprising that there are problems with reproducibility or that a whole range of emotional and personal factors need to be satisfied before the phenomenon is demonstrated under artificial conditions.[6]

Summary of the Evidence

It would be difficult to sustain the allegation that any of the three retarded children, Bo, Ilga and John, were accomplished stage magicians or frauds. The prosecution would argue that the fault lies with the investigators. The children did compensate for their disabilities but this took the form of 'super-sensory' cues derived from the tone and inflections of their mothers' voices. What was mainly true in the case of Ilga

K, was true for all. None of the three children were able to perform under the conditions which would be required for modern ESP experiments. Two required multiple guesses, which increased the probability that they would arrive at the target information purely by chance and, for the most part, Ilga's experiments were not even structured. When faced with the Latvian commission's controlled experiments, the 'telepathy' element simply disappeared.

Other results appear extraordinary but it is not beyond the bounds of probability that a child should guess twenty cards out of twenty-five. It is a rare event, but not one forbidden by the laws of probability. Like the spontaneous cases of 'telepathy', it is merely a coincidence which is later assigned a special meaning or importance.

The so-called medical evidence for telepathy is little more than supposition and conjecture, providing a 'magical' explanation for events which have other plausible explanations. Psychiatrists and psychoanalysts are prone to 'magical' theories to account for the behaviour and utterances of their patients. If telepathy is a reality, why is it not more common? Should not all dreams have a telepathic content? The cases of these three children only go to show that eminent psychologists and scientists are as capable of self-delusion as their colleagues in parapsychology.

In arguing the case for telepathy, the defence would ask the reader whether it is probable that John and his mother were using a code over the telephone. Again, how many sensory cues can be provided by the words 'no' and 'ready'? John was faced with guessing any one of ten numbers or twenty-six letters.

Might the reader not find it a little strange that the three recorded cases all feature a severely handicapped child. Not blind, deaf, crippled, or emotionally disturbed children but three very similar disadvantaged youngsters. Ehrenwald's hypothesis *is* based on anecdote, supposition and conjecture but it does seem to hang together. It predicts that we should see apparent instances of telepathy between parents and their young children. It predicts that children who remain dependent upon their mothers may maintain the telepathic link as compensation for their disabilities. It predicts that the surrogate mother-child relationship of patient and therapist should also give rise to telepathic exchanges. Two of the founding fathers of psychoanalysis, Freud and Jung, both related such encounters. Telepathy also explains phantasms of the living: dreams, visions and apparitions which coincide with crises. Finally, we also have an explanation as to why women are so often the participants in these experiences.

Indeed, Ehrenwald's hypothesis is just a bundle of interlocking conjectures but, as Professor Drake remarked at the end of his paper, '. . . no better hypothesis seems to be available and, until it is, some hypothesis is more desirable than no explanation at all.'

3

Psychokinesis and Poltergeists

Prosecution's claim is that human psychokinesis and poltergeist phenomena are trickery and the powerful delusion that events are occurring without any rational cause.

In 1951 a most unusual book, entitled *On the Search of the Unknown Man*, was published.[1] Written by a French police officer, Emile Tizane, it detailed the results of hundreds of investigations conducted by the French police into strange domestic disturbances between 1925 and 1950. Disturbances which could most easily be explained by the presence of a prankster – the 'Unknown Man' – an individual who always remained invisible and elusive. The police files recorded instances of houses being bombarded by stones; bangings and rappings against doors, walls and furniture; locked doors and windows opening by themselves; objects jumping off shelves or seemingly moving by their own volition; other objects passing through physical barriers such as ceilings and walls or passing in and out of locked cupboards; and, wonders of wonders, even objects which seemed to materialise out of thin air!

Stranger still, this discrete pattern of bizarre events has been reported for centuries.[2] The classical historian, Livy, reported numerous showers of stones during the Second Punic War (218 BC to 201 BC) which were interpreted as dire omens by the Romans. Jewish scholars and the early church fathers reported that similar strange events were associated with cases of possession.[3] The Jewish exorcist, Eleazar, would command the demon to upset a bowl of water as proof that the spirit had really been driven from the possessed's body. This association with the devil was confirmed by ecclesiastical writers such as the Jesuit, Martin Del Rio, who distinguished

Psychokinesis and Poltergeists

between different types of diabolical interference with humans in his *Disquisitionum Magicarum*, (1559).

Even today, these associations with the occult persist. In Latin American countries, possession and associated poltergeist activity are still identified with a demonic imp: 'El Duende'. Even the term frequently employed by the parapsychologist – 'poltergeist' – is an old German word which means 'noisy spirit'. There are still scholarly discussions as to whether some poltergeists have centred on living people or are spirit entities.[4] The truly amazing fact is that, when one considers certain cases, the evidence can be interpreted either way. However, most academic parapsychologists hold that poltergeist cases centre on living people, often disturbed adolescents, who bring about these miracles by Recurrent Spontaneous Psychokinesis (RSPK), a spontaneous and uncontrolled form of the same human force which, in the laboratory, may determine the roll of a dice or the ability to move objects at a distance.

But let us start at the beginning. Why should we even elevate this subject by lending credence to reports of any of these phenomena? Laboratory demonstrations of psychokinesis are subject to the same time-honoured objections which are raised against demonstrations of ESP. In poltergeist cases it is well established that the phenomenon appears 'shy' in that objects rarely move while watched by investigators. Surely, the explanation lies with man's propensity for fraud and self-delusion.

On a bright summer's morning I was given the opportunity to interview a man who has witnessed not one, but two miracles.[5] As a young post-doctoral chemist, Barrie Colvin decided that any scientific analysis of paranormal phenomena would require a guaranteed source of funds and life-long commitment. To this end, he established a chemical firm which today funds his research at a level well above that which even a researcher in the classical sciences might expect from a scientific research council.

Like so many other young scientists who became interested in parapsychology, Barrie Colvin's early investigations revealed little or no evidence of the paranormal. He first became fascinated by physical mediumship and, working quietly over a number of years, he exposed several famous mediums as frauds. On one notable occasion, Colvin, his hands secretly coated in blue dye, was invited to shake hands with a 'spirit' conjured by a medium at a seance. Later, pandemonium reigned when the lights were turned on and a very angry medium emerged from his booth, with his hands, props and clothes stained blue. Barrie's next recollection was that of picking himself up from the pavement outside the hall. But there were cases that he could not explain; like the Dutch medium who not only identified the reservoir in England where a murdered child's body had been dumped, but accurately described the surrounding countryside, down to inconsequential descriptions of local houses and their occupants.

Later he turned to poltergeist cases which represent some of the most numerous and accessible spontaneous phenomena. Extremely sceptical and cautious by nature, Colvin gathered around him a group of like-minded professional scientists who formed themselves into the Poltergeist Research Institute. Currently, the Institute is attempting to detect and measure energy fields, which may be associated with poltergeist disturbances, using a wide-band thermal camera. While still sceptical of reports of objects passing through barriers or materialising out of thin air, he is convinced that some events defy rational explanation. Investigating a case in the south of England, where rappings centred around a young girl, Colvin is convinced that he was treated to a dramatic example of spontaneous psychokinesis.

Colvin: What normally happened was, you could not get any rapping sounds if the young girl was not present. You got very good rapping sounds if the mother and the daughter, together, were present in the room ... later we got the rapping sounds to move away from the wall to other parts of the bedroom. Including, [picking up an exercise book] on this book as I held it and that was the most remarkable thing that ever happened. Those rapping sounds on this book.

Author: That is a most extraordinary observation because

> when I asked — — [another investigator] if he had really seen, without any doubt, an object move, that he knew was stationary and nowhere near a human being, he said 'no'.

Colvin: Well I actually have another case going back quite some years, where I did experience that ... There was a poltergeist case in Leeds where I was involved with this Peter — — [co-investigator] and one of the things that was happening was that eggs were being thrown against a wall and then smashing and running down the wall. Peter and I stood there talking with somebody else, so there were only three of us in the room and eggs would appear and be smashed against the wall. *And on several occasions, not just once but on three or four occasions, we saw it happen in front of our eyes.* And what was interesting was that it was typical of what other people have described, because Roll [a famous American parapsychologist] has described this thing. It doesn't take the normal trajectory, it is as though an invisible person is holding it there, because it was relatively slow and it was going in a straight line.

There have, of course, been cases of fraud. More importantly, seemingly genuine cases, like the Newark poltergeist investigated by W. G. Roll have later become tainted with fraud. Subjects associated with these disturbances, particularly children, may later resort to fraud to retain the expert's attention. However, cases of fraud are insignificant compared with the number of reported poltergeists which turn out to have a normal explanation.[6]

One very experienced investigator was asked to examine an alleged case of 'teleapportation' or objects literally moving through walls or physical barriers. The subject of these disturbances, an elderly lady, told him that the spirits played games with her. A large cactus growing in a pot on her windowsill would disappear for days, only to turn up later in its usual place. This always occurred at night, after the lady closed the curtains before retiring to bed. When the researcher reconstructed the events, he found that the cactus

The Sceptical Occultist

spines became entangled in the curtains as they moved in the draught from the open window. In the morning, when the curtains were drawn back, an accidental 'conjuring trick' ensured that the plant disappeared into the folds of the material. Later, the cactus would simply fall back on to the windowsill.

A more striking case concerned a widow who told an SPR investigator that her dead husband communicated with her by switching a bedside light on and off. The two retired to her bedroom and the light was switched off. After several minutes standing in the dark, the lady asked her husband to turn the light back on. To the investigator's very great surprise, the light came on and then extinguished itself again, apparently at the woman's command. All was revealed when the lamp was dismantled. It contained a heat-sensitive switch which responded to the warming and cooling of the light bulb. Wanting to believe that her husband was still with her, the good lady simply learnt to time her requests to the switch's delay.

Such stories are legion. In another case, a family was terrified by a rhythmic pounding which came from inside the walls of their house. Before considering the possibility of a poltergeist, the investigator looked for a purely physical cause. After noticing that the noise became louder when water was drawn from the taps, the parapsychologist was able to demonstrate, to the family's considerable relief, that the 'ghost' was a simple 'water-hammer' caused by an air-lock in the pipes. Another deserted property earned itself the title of 'the haunted house' after strange lights were seen in the rooms after dark. A cursory search quickly led to the arrest of an escaped convict.

One of the most unusual cases of this type concerned a terraced house in a northern English city. The wife was extremely frightened of the 'ghost' which appeared to haunt the house at night after her husband had left for his night-shift at a local factory. It was never seen but would open and close the living-room door, before walking across the room to open and close the kitchen door. Lying in bed, the woman was driven into a state of terror by the sound of the doors opening and closing downstairs.

The couple's account appeared to have a ring of truth as

Psychokinesis and Poltergeists

many hauntings are complicated by poltergeist activity. So with the terrified woman in bed, an investigator began his lonely vigil. Some time in the early hours of the morning, he awoke to the living-room door opening and closing. Nothing seemed to pass him as he sat in the darkness, but very soon the kitchen door opened and closed. In the morning, he examined the door hinges and made a study of the air currents in the house. The design of the house was such that gusts of air coming from outside created currents and eddies which were responsible for the two doors opening and closing. This apparent scientific rationalisation failed to convince the couple until the investigator demonstrated that the same thing occurred in several other houses in the street.

Other disturbances are not so easily rationalised. In the autumn of 1967, a series of strange events began to occur in a lawyer's office in Rosenheim, Germany.[7] Neon lights in the offices inexplicably went out. When examined, it was found that the tubes had become unscrewed from their sockets. Developing fluid in the photocopier leaked on to the floor. Electric light bulbs exploded, automatic fuses were blown and sharp raps came from the office walls. The final straw came when the lawyer received an astronomical bill from the telephone company. The local exchange had recorded hundreds of calls, many of which were itemised to 0119 – the number for the German 'speaking clock'. With the exception of the lawyer's own extension, the office telephones were disconnected, but still the phantom calls continued. An electrical fault was suspected so maintenance technicians connected a sophisticated line-recorder to the office's power-supply. At first, the technicians' suspicions seemed to be confirmed, the monitoring equipment recorded massive electrical fluctuations at the same time as other phenomena were reported. But when the power lines were disconnected and the office was linked to an emergency power unit which supplied a controlled current, the measuring instruments still recorded deflections and the rest of the phenomena continued unabated.

In November, a team from the Freiburg Institute for

Border Areas of Psychology, headed by Professor Hans Bender, were summoned to Rosenheim. Bender suspected a poltergeist case. Two physicists with the team, Dr F. Karger and Dr G. Zicha, set up equipment to control the power supply and began to eliminate normal explanations such as electrostatic charging, external magnetic fields, loose contacts and infrasonic and ultrasonic waves from vibrations within the structure of the building. They also carefully sealed their recorders and watched for any attempt to interfere with the equipment. The single telephone was also watched constantly by reliable witnesses but there was no evidence of fraud. Still the disturbances continued and the physicists were forced to conclude that no normal explanation could be found for the phenomena. Suspecting that these effects were due not to electrical disturbances but to RSPK, Bender asked for the line-recorder to be disconnected and linked to an internal 1.5 volt battery. The instrument continued to record maximal voltage deflections at the same time as paintings rotated on the wall, desk drawers appeared to open by themselves and a 400-pound filing cabinet moved away from the wall.

The parapsychologists found that all of the disturbances were associated with the presence of a new employee, a 19-year-old girl, Annmarie Sch. When she walked along the office corridor, the lampshades began to swing wildly behind her. She reacted to the disturbances with hysteria and muscular spasms which temporarily paralysed one of her arms. For the sake of her own health, Bender insisted that she be found a job in another lawyer's office. With her departure the phenomena ceased. Bender, who was a qualified doctor, proposed that he provoke and record the disturbances under hypnosis, with a view to ridding the girl of the unconscious conflicts which he believed were the cause of the poltergeist phenomena, but the girl's parents refused their consent.

Was Annmarie Sch. just a clever fraud? Perhaps, but sometime after the Rosenheim case, Annmarie became engaged to a young technician who was a keen amateur ten-pin bowler. During their visits to the local bowling alley, the electronic control system went berserk, refusing to reset the pins or record the scores in the bowling lanes. Journalists who had

Psychokinesis and Poltergeists

followed the Rosenheim case associated Annmarie's presence with these new disturbances and the girl once again found herself in the media spotlight. Her fiancé broke off their engagement.

Researchers at the Freiburg Institute have investigated five other major 'person-centred' poltergeist cases. The Vachendorf case (1948) centred around the 14-year-old daughter of German refugees living in a small mountain village in Bavaria. This case was unusual in that the disturbances largely involved 'extreme events' which physicists have very great difficulty in explaining. The Rosenheim case was in many ways a classical poltergeist case. Physicists working with Bender told him that they had no conceptual difficulties with a 'psychic energy' which was translated into kinetic or electrical energy. However, objects passing through physical barriers is altogether another matter. A coin, say, which dematerialised would release more energy than a hydrogen bomb and its reappearance later, still intact, is simply inconceivable; and yet at Vachendorf that is exactly what seemed to be happening.

One night the parents' and girl's adjacent beds were bombarded for hours by stones, coal, pieces of wood, litter and tools. When her father tried to switch the light on, he found that it was unscrewed from its socket. When he attempted to search the house, he discovered that the bedroom door was mysteriously locked. Later, the key was found hanging on the hands of a wall-clock. In the morning, the girl's mother replaced all the tools in their box and then sat on the toolbox saying 'Now you will stay here.' While she was sitting on the box, she later told investigators, one by one, the tools were scattered around the room.

At Neudorf in 1952, the 13-year-old son of the town's mayor was the focus of a case which included the apparent materialisation of objects out of thin air, showers of nails and the movement of objects. The Bremen-Freiburg case (1965–1966) centred around a 15-year-old apprentice who worked in the china department of a retail store. In his presence, dishes, cups and glasses literally jumped off the shelves. The boy was dismissed and referred to a psychiatric clinic where similar events occurred in the presence of bemused psychiatrists. At Nicklheim in 1969, Brigitte, the 13-year-old daughter of a working-class family, was the focus of a poltergeist case which included mysterious rappings, objects being displaced and the movement of objects from the interior of locked boxes and cupboards. Parapsychologists have attempted to analyse the types of objects displaced for their psychological symbolism. In this case, it is interesting that dolls were often undressed and placed in sexual positions.

American researcher, W. G. Roll, has investigated a similar series of poltergeist cases in America, the majority of which were also person-centred and again usually involved an adolescent or youth.[8] Like the Germans, Roll believed that psychological tests revealed underlying frustrations and conflicts in these individuals. The German parapsychologists were able to set up some controlled experiments at poltergeist sites. In one of these, a figurine was moved in a box which triggered electronic surveillance devices. However, both Roll and the Germans made one observation which may prove to be of the highest significance. When these children were brought in to the lab, they were totally unable to influence the outcome of PK experiments but in two of Roll's cases, and two reported by Bender (the Rosenheim and Bremen-Freiburg cases), the children proved to be high scorers in ESP tests. Perhaps, PK and ESP are manifestations of the same strange human capability or maybe both attributes are unleashed by the same psychological conditions?

There is another explanation, one favoured by more sceptical minds, and that is that the children, having fooled the parapsychologists into believing that they were investigating genuine poltergeist phenomena, then duped the investigators during the ESP tests. With these objections in mind, we shall examine two quite extraordinary recent poltergeist cases. The first case, which centred around a young girl, was investigated not by parapsychologists but by a team of very sceptical scientists. The second, which literally tore a small business apart in South Wales, consisted in part of those extreme phenomena which even hardened investigators have trouble in accepting. But there is another more pressing reason for examining these cases in detail. Like other scientific phenomena, poltergeists do not always fall into neat and tidy categories. In

Psychokinesis and Poltergeists

both of these cases, the phenomena manifested themselves in such a way as to force the investigators to consider the possibility of a discarnate entity.

In April 1974, the local press in a large town in southern England published an account of an apparently extraordinary series of events that was taking place in a council house. The house was occupied by Mr and Mrs Black (pseudonyms are used throughout) and their six children. The disturbances centred on a bedroom which 20-year-old 'Jane' shared with her 12-year-old sister, 'Susan'. The room was plagued with rappings of the type that were frequently reported at late nineteenth-century Spiritualist seances. They appeared to be produced by an 'intelligence' which would use a simple code to answer questions put to it by the girls. By means of this rapping code, the 'entity' had informed Susan that 'he' 'was a spirit named Eric Waters who was attempting to communicate with people in authority on earth in order to describe how he had been murdered'. The intelligent rappings were remarkably similar to the rappings associated with the Fox sisters in Hydesville in 1848, events which led to the founding of modern Spiritualism.

Very quickly, Barrie Colvin concluded that the activity appeared to centre on Susan and was therefore not remarkably different from the cases described by Bender and Roll, which focused on adolescents. He researched the literature and discovered another seven cases which appeared to focus on young girls. But what about 'Eric'? Was this a classical person-centred poltergeist case or was there really a discarnate entity?

Like all seasoned investigators, Colvin wanted to exclude normal explanations for the rappings. The apparent 'intelligence' appeared to rule out such obvious explanations as airlocks in water pipes, underground noises and the creaks and groans produced by the subsidence of a building. The rappings were only produced when the girl was in the room, lying down on the bed. 'Despite several attempts, it was not possible to obtain rapping sounds when [Susan] was in a standing position. Success was generally obtained when [Susan] lay on her side, facing the adjacent wall, with a light cover over her.'

The Sceptical Occultist

Fraud, of course, was the other serious possibility. Although it was not clear how the girl could be producing the noises while lying on the bed, parapsychologists have learnt to their cost that trickery, even the simple devices used by children, remain 'invisible' to the investigator who has become convinced that he is seeing genuine phenomena. Colvin knew that if he was to make any progress, he would have to persuade 'Eric' to produce more dramatic phenomena. Furthermore, Colvin wanted to do this in the presence of sceptical observers, one of whom was Dr Reinhart Schiffauer, a senior research physicist and a man extremely sceptical of paranormal phenomena.

I did take with me, well, a number of people really, including a chap called Reinhart Schiffauer, a chap who had a good scientific background and I took him because he was the most sceptical person I knew. And he was there on three occasions and is, to this day, absolutely convinced of the genuine nature of the case. Mainly because we were able to get it to move the knocking sounds away from the wall. I think if we had not done that, well, you are always going to say, maybe there was something behind that wall. But when you get it to knock on the bed-head and shake the bed-head whilst its doing it and you are there within a foot of it! Well, that one case convinced me that the poltergeist force is genuine.

The third occasion that Reinhart Schiffauer went was 2 p.m. on a very hot sunny day. Plenty of light about and we went upstairs to the room. 'Susan' was lying on the bed and when it did tap it tapped very occasionally, and it was very light. Reinhart then said, 'let's see if we can get it upset'. And he got the other children, Susan's brothers, to start calling it all sorts of names and saying, Eric, we don't believe this story, we don't believe that story. Because the family had done this previously and it had really started banging. Banging so loud that the family decided to leave the house. It got beyond control. So we decided to do the same and I can only say that Reinhart and I were absolutely amazed. It was so loud that you could put your hand on the wall and feel the wall vibrating. We went outside to the ground floor below her bedroom window, and you could feel the vibration. It was so loud it was just incredible. In fact, we walked down the road and we could still hear it, some 50 metres away. That was another really momentous event. We could find no normal explanation for that.[9]

Psychokinesis and Poltergeists

Subsequently, Colvin and Schiffauer got the rapping sounds to move to different parts of the bedroom on request, including the exercise book in which he was writing the case notes. It marked a water-shed in the attitudes of both men to poltergeist phenomena and human psychokinesis. But more surprises lay in store for the investigators. Although the rappings only occurred in the presence of Susan, it was noticed that the regularity and intensity increased when her mother was in the room. It gradually began to dawn on Colvin that the mother was contributing to the psychokinesis. When the mother was in the room it became a group phenomenon.

> You could ask questions and 'Eric' would rap back messages. When you asked it to spell out a sentence it would rap the number of the next letter in the alphabet. For example, one rap for 'A' or 13 raps for 'M'. You would count through the alphabet and you would say, 'M' and it would give one rap for 'Yes', two raps for 'No' and three raps for 'don't know'. This was just what they had worked out with it. So when it was spelling out a sentence, and one I remember quite well was 'I am here to rest and stop my bones from rotting', you can imagine that takes an awful long time. It goes on and on and on. The mother would often go through the alphabet until she reached the next letter in the message. Lets say it was 'P', she would enquire 'N'? and it would give two raps for 'No', 'O'?, followed by two raps and she would just be about to say 'P'? and it would rap once for 'Yes' at the moment she was about to say it. And on some occasions I believe it was just *before* she came out with the letter.

For Colvin this suggested that the mother's unconscious was contributing to the rappings. The 'entity' was able to rap 'Yes' to the question as it was being formulated by the woman, but still unspoken, because it was partly a product of her unconscious mind.

The other explanation is that Susan or her mother, or perhaps both, were enjoying transient telepathy. As mentioned above, the focus of poltergeist activity can often produce high scores on ESP tests. Colvin attempted three experiments with the numbers 1 to 10 pasted on to cards. There were forty cards giving four of each number in the pack. Cards were drawn from the deck randomly. In the first experiment, the target cards were viewed by everyone in the room (Susan, her mother, her two brothers and Colvin). 'Eric' was persuaded to rap out six calls, all of which were correct. In the next two experiments, the target cards were only seen by Colvin. 'Eric' made a total of eighteen calls, sixteen of which were correct. This result, which was far better than what might have been expected on the basis of chance-coincidence, is indicative that the phenomena had a telepathic component. In the last experiment, the target cards were seen by nobody in the room but as 'Eric' made only six calls, two of which were incorrect, there was insufficient evidence to implicate pure clairvoyance.

Was 'Eric' living or was he dead? The balance of the evidence suggests that 'Eric' was just a dramatised vehicle for the expression of spontaneous psychokinesis produced by Susan – with contributions from her mother. Like other children identified as poltergeist foci, Susan was a frail, shy child who was anxious in the presence of strangers. She was lonely and 'Eric' was seen as a comrade, rather like the imaginary friends created by many children. The poltergeist activity was totally dependent upon Susan's presence. In fact it was only produced when she was lying on her bed and the activity peaked just as she was falling asleep. Once Susan was asleep, the rappings ceased completely.

The statements made by 'Eric' were banal and often inconsistent. 'He' claimed to have been Eric Waters who had been murdered at the age of twenty. When asked how long ago he had died, the raps continued to fifty and then faded out. 'He' appeared simple-minded and child-like, more the fragment of a personality than a disembodied intelligence.

Colvin made extensive enquiries amongst both branches of the Waters family in the town; he contacted newspaper archives, sought the help of amateur historians, checked registers of births and deaths and the genealogies of the Waters family and even advertised for information. He never found a shred of evidence that Eric Waters had been an historical person or that anyone had been murdered on or near the site of the council house.

Colvin's investigation showed how a person-centred poltergeist case could masquerade as a ghost. More importantly,

Psychokinesis and Poltergeists

it suggested that other people close to the focus might contribute to the activity. To just what extent a group might unconsciously produce poltergeist activity is a question central to the next case. Are all poltergeists person-centred or are some the manifestations of discarnate entities?

It is rare for an academic psychologist to be presented with a series of events which will overturn the way in which he thinks about the world. For Professor David Fontana, a member of staff at the University of Wales, these experiences began with a telephone call in June 1989.[10] On the line was John Stiles, the Honorary Spontaneous Officer for the Society for Psychical Research. After the usual exchange of pleasantries, Stiles came quickly to the matter in hand. A businessman in Cardiff had telephoned the Society on the advice of his insurers, as his premises appeared to be plagued by a poltergeist which was bombarding the staff and customers with missiles. The insurance company wanted the case investigated in the event that any of the customers, hit by a flying object, decided to sue. There were also some very strange aspects to the case. Just how strange, Fontana was soon to discover.

The disturbances were taking place in a small engineering workshop established by 'Jim', a mechanic by trade. Most of his employees were part of a tightly knit family group which included Jim's wife Ann, Ann's brother Paul, a plumber who had taken early retirement on health grounds and who offered his services voluntarily and Paul's wife Yvonne. The firm had three other employees: Ron, who worked part-time, Michael, who later became Jim's partner, and Alex, who had left the firm before Fontana's investigation.

It appeared to be the archetypal family business most likely to survive the looming recession. Jim had managed to acquire premises in a popular Cardiff high-street. The small retail area in the front was connected to the large workshop by a single door. A small kitchen and toilets were located at the rear of the building. A door in the side of the workshop opened on to a small alley which connected with the street and a yard behind the building, allowing plenty of access for vehicles. Above the shop was a solicitor's office and the two businesses were soon on good terms. However, there was a totally unforeseen complication – they appeared to be sharing the premises with the sort of prankster that Emile Tizane called the 'unknown man'.

The disturbances began soon after the premises were occupied at the beginning of 1987. Small stones, coins and bolts began ricocheting off the walls of the workshop and the retail area. It seemed incredible that either Jim or his customers could have thrown them. The objects were only seen as they landed and very rarely in mid-flight. Frequently Jim would be alone with the customers or sales representatives in the front of the shop when the phenomena occurred. There were other strange occurrences: objects would simply disappear and reappear as if by magic. On one occasion, a paint scraper went 'missing' and suddenly reappeared but, when he picked it up, Jim soon dropped it again, it was so hot 'as if it had been heated for some minutes by a blowlamp'. This has been a common finding in poltergeist cases. Recently, one member of a team investigating disturbances in Leamington Spa, picked up a cup which had been propelled across the room without breaking. It was so hot that it left blisters on his fingers. The blisters were photographed.

Very soon, however, much more sinister events were witnessed. Objects mysteriously began to appear as if by the men's commands, usually falling on the floor at their feet. When Jim spoke of recording the events, a pen fell beside him, followed by a sheet of headed notepaper which had come from the solicitor's office on the floor above. The men, still undisturbed by these events, christened the apparent entity 'Pete'. When they jokingly told 'Pete' to bring them money, old pennies and half-pennies fell on to the floor. When Paul asked for a sovereign, a Jubilee crown had dropped beside him. The pennies had apparently come from a collection in the office, but the Jubilee crown was taken from a drawer in Jim and Ann's house. On another occasion, when Paul had requested money, three old pennies, all dated 1912, had appeared on the floor beside him. Their source was never traced.

Psychokinesis and Poltergeists

As the momentum of the disturbances increased, the outside of the building was showered with stones, on one occasion forcing Jim and Michael to abandon a televised rugby game. Tools started to swing in their tool racks without any apparent cause. A diary disappeared from the solicitor's office and was accidentally discovered on the roof of a neighbouring building. A fluorescent light exploded and, more than once, the women found themselves locked in the toilets. A single spoon was kept in the kitchen to stir the cups of tea and coffee but this was joined overnight by two other spoons and, again overnight, the three spoons, cups and saucers would be removed from the cupboard and laid out on the counter.

The most chilling episode began with an experiment. Jim was exasperated and angry as he suspected that someone on the staff was trying to sabotage the firm. The problem was that the disturbances did not appear to centre on any one individual and continued during those periods when members of staff were sick or on vacation – and, indeed, when the workshop had been locked and secured overnight and during weekends. The police had been involved on numerous occasions and had patrolled the alley and yard but had been unable to catch a prankster. Jim wanted a final proof one way or the other.

One evening when Jim, Paul and their wives were closing the shop, Jim placed a carburettor float on the gas fire in the workshop and 'challenged' it to be moved by the morning. After the others had left, Jim took a last look at the float, still on the fire, before leaving and locking the outer door. At this time, Jim held the only set of keys to the premises. On the way home, Jim and Paul, accompanied by their wives, stopped the car for Paul to buy cigarettes. As Paul picked up his change from the counter, he discovered, to his horror, that it contained the carburettor float. The two couples returned immediately to the workshop and found that the float had disappeared from its position on the gas fire.

Jim and Ann now became the focus for these strange events. Their home telephone would ring day and night but when the telephone was answered the line was dead. The same thing happened at the workshop but British Telecom engineers were unable to discover a fault or identify a nuisance caller. A brass shell case, which Jim kept as a souvenir, was propelled around the workshop. Jim angrily grabbed hold of it and placed it in the yard at the back of the workshop but, as he walked back into the premises, it fell at his feet on the side furthest from the door into the yard. Sometime later, one of the men challenged 'Pete' to 'fire the shell' and immediately blue flames appeared from the top of the case. In the evening, when Jim and Ann returned home, they would find carburettor floats impaled in their ceilings. The floats began appearing everywhere, in their clothes, on their chairs and once impaling a garden parasol they were sitting under. Paul and Yvonne suffered similar attacks.

The most extraordinary phenomena began when Jim, incensed by the stone throwing activity, picked up a stone and hurled it angrily into a corner of the workshop. *A moment later, it was thrown back and landed at Jim's feet.* From that moment onwards, stones and other objects thrown into that corner of the room were usually returned immediately.

Poltergeist phenomena are usually 'shy', refusing to perform in front of investigators. This has often added credence to the sceptic's cries of fraud. This was not the case with the Cardiff poltergeist and Professor Fontana recorded his personal experiences of more than seventeen different events. In his first paper, he described the stone throwing.

> On a number of occasions, I was present when this happened, the stones being thrown either by Jim or Ann. (Ann incidentally, informed me that she had a much more active response from 'Pete' if she called out insults to 'him'.) In each case I watched the flight of the stone thrown by the individual concerned, witnessed it land, then a moment later (with the stone thrower in my full view) heard the familiar clatter as it was 'returned' against the wall on either side of the workshop.
>
> Perhaps more significantly still, I found that I was able to reproduce this phenomenon myself, and did so on a number of separate occasions. There was no question of my own stone bouncing back and being mistaken for that 'thrown' by 'Pete'. I experimented deliberately at obtaining rebounds of any kind, and succeeded in achieving them only on a small number of occasions, with the rebound never travelling for more than two

or three feet, and the trajectory fully obvious each time. In 'Pete's' case the stones impacted on the wall at a distance of some twenty feet away from the point at which my stones struck, with no apparent trajectory.

Two instances of my own experiences with reciprocal stones are of special interest. On my visit of 19 September (unannounced) the four principal witnesses (Jim, Ann, Paul and Yvonne) were all away on holiday. Michael was alone in the workshop. I asked him if any phenomena had occurred, and he reported that, apart from some sudden gusts of wind ('as if the retail shop door was open, but it wasn't') nothing had happened. He gave it as his opinion the 'energy of two people' might be needed if any phenomena were to occur.

I then suggested I try throwing stones into the 'active' corner, and when I did so, I immediately obtained the usual response. Feeling this supported his theory, Michael then suggested he withdraw into the yard, leaving me alone in the workshop. In his view, phenomena would then cease. We duly carried out this experiment, but once more my stones were followed by the clatter of returning ones. I was thus alone in the workshop at this time, though the door to the yard was open. The retail shop was empty.

The second instance took place after Jim's return from holiday. He and I stood in an otherwise empty retail shop and both threw a number of stones into the corner adjacent to the 'active one' (and which also was a focus of activity). Our stones were frequently 'returned', hitting the wall to either side of us but invisible in flight.

One year later, Jim's partnership with Michael was dissolved. Michael, who had something of a reputation for practical jokes, had also been a key focus for many, although certainly not all, of these strange events. But if Michael had been an accomplished practical joker who was manufacturing the poltergeist – and there is not a shred of evidence to suggest that he was – Michael was gone. The shop was redecorated and underwent structural alterations – and the disturbances ceased. The 'active' corners of the workshop were silent and stones were no longer returned. The business returned to normal. And then, within weeks, David Fontana was again telephoned by Jim. The poltergeist had started up again, only now it was different. What was more, it had begun to persecute Ann's brother, Paul.

Sacks of fertiliser and grass seed which were being stored in the workshop were emptied and the contents scattered across the floor and over the counter of the retail shop. The engine of a powerful commercial lawnmower was set running overnight, filling the shop with petrol fumes. Dishes in the retail area were smashed, but the pieces lay perfectly together. Most of this happened overnight when the shop was locked but one day, while Paul was serving a customer, he looked up and was horrified to see a dark cloud of fertiliser hanging over the man, which just as suddenly rained on to the customer's head and shoulders. Paul remembered that the man had fled without waiting for his change.

The carburettor floats from the workshop again began to serve as a focus of activity and would ricochet around the walls of Paul's living-room. Three floats were thrown through the open window of his car as he waited for his wife in a supermarket car-park. During another incident, Ann and Paul were bombarded with floats as they stood talking on the pavement across the road from the shop.

But the strangest phenomena started to occur when Paul once again taunted 'Pete' with requests for money. This time, instead of pennies falling on to the floor, rolled bundles of bank notes were found conspicuously pinned to the walls by the ubiquitous carburettor floats. Again, these would often appear overnight to be found when the shop was unlocked in the morning. And the money kept coming. Paul found one £10 note pasted to the windshield of his car as he and his wife left to drive home at the end of the day. One night Paul was hit by a shower of coins as he crossed the darkened hallway of his home. When interviewed by David Fontana, Paul insisted that they had not simply bounced off the inside of his front door but that he had seen the coins *actually pass through the door as if thrown from outside the house*. In total, around £70 appeared in this way, most of it as rolled up £5 notes.

If 'Pete' really was an entity he may now have decided to make himself known to Paul. Alternatively, Paul's subconscious may itself have begun to conjure a visual identity for the poltergeist in the form of an hallucination. We will never know. The facts are that when Paul opened the shop one morning, he saw the apparition of a small boy sitting on one of the shelves close to the ceiling in one of the 'active' corners. The apparition was dressed in short trousers and peaked school cap but, apart from an 'oval shape', there was no face under the cap and Paul had no impressions of arms or legs. Paul later told Fontana that he had not been afraid, 'In fact it was quite a pleasant experience, as if seeing a real child.' Paul said 'Hello! What are you doing here?' Almost immediately, a float was thrown towards him from the direction of the apparition, whereupon the 'boy' vanished.

The second time Paul saw the apparition, he was working with Jim on a piece of machinery. Looking up from his work, he caught sight of the 'child' and shouted to his boss, 'Look behind you.' The apparition vanished and immediately a stone struck the machine with such force that both men were shaken.

On the third and final occasion that the apparition was seen, Paul was preparing to leave the workshop for the day. He was the last to leave. After extinguishing the workshop lights, he was walking towards the rear exit, when he caught sight of the 'child' standing in the open door to the washroom, silhouetted in the light from the washroom's windows. Once again Paul was unable to discern the figure's face and hands. He estimated that the apparition was about two and a half feet tall and again appeared to be wearing short trousers and a peaked cap 'braided down the sides as the caps worn by Wolf Cubs used to be'. This time the 'child' appeared to be waving 'as if saying goodbye'. Paul was very disturbed by this experience and for sometime after refused to talk about the apparition or the other disturbances.

The poltergeist phenomena began to decline. The last events recorded by Fontana in his papers concerned a child's teddy bear and large rubber ball that were kept at the workshop. One morning, the men discovered that these toys had vanished overnight but as so many objects had disappeared in the past two years, it passed without comment. Sometime later, Jim and Paul were being driven mad by a regular bumping which appeared to come from the ceiling. Finally, the men decided to investigate and, removing the tiles, gained access into the space above the ceiling. Carefully hidden away in the ceiling space were the teddy bear and the rubber ball. The two men reflected that the sounds they had heard were the ball being bounced on the inside of the ceiling.

Few who read this case in its entirety can fail to be touched by the account of the apparition of the little boy, Paul's reaction to this experience and the displacement of the rubber ball and teddy bear. The Cardiff poltergeist, painstakingly documented by David Fontana, who was himself an eye-witness to many of these events, may seem, for many, to provide the final proof that some poltergeist disturbances are caused by discarnate entities.

It remains to enquire whether we can account for all of these manifestations in terms of human psychokinesis and what is now known about hallucinations and apparitions. A possible explanation lies with the psychokinetic energy produced not by a single individual but by a *group* of people. Barrie Colvin's case implicated the mother in unconsciously contributing to the rappings; and some academic parapsychologists believe that demonstrations of PK in the laboratory are dependent on contributions from *both* the subject and the experimenter. What would be learnt if we could create an artificial poltergeist?

Clinical psychologist, Kenneth Batcheldor, and his colleagues did just that in the early 1960s. Batcheldor was interested in some of the physical phenomena reportedly produced by famous mediums such as D. D. Home and Eusapia Palladino. It is an area steeped in fraud and Batcheldor decided that his only approach lay in attempting to reproduce the phenomena with a small group of friends. They met regularly and the sittings were conducted in a relaxed and friendly atmosphere. One member was chosen to act as the 'medium' and he and the others sat in the traditional circle with their hands on the surface of the table. In later experiments, the legs of the table were equipped with switches, connected to a circuit and red indicator light, which came on when all four of the table's legs lost contact with the ground. Batcheldor later described their experiences in a series of papers.[11]

Psychokinesis and Poltergeists

I was myself, formerly sceptical, but I shall now be writing from the point of view of personal belief based on first-hand observation. Neither I nor either of my two friends had had any previous experiences of this nature, or had any claim to 'mediumistic power'. We were all the more surprised at the remarkable phenomena that began to manifest soon after we began sitting in darkness or dim light with our hands on the table . . .

. . . The first total levitations occurred in total darkness and were detected only by our sense of touch and by the sound of the table falling back to the floor. After many hours experience of the feel of the table this was not as unreliable as it may seem, but it clearly left room for faulty observation and we thought it very desirable to have some instrumental means of checking the reality of the levitations. For this purpose I equipped the table with a simple electrical apparatus consisting of four switches, one on each foot, joined in series to a battery and lamp. . . . The lighting of the little red lamp not only confirmed our tactile impressions that the table was off the floor, but added visible evidence that it was (say) at chest height, and that all hands (fingers and thumbs) were on *top* of the table. The fact that onlookers witnessed the lighting of the lamp helped reassure us that we were not hallucinated, but the possibility remained – however improbable – that everybody present was collectively hallucinated. The latter hypothesis was ruled out a few sessions later when the idea suggested itself of replacing the lamp with a buzzer. By this means every total levitation was clearly registered on the tape-recorder as a buzzing, superimposed on the conversation of the sitters: thus we had an automatic record independent of our senses . . .

. . . As the sitting proceeded the movements of the table usually increased in power and extent. Under these circumstances it was often impossible to remain seated, and chairs were pushed back and we continued standing. Sometimes we had to go at a brisk pace from one end of the room to the other, even with a heavy (40 lb) table. On many occasions (more frequently in earlier meetings) the table was totally levitated, sometimes remaining suspended in the air for twenty seconds (15 lb table, timed with stopwatch from recorded buzzer). When the power had built up, various experiments were tried for the remainder of the sitting. Sometimes we took our hands off and watched the table moving without contact.

Batcheldor and his friends wanted to reproduce the physical phenomena occasionally reported at Spiritualist seances, but they also reported some of the phenomena associated with poltergeists. Rappings were heard, not only on the table but from the wall and furnishings. The table would sometimes become 'glued' to the floor and impossible to shift. They also reported spots of intense cold and cold breezes, also associated with poltergeists and hauntings. The group also recorded events of the type which so plagued the Cardiff workshop.

> In one recent sitting a stone was thrown across the room, and in another a box of matches was sprinkled about (falling on me). These incidents resemble the so-called 'apport' phenomenon. The stone, which I have kept, is like some in my garden. The matches were of a brand kept in the kitchen.

In his paper, Batcheldor remarked, 'No sceptic worth his salt would for a moment admit that our experiments provide him with good grounds for changing his opinions.' Happily, the reader will not be asked to form an opinion simply on the basis of this paper. Some ten years later, one of Ken Batcheldor's papers was read by a member of the Toronto Society for Psychical Research. It provided the missing jigsaw piece which catalysed a similar series of experiments, only this time they were captured by a film, two live television broadcasts and photographs taken during demonstrations, including two in front of psychologists at American universities.

Iris M. Owen's account of these experiments, was detailed in her subsequent book, *Conjuring Up Philip*.[12] Her husband, a noted scholar and himself the author of a standard text on poltergeists, described it as 'one of the most unusual and interesting books ever to be published'.

Their story began with a haunting. One night, during a vigil, several of the Society's investigators together witnessed the appearance of the ghost. Collective apparitions pose an interesting problem. The most convincing explanation is that they are hallucinations; but then how are hallucinations – by definition, private experiences – seen by more than one person? Of course, there is the idea that one person experiences an hallucination (the 'ghost') which is then shared telepathically with other observers (see Chapter Four). With this in mind, the Society established a research group which would attempt to produce an 'experimental ghost'.

Psychokinesis and Poltergeists

The group was carefully selected. Members had to be compatible and capable of establishing close emotional ties to each other. Meeting every week, they fashioned a biography for their 'ghost'. He was called 'Philip', an aristocratic landowner and Cavalier who had fought with the Royalists during the English Civil War and then died a romantic but violent death. In fact, much the same sort of biography as some ghosts in hauntings, but with one important exception: 'Philip's' biography was pocked with historical inaccuracies. If 'Philip' appeared, if one person in the group actually created an hallucination of 'Philip' and in a flash of telepathy shared it with other members of the group, they would know that it was their own creation; that it was an 'artificial entity'. At their weekly meetings they talked about 'Philip', drew pictures of him and met in a room filled with Civil War memorabilia. Part of each session was spent in meditation, which it was hoped would provide the necessary conditions for an hallucination. It never worked.

After a year of research, the group had never managed to conjure an apparition; never mind a collective apparition. Then, a member of the group saw one of Ken Batcheldor's papers and their approach changed tack. Instead of meditating, they sat around the table and, in a friendly jovial atmosphere, talked and sang songs. There was only one detail of Batcheldor's experimental protocol they wanted to change: the Canadian group would always work in full light. They were still expecting a full visual apparition when the table started to tremble and buck and rappings were produced under the hands of the sitters. Iris Owen recalled their surprise,

> During these first sittings the group members were somewhat nonplussed. They were not sure how to deal with this strange twist to their experiment, although they were aware of the possibility of the manifestation of this type of phenomena. While this speculation was going on aloud about the cause of the table rappings, Dorothy exclaimed, 'I wonder if by chance Philip is doing this?' Immediately there came a very loud rap from the table – so Philip had come, though in a different form from that which we expected.

Like the poltergeist investigated by Barrie Colvin, 'Philip' would respond to the sitters' questions with a rapping code. From the questions and answers, it became very clear that 'Philip' was simply a manifestation of the group psyche. If the group believed, rightly or wrongly, that an aspect of English history was the case, 'Philip' believed it also. Parapsychologists have demonstrated that the foci of poltergeist cases are granted, for a time at least, the facility of ESP and the 'Philip' experiments were seemingly associated with a single instance of this type. One evening, Iris's husband, Professor Owen, joined the group. The conversation was revolving around 'Philip's' grand tour of Europe as a young man. 'Philip' had claimed not to have known Prince Rupert, the commander of the Royalist Cavalry during the Civil War.

Sid asked, 'Did you go to Bohemia?'
(Rap) 'Yes.'
'Did you know Elizabeth, the Winter Queen?' Dr Owen asked.
(Rap) 'Yes.'
'That's odd,' Dr Owen said. 'He says he knew Elizabeth, and yet previously he never said he knew Rupert, her brother-in-law.'

Dr Owen continued to assert that Rupert was Elizabeth's brother-in-law, and 'Philip' continued, by a series of double raps, to deny that he was. Nobody else could recollect hearing of Elizabeth and Rupert together, nor of their relationship to each other. Dr Owen retired to look up the matter in an encyclopaedia. He discovered that Rupert was not Elizabeth's brother-in-law.

It is not clear whether Owen discovered the true relationship, but Prince Rupert, nephew of Charles I and commander of the Royalist Cavalry, was the *son* of Elizabeth of Bohemia.

The Canadian group also produced rappings on the walls and furniture, cold spots and the sort of electrical disturbances that were seen at Rosenheim; lights were apparently extinguished or flickered at the sitters' command. During sittings the table would tremble, buck, levitate, stand with three legs off the ground and march across the room. The table would move without contact with the experimenters and when one of the sitters arrived late, it moved quickly across the room to greet him.

Psychokinesis and Poltergeists

On one occasion they produced phenomena of the sort frequently reported in the Cardiff case. Initially the group had worked with a wooden card table in one of the experimenters' homes. Then they decided to move permanently to the headquarters of the Society's offices in Toronto. They began again with a new table but the phenomenon was slow to appear and the experimenters wondered if 'Philip' had come with them. Soon, however, the table began waltzing across the floor and even lay on its back, with its four feet in the air at the sitters' request. The original table back at Al's house was also moving,

> When Al left home that evening Philip's table was in its usual place at the far end of his living room, against the window, with a chair against it. When Al returned that night, the chair was overturned and the table had travelled across the room, and was in the hallway. There was no evidence of a break-in. Al said that when leaving that evening, he had said to himself, 'Come on Philip, you've got to go to your new home tonight.' He had then locked the door and gone out. It is impossible to say *when* the table actually made the movement, whether at the moment of Al's leaving, or during the initial period when the group was trying to summon Philip.

In early 1973, the Toronto Society established a second group which was to attempt to repeat the 'Philip' experiments. It was a success. The group, basing their 'ghost' on 'Lilith', a Second World War heroine shot by the Germans, managed to reproduce much of the original phenomena. Meanwhile, the 'Philip' group, used to performing under the gaze of observers, was invited by the Canadian Broadcasting Corporation in November 1973 to become the subject of a *Man Alive* documentary. Under the glare of television arc lights, millions of Canadian viewers watched as the table reared on to one leg and shot across the room, leaving the sitters to follow as best they could. At the end of 1974, 'Philip' and the sitters became the subject of another documentary, *Philip, The Imaginary Ghost* (George Ritter Films Ltd). Another live television broadcast – Toronto City TV's *World of the Unexplained* – followed, only this time the group asked to work in the studio, in front of a live audience and a chosen panel of psychologists, physicists, reporters and other interested parties.

Philip has become a star of film and TV and – appropriately – has demonstrated that he is a terrible ham. At a televised talk show, the Philip group was situated in a corner of the studio, ready to perform, while a panel of experts occupied the main stage – a raised dais. Philip quickly made it obvious that he felt his place was on the dais with the speakers' panel, rather than in the corner of the studio, and his efforts to mount the dais and take his rightful place were hilarious. ... Both the audience and the studio staff were in fits of laughter as the table lifted first one leg, and then another, and then swung around, wriggling and pushing to get to the forefront of the show.

The 'Philip' experiments caused a sensation in America and amongst scientists and parapsychologists across the world. Any reservations that might have remained regarding unconscious fraud were seemingly laid to rest by two university investigations.

At an invitation to demonstrate the phenomena to a group of psychologists and physicists in Cleveland, Ohio, only four of the group were able to be present, and the table supplied was an antique, heavy wooden chess table with wheels on castors, one of which squeaked when the table was pushed. Philip however easily made his transition to this unfamiliar terrain and the table glided around the carpeted floor without the wheels squeaking and without leaving tracks on the carpet. On two occasions, one of the men present sat on the table and was thrown off, once quite violently.

A year later, the group was invited to Kent State for two days of experimentation, when the entire proceedings were videotaped and recorded. A strain gauge measured the upward thrust of the table, registering a force of more than twenty pounds, thus showing that the table was indeed pushing upwards, although all the sitters' hands were resting on top of it.

The sitter-type experiments apparently represented one of the most significant advances in understanding human PK and poltergeist phenomena and yet, within ten years, this whole area of research seemingly dropped into a void. As Julian Isaacs later explained in a paper, it did not translate into the laboratory, with all the human, financial and psychological considerations which hedge scientific research.[13] The experiments called for a huge investment of time and motivation and this was not to be found amongst volunteers. There were problems in obtaining the social skills necessary for the emotional bonding within the group. Some got fed up and left, others became frightened, 'Most galling of all, some got cold feet just as really striking ostensible PK developed, leaving amidst a cloud of weak excuses.' Of course, there was also the force of the 'lesser miracle'.

Security against fraud was an insoluble problem since, although I felt I could trust my fellow sitters, it was an inescapable fact that even if my groups were successful and I reported positive results, the parapsychology community would certainly write them off as probably fraudulent. This is a crucial deterrent preventing newcomers from venturing into this field.

Summary of the Evidence

The extreme sceptic would agree with the philosopher David Hume; the movement of objects by an unknown human force runs counter to everyday experiences. Poltergeist phenomena are a human folly created by fraud, and fed by fear and superstition. Scientists who investigate poltergeists and lend their authority to the authenticity of the phenomena have become sucked in to the group's delusions. Poltergeist phenomena break the laws of nature: objects simply do not disappear from closed spaces or pass through walls and doors. When a group of people or experimenters choose to disregard cause and effect, they will 'see' what they expect to see. Every year a large number of poltergeist cases, which are investigated by parapsychologists, are shown to have a normal explanation. In seemingly 'authentic' poltergeists this explanation still awaits discovery.

The defence would argue that poltergeist phenomena are a discrete package of phenomena which have been described since the beginning of recorded history. The laws of nature are of course *descriptive* and not proscriptive: they cannot be 'broken'. Poltergeist phenomena hint at both unexplained human potentials and unsuspected aspects of reality. In the final chapter, we shall provide a psychological explanation for group Psi and poltergeists and suggest how objects might be able to move through physical barriers. We shall then be in a position to ask whether the Cardiff poltergeist was due to group Psi masquerading as a ghost or whether there are still aspects of this case which remain unexplained.

4

Ghosts

Prosecution's claim is that ghosts are just complex hallucinations and illusions peppered with fraud and self-delusion.

If we can be persuaded of the reality of just one ghost story, we are forced to accept the survival of the human personality after death and a wholly different reality complementing that described by science. The French scientist and philosopher, René Descartes, held that the human being is a two component item – the body dies but the soul, the human personality, survives death and lives on. While in everyday life many of us remain intuitive Dualists, this is no longer a popular idea. It has even been said that science has proven that there is no life beyond the grave. Professor John Taylor, a physicist who was once a keen investigator of the paranormal and now an avowed sceptic, has written,

> So we come to the realisation that there can be no immortality in a physical world. In a nonphysical universe, anything is possible, but since we cannot be sure that anything makes sense, we cannot consider it usefully. *According to modern science there is only death after death* [Author's italics].

This is, of course, quite wrong. Conventional science has nothing to say about life after death, addressing as it does questions of a totally different order. It may concern itself with the medical and human needs of the dying, even exploring the biochemical changes in the brain which may account for Near Death Experiences. After death, the pathologist may be asked to describe the mechanisms that brought about the individual's demise but this ends normal scientific enquiry.

In contrast, philosophy has much to say about the human

mind and personal identity which has ramifications for the survival question; but the more popular idea amongst philosophers is that human beings are only bodies: consciousness being a mere by-product of the processes of the brain.

The parapsychologist's interests include survival but, in reality, most professional parapsychologists adhere to the 'supernature' worldview, choosing to investigate in their laboratories the neat and tidy phenomena of extra-sensory perception and psychokinesis which are ascribed to undiscovered laws of nature or unsuspected human abilities. Ghosts and the question of survival are less accessible problems and rely on human testimony.

The first and most formidable problem is differentiating ghosts from hallucinations and illusions. To paraphrase the remarks of Professor Antony Flew, our real problem is not directed at the question of whether ghosts have appeared to people but the question of whether, and if so how, we can know that they have and when and where they have.

The prosecution has an easy task. It needs only to introduce expert witnesses who can convince the reader of the awesome power of illusions and hallucinations to subvert reality. To this end, the first witness will relate a detective story which demonstrates just how well a complicated illusion can counterfeit experience. Ronald K. Siegal is a professor of clinical psychology and a scientist in the mould of the great fictional detectives. In his book *Fire in the Brain*, he has given an account of some of his most fascinating cases. Perhaps, not surprisingly, a number have paranormal overtones. One will suffice as an example.[1]

Mr Jack Wilson was the very model of the rugged and tanned American outdoor man. At fifty-two years of age, Wilson, a veteran of the US Navy, lived in San Diego, California, close to his 24-year-old son Peter. Psychological tests and interviews were unremarkable and presented a picture of a well-balanced, self-sufficient individual who seemed reliable and truthful. He was also a very frightened man with a most extraordinary story to tell.

Jack and Peter had driven back to California after visiting relatives in Florida. They had crossed the Arizona border at

Ghosts

night, stopping to take on extra fuel and water before entering the badlands. Sunrise found them on an isolated stretch of highway that cut its way through high desert chaparral and the southern Rocky Mountains.

The trouble began with a mechanical noise at the rear of the vehicle. Wilson stopped the car, intending to go back and take a look but, as he stepped on to the hard shoulder, he became dizzy and began to feel faint. Suddenly, there was a blinding light and a 'little grey man' appeared in front of him. The 'humanoid' was only three to four feet tall. Jack Wilson told Siegal, 'He was inside a force field that made him appear blurry. A halo of glowing lights was surrounding his head.' As Jack retreated towards the safety of his car, the alien followed him. Suddenly, he felt paralysed, his body became very light and Jack found himself transported into some sort of hovering vehicle. Just in case his psychologist was not getting the message, Wilson spelt it out, it was a ship, 'a god-dam gen-u-ine UFO'.

In the 'loading-dock' of the craft, Wilson found himself floating down a corridor honeycombed with panels. The corridor led to an 'operating theatre' where more grey figures surrounded him. One touched his head and Jack reported being knocked out and seeing the little stars experienced when someone is punched in a fight. The aliens then proceeded to 'drain his brain of memories', which Wilson saw in flash-back as if they passed across a television screen. When Siegal suggested the obvious explanation, that his patient's experience was just a vivid dream, the hypothesis was immediately shot down in flames,

> 'Friend, it was no dream,' he began. 'My son Peter was with me. They drained him, too.' This caught me off guard. Apparently there was an independent witness and co-abductee. The dream interpretation was no longer an obvious explanation.

With Jack Wilson admitted for a full clinical workup, Siegal started his investigation. Wilson's car was dirty but it was mechanically sound and no faults were discovered in the electrical wiring. It therefore could provide no clue as to the nature of the mechanical noise which had initiated the experience. But neither were there any scorch marks on the roof, or paint or chrome stripped from the outside of the vehicle, as had been claimed in stories about other UFO encounters and which might be expected to result from a close encounter with a hovering spacecraft. But there was one windfall. The professor found Jack's road map in the glovebox and borrowed it to try to build up a picture of the position and direction of the car with respect to the surrounding terrain and the rising sun at the time of the experience.

Meanwhile, his patient's medical tests showed no interesting features apart from a mild photophobia (inability to withstand bright light). Blood chemistry was normal and there were no traces of drugs or anaesthetic gases. Nurses and doctors reported that Wilson had been calm and relaxed during the examination. An independent psychologist gave his opinion that Jack was of average intelligence, unimaginative, not particularly creative and with little or no interest in UFOs or the paranormal.

Siegal's next destination was San Diego to interview the co-abductee, Jack's son Peter. For the most part, Peter's story corroborated that of his father but it differed on several essential points. He told Siegal that they had been driving for nearly thirty hours before they crossed the Arizona border. They had rotated drivers but neither man had slept well. Jack Wilson had been at the wheel for approximately eleven hours when he stopped the car. But yes, both men had seen the little grey humanoid. However, Peter told the psychologist that his father did get back in the car and Jack and his son discussed the experience, wondering if it had been a ghost or perhaps some sort of 'radioactive animal'. Peter, too, could recall the spaceship but when both men regained consciousness, they were still in the car and seven hours had elapsed.

Professor Siegal now had most of the pieces of the jigsaw puzzle. One key piece was missing and, after driving back to Los Angeles and working through the night, he discovered the missing piece of information in a textbook on atmospheric physics.

Early the next morning, Siegal collected his patient and the two men drove to a diner for breakfast. Jack Wilson was irritable and impatient and in no mood to be fobbed off with

Ghosts

further tests or medical generalisations. It would prove a difficult interview. As soon as they had ordered, Siegal started to debrief his patient with his reconstruction of what had probably happened out there in the desert.

When Wilson stepped out of the car he began to feel faint but the patient himself had offered a history of orthostatic hypotension: a common minor complaint where dizziness occurs on standing after the person has been sitting down for a long period.

The car was facing west and when Wilson turned to the back of the car he was staring into the rising sun. This was the blinding light and his almost instinctive reaction would have been to turn around and face west. When he did turn around, Jack Wilson would have been staring at the anti-solar point: a location in space directly opposite the sun. The meteorological report for the area on that day reported a light ground mist which persisted for two hours after sunrise. The mist at the anti-solar point would have focused the sun's rays to produce a halo composed of the colours of the rainbow. It is also known as a glory. The anti-solar point has been given another name by atmospheric physicists, one which was more relevant to Siegal's investigation. They give it a German name: *Heilgenschein*, meaning 'Holy Light', so-called because of the many instances of people mistaking the anti-solar point for visions of angels. Siegal reasoned that the 'little grey man' was Jack's shadow cast in the direction of the anti-solar point. The shadow, with the glory around its head and the outlines blurred and softened by the mist, produced the 'little grey humanoid' within the 'force field': a real object seen by both men. Back in the car, they discussed the strange experience and fell asleep for seven hours.

It was sleep born of exhaustion, and both men are likely to have dreamt and experienced the vivid images that occur between sleep and awakening. Peter had also dreamt about the 'grey man', the spaceship, floating inside a 'long hallway' and had experienced flash-backs from their holiday in Florida. Although there were marked differences in the two men's dreams, for the rest of the trip they continued talking excitedly, filling in gaps 'until the fleeting images of the dream coalesced into a solid abduction story'.

Peter had realised that the two men had fallen asleep inside the car but had chosen to believe that the aliens had experimented with their astral bodies. Driving back to Los Angeles, Siegal had run the interview back through his mind, 'Silently I wondered what self-respecting visitor to another planet would be satisfied with examining the astral body of an inhabitant when they could have had the real thing instead.'

There is one nagging doubt not covered by Ronald Siegal's investigation. Jack and Peter's descriptions of the spacecraft were strikingly similar. Siegal suggests that, in sharing the accounts of their respective dreams, Jack and Peter unconsciously forged a 'solid abduction story' and yet both men seemed in touch with reality. Both described the 'little grey man'. It was a sensory mistake but both recounted it accurately. Peter corrected Jack's account of being taken up into the spacecraft immediately after the encounter with the 'little grey man'; his father had returned to the car where he and his son had discussed the incident. And then both described the craft's 'loading bay', the corridor and the flashbacks. Surely, unless they had dreamt much the same dream, it would have been impossible to have found any common ground in order to produce a single story. Perhaps there really was an alien spaceship!

One answer to this question is to be found in the results of an experiment conducted by John DeHerrera, working on behalf of an American UFO investigative organisation, and Dr W. C. McCall of Anaheim, California. These investigators advertised for volunteers with high levels of creativity and verbal skills. Of those members of the public answering the advertisement, the investigators selected eight subjects who met their criteria and who claimed to have little knowledge about UFOology or the cult literature. The subjects were then provided with a questionnaire which asked them to describe an imaginary encounter with an alien spaceship, the interior of the craft and the sort of message that might be given to them by the aliens. Incredibly, the resulting fancied confrontations were highly detailed and virtually indistinguishable from accounts of alleged 'real' abductions.

Where then do these ideas come from? Towards the end of

his life, the famous psychoanalyst, Carl Jung, suggested that flying saucers corresponded to the 'Mandala', one of the fundamental archetypes which he believed were present in the subconscious of all human beings and which could give rise to corresponding hallucinations. In short, all accounts of encounters with UFOs could be imaginary.

As the supervisor of research students, Ronald Siegal likes to bring home the power of illusions and hallucinations in a dramatised form. During one tutorial, he had technicians construct two 'spacecraft' out of plastic bags, straws, tape and birthday candles. The little hot-air balloons were then released into the sunset and the technicians stood around watching their antics, hoping to attract the attention of passers-by. Soon quite a crowd gathered. As part of the 'theatre', a student arrived late for the tutorial and, after a well-scripted ticking-off from his supervisor, began to relate details of the UFO sighting. With Siegal's permission, his students tumbled out of the building and joined the crowds in the street below. Very soon, and with considerable satisfaction, Siegal was listening to graduate psychologists remarking how the 'glowing eggs' seemed to be chasing each other, darting so quickly across the sky as to defy the laws of aerodynamics. One student thought she saw shapes moving inside the 'glowing eggs' and became convinced she was seeing spacecraft manned by aliens. The exercise ended on a high note. When the candles finally burnt themselves out, the spaceships 'suddenly vanished'.

Professor Siegal's tutorial and Jack Wilson's 'little grey man' were examples of an illusion – a sensory mistake. There *is* something in the sensory field but it is misinterpreted. An illusion is public, all the onlookers can share in it. A stick appearing to bend when it is placed in water is an illusion. A mirage or the shimmering heat rising from hot sand produces the illusion of a lake or a sea to beguile the desert traveller. Lovers looking into the night sky and believing that they are watching the stars are in a sense also experiencing an illusion. We actually see the light from stars, light which left many of these suns before there was even life on earth. In the interim, many stars have been extinguished and others born. If we could really see the stars as they are today, the night sky would look very different.

Nearly all of us have experienced an auditory illusion when listening to music over the noise of a machine (such as a vacuum cleaner or the road noise in a car). When the music ends we may continue to 'hear' it for a short time. Auditory hallucinations are very common. Doctors have treated thousands of sane people who are forced to listen to the incessant chatter of internal voices.

In contrast, a visual hallucination takes place in the mind's eye. Taken simply, it is a creation of the brain that is then projected out into the sensory field. Imagine that a television has been turned off. Now if a shaft of sunlight playing on the screen convinces a person that he is watching a television picture – that is an illusion. But if there is no shaft of sunlight or any other type of sensory information available to give rise to a perceptual mistake – the resulting picture has been created by the brain; it is an hallucination.

It should not be surprising that we are prone to hallucinations. Our experience of the world is a hybrid construction woven from sensory information and our brain's interpretation of that information. In other words, we do not experience 'real objects' directly, but are forced to work with a biological 'computer simulation' of reality which is projected out into the world of tables and chairs. Philosophers call the raw sensory information 'sense data'. In psychology experiments, subjects have been given glasses which turn the world upside down. After several weeks of adjusting to their new topsy turvey world, the subjects remove the glasses, but for them the world remains upside down until their brains have learnt to reorganise the sensory information and correct the simulation.

Extraneous impressions worming their way into the simulation can subvert it to produce hallucinations so complete that it is impossible to know the difference between hallucinations and the real world. Illusions and hallucinations can sometimes merge. In a series of experiments conducted by early SPR investigators, a subject under hypnosis was told that there was a child's top spinning on a white piece of paper in front of him. The subject reported that he could indeed see the spinning top and was asked to point to it. The man then pointed to a tiny speck of dirt on the paper.

Many of us may experience hallucinations without being aware of it. Sometimes they seem to be an encounter with a ghost. The following account was related to Edmund Gurney by a distinguished officer in the Indian Army.[2]

> I had been taking luncheon with some friends, and after it was over, my host proposed that I and my fellow guest should accompany him to see some alterations he was making in his grounds. After we had been out for some little time, looking at these changes, a native servant approached me with a message from my hostess, asking me to go into the house to speak to her. I at once left my friends, and accompanied the man back to the house, following him through the verandah into the room where the luncheon had been laid. There he left me, and I waited for my hostess to come, but no one appeared; so after a few minutes I called her by name, thinking that she might not be aware that I had come in. Receiving no answer, after once again repeating her name, I walked back into the verandah, where, on entering, I had observed a durzee (or tailor) at work, and asked him where the man was who had come in with me. The durzee replied, 'Your excellency, no one came in with you.' 'But', I said, 'the man lifted the chik (the outside verandah blind) for me.' 'No your excellency, you lifted it yourself,' the durzee answered. Much puzzled, I returned to my friends in the grounds, exclaiming, 'Here's a good joke,' and then, telling them what had happened, and what the durzee had said, I asked them if they had not seen the servant who called for me shortly before. They both said they had seen no one. 'Why you don't mean to say I have not been in the house', I said. 'Oh, yes, you were in the midst of saying something about the alterations, when you suddenly stopped, and walked back into the house; we could not tell why,' they both said. I was in perfect health at the time of the occurrence, and continued to be so after it.

We seem to be moving closer to ghosts when we consider those apparitions that are seen by more than one person. Illusions can give rise to collective apparitions, like Jack and Peter Wilson's 'little grey man' but in many cases we are really unable to say how the 'illusion' was produced. Rubber-stamping all collective cases as 'illusions' is a sop to prejudice and not a guide to investigation. As will be discussed in a later chapter, a most extraordinary event took place between 1968 and 1971, above a coptic church at Zeitoun, a suburb of Cairo. Many thousands of onlookers reported seeing an apparition of the Virgin Mary which appeared by night and was seen to walk around the central dome of the church. When a sociologist also reported seeing 'something', papers in academic journals stopped referring to the apparition as a 'mass hallucination' and began describing it as an 'illusion'.

One objective fact would seem to question the illusion hypothesis of Zeitoun. Photographs had been taken of the apparition which, on inspection, appeared to reveal a figure seemingly composed of light, in long flowing robes and with a halo of light around the head. The apparition's appearance was similar to contemporary statues and icons of the Virgin Mary and appeared to show what many people in the crowds had described. Now, there are a great many reasons for arguing that the apparition could not have been the real presence of the Mother of God, but there are also many reasons for arguing that this was not an illusion either.

'Mass hallucination', often used by academics and psychiatrists to explain the seemingly inexplicable, is another strange term.[3] By definition, hallucinations are private experiences. As the Oxford philosopher, H. H. Price, once remarked, 'The notion of *public* hallucination is a very strange one, almost as strange as the notion of a public dream.'

When two or more people claim to have experienced simultaneously an apparition, we are presented with a real and intriguing problem. It is obvious that simply labelling the experience an 'hallucination' constitutes, at best, only part of an explanation. An investigator seeking to determine whether any one of these experiences is more than an hallucination must first address the problem of what is happening in collective apparitions. There are basically three hypotheses.

The first, favoured by many psychologists and doctors, and the 'lesser miracle', is that the people concerned do *not* see the same thing. One person experiences an hallucination and reports it to the others who then delude themselves that they too can see the figure. In some rare cases, an atmosphere of

Ghosts

fear and expectancy, as might be found in a house reputed to be haunted, may prompt the participants to experience *private* and *individual* hallucinations. It is only later, after much excited discussion, that these experiences are combined into a single report of a ghostly figure. This hypothesis, then, holds that there are no ghosts; simply hallucinations and self-delusion.

The second hypothesis, and one held by a great many people, is that the deceased do appear to the living and that during these experiences the ghost assumes a quasi-physical body. Ghosts can be seen by groups of people because, for the duration of the experience, they are as real as the tables and chairs.

The third hypothesis, and the one which formed the basis of the early 'Philip' experiements (Chapter Three), is that collective apparitions result from infectious hallucinations. One person creates an hallucination, which is then communicated to other onlookers by way of telepathy. Like the first hypothesis, this equates most collective apparitions with hallucinations. But surely, if telepathy is involved, the telepathic 'telegram' may originate in a deceased consciousness. Might not some collective apparitions result from telepathic messages sent by the dead?

Some cases do seem to provide evidence for the first hypothesis. Charles McCreery and Celia Green analysed such a case in their book *Apparitions*. It is a well-known story of a ghost first recounted by Sir Ernest Bennett in his book *Apparitions and Haunted Houses*.

On an afternoon in February, 1926, Miss Godly, her steward and her masseuse set off to visit an old farm labourer living on her estate. On their way back, the party seemed to see his spectre rowing across Killegar lake. Upon returning home, they learned that the old man had just died. Miss Godly related the incident to Bennett,

> One afternoon in February 1926 I went to visit a former old farm labourer of mine, Robert Bowes, who lived about a mile away, but inside the place. It was about 2.30. He had been ill for some time but was not any worse. I had lately broken my leg and was in a donkey trap, the steward was leading the donkey

and my masseuse walking behind. I talked to Robert through the open window and he sat up and talked quite well, and he asked me to send for the doctor as he had not seen him for some time. I then came straight back. The road runs along the shores of a big lake and, while the steward stopped to open a gate there, he asked me, if I saw the man on the lake. I looked and saw an old man with a long white beard which floated in the wind, crossing to the other side of the lake. He appeared to be moving his arms, as though working a punt, he was standing up and gliding across but I saw no boat. I said, 'Where is the boat?' The steward replied 'There is no boat.' I said, 'What nonsense! there must be a boat, and he is standing up in it,' but there was no boat and he was just gliding along on the dark water; the masseuse also saw him. The steward asked me who I thought he was like. I said, 'he is exactly like Robert Bowes, the old man.' The figure crossed the lake and disappeared in among the reeds and trees at the far side, and we came home. I at once went to take off my hat and coat and to write a note for the doctor, but before I had left my room, the bell rang and the doctor came in. I said I was glad to see him as I wanted him to go and see Robert Bowes; he said, 'I have just been there' (he went in a car by a different road to the one I had been on) 'and the old chap is dead.'

The steward, the first person to see the apparition, also gave an account of the experience.

Miss Anna Godly, Miss Goldsmith and I were visiting a sick man on the estate. We had no idea that he was so near passing out of this earthly life, but on parting from him on his sick bed, and on our way home we were amazed when passing Killegar lake, at the close of the same day, to see him walking on the surface of the water. His whiskers were floating in the breeze and when near the shore, in the shadow of the wood, he completely disappeared. We all three beheld the same sight.

In contrast to these two accounts, Miss Goldsmith, the masseuse, appeared to have seen something different, a 'shadowy bent form' in a *boat*,

We had just left the cottage where the old man was lying in a terribly weak condition, and on walking back, we were impelled to glance towards the lake, and saw a shadowy, bent form step from the rushes, and into a boat, and after an interval of time just disappear. We learnt later on that the old man had passed away at that moment. Though not in the least given to seeing visions, but being of an extremely practical nature, I certainly saw the spectre as I describe it.

Miss Godley remarked on the boat in her masseuse's account,

> There was no boat on the lake when we saw Robert Bowes crossing. My masseuse thought he was standing up in one, but he wasn't; there was nothing except what looked like a pole being used by him to help himself across.

What really happened that afternoon beside Killegar lake? Did the wind scudding across the black water prompt an illusion, which each of the three individuals interpreted differently? Maybe they really saw the old man's astral body or soul on the water, but then why did Miss Goldsmith's account differ so strikingly? The old man's final journey across the water appears to be a symbol for his death. Perhaps the steward of the estate, unconsciously anticipating the demise of his former employee, conjured a symbolic hallucination. When he mentioned it to his companions, they were able to convince themselves that they also saw a figure on the lake. Hallucinations, illusions, dreams, fantasies and thoughts form a continuum and thus are not always sharply distinguishable from each other.

However, in a great many cases, the evidence suggests that the participants do see the same thing. In the next case, a husband and wife experience a point-blank encounter with an apparition after they have retired to bed.[4] The reality of the figure, and the couple's fear and incredulity lend authenticity to the story and suggest that both experienced much the same thing. The apparition brings a pressing personal problem to a climax and resolution. The wife's letter to the Society for Psychical Research reads,

> June 16th 1885
> In the year 1867 I was married, and my husband took a house at S—, quite a new one, just built in what was, and still is probably, called 'Cliff Town', as being at a greater elevation than the older part of the town. Our life was exceedingly bright and happy there until towards the end of 1869, when my husband's health appeared to be failing, and he grew dejected and

The Sceptical Occultist

moody. Trying in vain to ascertain the cause for this, and being repeatedly assured by him that I was 'too fanciful', and that there was 'nothing the matter with him', I ceased to vex him with questions, and the time passed quietly away till Christmas Eve of that year (1869).

An uncle and aunt lived in the neighbourhood, and they invited us to spend Christmas Day with them – to go quite early in the morning to breakfast accompanied by the whole of our small household.

We arranged therefore to go to bed at an early hour on the night of the 24th, so as to be up betimes for our morning walk. Consequently, at 9 o'clock, we went up stairs, having as usual attended to the bars and bolts of the doors, and at about 9.30 were ready to extinguish the lamp; but our little girl – a baby of 15 months – generally woke up at that time, and after drinking some warm milk would sleep again for the rest of the night; and as she had not yet awakened, I begged my husband to leave the lamp burning and get into bed, while I, wrapped in a dressing gown, lay on the outside of the bed with the cot on my right hand.

Mrs P. then provided a diagram and description of the bedroom. The bed faced a chimney with a settee situated in between. The door was to the left of the bed and to the right the baby's cot stood between the bed and the wall. To the right also was a large bay window. Various pieces of furniture stood either side of the fireplace.

This takes some time to describe, but it was still just about 9.30, Gertrude not yet awake and I was just pulling myself into a half-sitting posture against the pillows, thinking nothing but the arrangements for the following day, when to my great astonishment I saw a gentleman standing at the foot of the bed, dressed as a naval officer, and with a cap on his head having a projecting peak. The light being in the position which I have indicated, the face was in shadow to me, and the more so that the visitor was leaning upon his arms which rested on the footrail of the bedstead. I was too astonished to be afraid, but simply wondered who it could be; and instantly touching my husband's shoulder (whose face was turned away from me), I said, 'Willie, who is this?' My husband turned, and for a second or two lay looking in intense astonishment at the intruder; then lifting himself a little, he shouted 'What on earth are you doing here, sir?' Meanwhile the form, slowing drawing himself into

Ghosts

an upright position, now said in a commanding, yet reproachful voice, 'Willie! Willie!'

I looked at my husband and saw that his face was white and agitated. As I turned towards him he sprang out of bed as though to attack the man, but stood by the bedside as if afraid, or in great perplexity, while the figure calmly and slowly moved *towards the wall* at right angles with the lamp in the direction of the dotted line. [On the diagram with her account.] As it passed the lamp, a deep shadow fell upon the room as of a material person shutting out the light from us by his intervening body, and he disappeared, as it were, into the wall. My husband now in a very agitated manner, caught up the lamp, and turning to me said, 'I mean to look all over the house, and see where he is gone.' I was by this time exceedingly agitated too, but remembering that the door was locked, and that the mysterious visitor had not gone towards it at all, remarked, 'He has not gone out by the door!' But without pausing, my husband *unlocked* the door, hastened out of the room, and was soon searching the whole house. Sitting there in the dark, I thought to myself, 'We have surely seen an apparition! Whatever can it indicate – perhaps my brother Arthur (he was in the navy, and at that time on a voyage to India) is in trouble: such things have been told of as occurring.' In some such way I pondered with an anxious heart, holding the child, who just then awakened, in my arms, until my husband came back looking very white and miserable. Sitting upon the bedside, he put his arm about me and said, 'Do you know what we have just seen?' And I said, 'Yes it was a spirit. I am afraid it was Arthur, but I could not see his face' – and he exclaimed, 'Oh! no, it was my father!'

My husband's father *had been dead for fourteen years*: he had been a naval officer in his young life; but, through ill-health had left the service before my husband was born, and the latter had only once or twice seen him in uniform. *I* had never seen him at all. My husband and I related the occurrence to my aunt and uncle and we all noticed that my husband's agitation and anxiety was very great; whereas his usual manner was calm and reserved in the extreme, and he was a thorough and avowed sceptic in all so-called-supernatural events.

As the weeks passed on my husband became very ill, and then gradually disclosed to me that he had been in great financial difficulties; and that at the time his father was thus sent to us, he was inclining to take the advice of a man who would have certainly – had my husband yielded to him (as he had intended

The Sceptical Occultist

before the warning voice) – have led him to ruin, perhaps worse...

In her classic paper *Phantasms of the Dead*, Mrs Eleanor Sidgwick, a notable academic and leading light of the early SPR, urged that seemingly evidential cases of ghosts should be analysed to exclude commonsense explanations such as 1) hoaxing, 2) exaggeration or inadequate description, 3) illusion, 4) mistaken identity, 5) hallucination.

Certainly, Mr and Mrs P. do not appear to be engaging in a hoax. The letter was written only at the behest of their friends, Dr and Mrs C., and was submitted with signed statements from friends with whom they had discussed these events closer to the time of occurrence. When compared with similar cases, the narrative does not appear to be exaggerated as we are not told that the ghost performed 'impossible' feats such as lighting candles or opening locked doors or holding forth with long Shakespearean speeches. Similarly, Mrs P. can hardly be accused of providing an inadequate description of these events. It is also clear from the locked bedroom door, and the sudden disappearance of the figure, that it is unlikely that a living person was mistaken for a ghost.

The apparition was seen by two people at close-range and we must therefore consider the possibility of an illusion. Illusions occur when several predisposing factors are satisfied. For example, Jack Wilson's 'little grey man' was the product of his shadow and the early morning mist seen in conjunction with the anti-solar point. If this ghost was an illusion it seems rather odd that, of all the nights which the couple had spent in their bedroom, applying themselves to the nightly regime demanded by their infant daughter, the predisposing conditions for the illusion (e.g. lighting, reflections, fatigue) were only satisfied on just *one* occasion. Consequently, an illusion seems to be a poor explanation of these events.

But is it not strange, readers may ask themselves, that Mr P.'s father, returning from the dead after fourteen years, risked not being recognised by choosing to appear in the uniform of a naval officer, a form of dress he had worn on only a few occasions while his son was still very young? But it is not so strange if we consider this experience to have been an hallucination. After a long period of

Ghosts

financial worry, Mr P. was faced with a decision which involved a large element of risk – *a decision he was unable to bring himself to make*. Might not Mr P.'s subconscious have arranged for a drama to resolve the conflict. The warning ghost is tainted with suspicions of regression to childhood memories, where the ultimate authority figure and the wellspring of moral action within the Victorian family, Mr P.'s father, is invested with further authority by virtue of his military uniform. To Mrs P. the 'ghost' appears to have very little to say, but its admonishment 'Willie, Willie!' is fully understood by her husband within the context of his present difficulties. In other words, might not Mr P.'s father, fashioned from childhood memories, have returned to help make his son's difficult moral decision?

There is another important reason why this case cannot be accepted as evidential. Mrs P. (Mrs Percival of Cape Town) supplied the SPR with not one but *two* first-hand accounts of apparitions. The second forms the basis of another famous case, which is often treated separately but which is linked to the first case in Ernest Bennett's *Apparitions and Haunted Houses*. This case refers to Mrs P.'s rather lonely childhood and deep attachment to her father. When he died suddenly, the woman was thrown into the deepest despair and, in the very darkest hour of her grief, experienced a realistic apparition of her father. This raises the possibility that Mrs P. was predisposed to experience hallucinations. It was Mrs P. who saw the figure of the naval officer first and a careful reading of the case indicates that, initially at least, Mr P. did not recognise the apparition. Is it not possible that Mr P.'s later identification of the figure was no more than a rationalisation that sat well with his ongoing preoccupations?

Many readers who hold a belief in ghosts and survival will, I am sure, feel that the author is simply splitting hairs, but we must gently remind ourselves that our problem here is not whether ghosts have ever appeared to people but rather how we can *know* that they have and *when* and *where* they have.

The possibility that the apparition was an hallucination is too strong for this case to stand as evidence for ghosts, but we are still left with the problem that if the above apparition was an hallucination produced by the husband or wife, how was the other able to share in this private experience?

Celia Green has suggested that there is no point in discussing whether the participants to a collective apparition see exactly the same figure since the experience is hallucinatory. We must reject Ms Green's argument for two reasons. Firstly, we see 'real objects' such as tables and chairs by virtue of a simulation *vis à vis* 'sense data' and it is very unlikely that two people looking at the same chair see exactly the same thing. Consequently, Mr and Mrs P. would not have enjoyed *exactly* the same experience, even if the figure at the foot of their bed had been a *real intruder* (a point not lost on police officers and lawyers). Secondly, if both husband and wife experienced separate and private hallucinations, why did these occur at the same time and how were they co-ordinated to resemble the actions of a single figure?

The first hypothesis, the idea that participants in collective apparitions do not have the same experiences, is difficult to sustain when considering cases like that described by Mrs P. In a collective apparition considered later in this chapter, not only is the figure seen by three people in a room but two spontaneously identify it as the recently deceased mother (the third participant, paralysed with fear, later concurred with the identification).

The second hypothesis revolves around the traditional idea of a ghost. Hollywood has made a great deal of money from the idea that ghosts have semi-physical bodies and rampage through the world, terrifying, and even inflicting harm upon, the living. During the Spiritualist craze of the nineteenth century, the faithful believed that physical mediums could conjure their departed loved-ones, who would appear to walk amongst the audience, speaking with, and even embracing, their relatives. Magicians and occultists believe that they can leave their bodies inside an 'astral body'; which is neither body nor soul but something in between. If the dead can avail themselves of quasi-physical bodies, then perhaps Mr and Mrs P. really did see a ghost.

Is it possible that ghosts can acquire a physical body and what would happen if you could touch a ghost? In fact, there are very few cases of individuals managing to grab hold of a spectre – or, for that matter, even wanting to.

In August 1891, Agnes McCaskill and her cousin Miss L.V. were sleeping in a room in Cassel, Germany.[5] They had been told that their room was haunted by the ghost of a knight who had hanged himself there and whose portrait formed one of the stained glass windows. The ghost was reputed to return to the scene of his suicide every ten years and that particular night was one of the decanniversaries. Armed with this cheerful intelligence, the two ladies retired for the night, taking care to lock their bedroom door. Just after midnight, Miss L.V. saw a strange light emerge from either the wall or the stained glass window. It materialised into a tall figure, completely draped in white, with the face concealed except for two piercing green eyes which appeared to glitter in the light from the lamp. Miss L.V., not unnaturally, screamed, prompting Agnes McCaskill to turn and she also saw the figure. The apparition was clearly defined but transparent, allowing the wall and other objects to be seen as it walked silently across the room directly towards Agnes's bed. When it came near enough, Agnes reached out and grabbed hold of it: 'as soon as it came close to my bed, I seized it, and seemed to take hold of something soft, like flimsy drapery, but whatever it was seemed dragged from me by some invisible power . . .'

Far from having a real body, the spectre in this case has many of the features of an hallucination. The scene had been set by the legend of the haunting and the 'ghost' appeared at midnight, the traditional 'witching hour'. It materialised close to the stained glass portrait, which may have catalysed the experience. Like many hallucinations, the figure was primarily experienced by only one sense (sight). The sensation of touch could also have been hallucinated.

Some participants have suffered shock and a fear-induced paralysis but, on coming to their senses during such experiences and advancing on the figure, find that it suddenly disappears. This can be explained by the brain processes which produce the hallucination suddenly being interrupted by a stream of consciousness as the person recovers his equilibrium.

In other cases apparitions have seemed 'shy' and have managed to keep out of the participant's reach. It might be argued that apparitions do not want the living to touch their 'astral bodies'; however a rather more compelling explanation is offered by Tyrrell, who reasons that the aversion to being touched results from a potential psychological conflict. That part of the person's subconscious which is organising this drama strives after consistency. A tactile hallucination of a 'solid' apparition would be contradicted by the visual hallucination of watching one's hand pass through the figure. Indeed, this was reported to have occurred in a haunting related by Sir Ernest Bennett in his book *Apparitions and Haunted Houses*.

The most impressive argument against the idea of a ghostly body comes from those cases where several people in a room report seeing the apparition, while the others present see nothing. In sending an account to the SPR in July 1886, a Mr Z. writes,[6]

> I had often heard peculiar noises in the house, and the servants called the place 'haunted' but nothing ever occurred to establish the fact until last winter, when the butler saw the shadow when putting coals on the fire. One fact seems to be satisfactorily established, and that is two or three people out of a room can see a spirit, and the others remain in ignorance of its presence. I have tried on four occasions to see it when it has appeared. My wife, a lady friend, and the butler could see it, but four other people present failed to do so.

I put this argument to a sensitive in a Buckinghamshire public house. It was very obvious that she thought that I had become deluded by my scientific training. I asked her to look at a lamp which stood on a small table close to ours. All of the people in our party could see the light and I offered to ask the other people in the pub whether they too saw the lamp. 'Real' objects, such as the ornate light in the pub, are 'out there' by consensus: we all agree that we see them. Documented experiences of apparitions demonstrate that *ghosts are not like 'real objects'. The consensus breaks down; some people see the ghosts but other people in the same location see nothing.*

There are two further arguments against the idea of ghosts

having quasi-physical bodies. Firstly, apparitions of the dead are qualitatively identical to apparitions of the living and secondly, even if the apparition is composed of 'flimsy drapery' it is still difficult to understand how it can pass through walls and other objects.

It is difficult to sustain either of the first two hypotheses on the basis of the evidence provided by people who have experienced collective apparitions. The third hypothesis introduces the contentious concept of telepathy, but the reader may decide that it offers the best explanation as to what is taking place in collective apparitions. The idea of telepathy appears to be borne out by our next case, which comes from the pen of a psychiatrist who was confronted by a patient who could create apparitions at will and who could, under certain circumstances, share them with animals and other people.

'Ruth' and her husband Paul were Americans living in Britain in the mid-1970s.[7] They had been married for six years at the time of Ruth's breakdown and had three young children. Ruth's initial distress centred around a difficulty in coping with life and relationships. She had become very agoraphobic and also suffered from frightening dreams. Immediately after her first consultation with American psychiatrist Morton Schatzman, she experienced an apparition of her father's face superimposed on that of her youngest child. At the time the baby was crying but she was unable to bring herself to pick it up.

This hallucinatory experience, representing a serious deterioration of his patient's condition, prompted Schatzman to admit Ruth to the Arbours Crisis Centre in London. The refuge was friendly and staffed by two clinical psychologists available to handle the further acute episodes which the psychiatrist suspected would soon occur. Schatzman was right; within days of being admitted to the centre, Ruth walked into the kitchen to experience a full-blown persecutory apparition of her father drinking coffee and laughing at her. Ruth realised that this and subsequent apparitions were hallucinations. Her father was still alive and would never be able to afford the airfare to come to Britain but, more importantly, Ruth was sufficiently in touch with reality to realise that the coffee cups and cigar ash associated with the figure of her father simply disappeared when the hallucination was over.

This was important to Ruth's sanity as successive hallucinations would become indistinguishable from real human beings. When the figure moved, Ruth would hear the footsteps and the rustle of its trousers. The figure looked firm and three-dimensional; it was also solid to her touch and Ruth could even smell her 'father's' unwashed body odour.

During consultations, Ruth's psychiatrist was able to build up a personal and clinical history of his patient. Schatzman and other psychiatrists have continually stressed that patient memories are often a patchwork of fact interwoven with fiction, but Ruth's alleged childhood does bear a striking resemblance to those of patients with other serious complaints, such as multiple personality disorder, which are thought to arise from severe childhood trauma.

Ruth was one of four children born to a poor white Californian family. Her father had a history of alcohol- and drug-abuse. His often violent outbursts had resulted in periods of imprisonment and several committals to a state psychiatric institution. The medical diagnosis was unclear but his behaviour showed features of schizophrenia and a severe personality disorder. During some of these periods, the children were taken into care and Ruth spent a long period in a children's home. When Ruth was ten years old, her father raped her. Ruth's mother chose not to believe her daughter's account of these events, probably because her husband had already abandoned the family several times. The mother was clear about one thing, her daughter could no longer stay under the same roof as her husband so Ruth was returned to the orphanage where she remained until she was seventeen years old. On her return home, her father's assaults continued and even occurred on trips home after she was married. More recently, he had discharged a shot-gun at Ruth and her eldest child, later claiming that it was an accident.

The extraordinary element which emerged from Ruth's biography was that she had the ability to create hallucinations of figures at will. Other apparitions, often frightening and sinister, were created outside Ruth's conscious control.

Ghosts

Schatzman speculated that she may have mistaken many of these apparitions for real people during her childhood and adolescence. So real were Ruth's apparitions that they were reflected in mirrors. If they walked in front of a light, the ambient illumination diminished and when they were speaking, Ruth found it very difficult to hear real conversations. Paul's job sometimes took him away from home but, in his absence, Ruth was able to enjoy full sexual relations with an hallucination of her husband.

This talent for conjuring apparitions may already have been well developed in early childhood and it appeared to be independent of the terrible experiences Ruth had suffered as a child. Under conscious control, many of the hallucinations may have been comforting or developed in play, but this talent was to prove a double-edged sword. It took on a more frightening aspect and moved outside Ruth's control during periods of heightened stress, such as when Ruth was placed in the orphanage or during her first pregnancy. Finally, as Ruth's defences against the ghastly memories of her past began to weaken, the apparitions once again became persecutors.

In therapy, Morton Schatzman had two problems. Firstly, he had to bring Ruth to terms with her ghastly memories and to help do this he utilised his patient's gift. Ruth was able to create an apparition of herself which would answer questions about her childhood. When she superimposed her body with the apparition and they 'merged', she was able to be regressed back to childhood. She appeared to be in a dissociative state, suggesting a type of auto-hypnosis, a trance state where she appeared to be 'possessed' by the younger versions of herself or by other people. That this therapy was successful is suggested by the later reconciliation with her father.

Secondly, Schatzman had to teach Ruth to control her faculty for creating apparitions. Part of the treatment involved bringing the hallucinations into existence and then getting rid of them, at will. They also appeared in Ruth's dreams, so Schatzman used a technique accredited to the Senoi Aboriginals in Malaya where the children are encouraged to discuss their dreams and are taught to defeat their dream enemies

The Sceptical Occultist

and then make them give them gifts. Ruth enlisted the help of a dream apparition of Morton Schatzman to defeat the dream apparition of her father. As Ruth learnt to control her apparitions and her family prepared to return to the United States, Morton stopped taking fees and, with Ruth's permission, began exploring the experimental aspects of the case.

Of course a central question remains. How do we know that Ruth really possessed this extraordinary gift? In order to test Ruth's ability, Morton Schatzman approached Peter Fenwick, a consultant in neuropsychiatry at the London Institute of Psychiatry and St Thomas's Hospital. They decided on tests used to diagnose hysterical blindness and deafness. In one, the patient is exposed to bright flashing lights or a television showing a chequerboard of interchanging squares. Although the hysterical patient may claim not to see the lights or the television screen, the images produce an involuntary electrical response in the brain ('visually evoked response') which is detected by electrodes on the patient's scalp. This electrical activity is traced on to a paper chart producing an electroencephalogram.

What would happen, the two investigators asked, if Ruth conjured an apparition between herself and the lights or television screen? Surely, being imaginary, they reasoned, it should have no effect on the visually evoked response. In fact, when Ruth created an apparition, the electrical signal in her brain was reduced, just as though a physical object had blocked out the light. Other tests showed that this occurred in the brain and not at the level of the retina: the light-reactive tissue in the eye. In other words, when the figure moved in front of the test signal, Ruth's *eyes* continued to register the light but the resulting electrical response was suppressed by her brain. It seems that the brain enters into the drama of creating the apparition at a number of different levels.

Auditory tests gave the same result. Ruth conjured an apparition of her daughter who appeared to turn down the volume on a machine which fed clicks through a pair of earphones. The resulting auditory evoked response was completely absent. Tests measuring Ruth's apparition's ability to block taste (lemon juice) and touch (alcohol cooling on the skin) gave similar results. Peter Fenwick concluded that Ruth had an unusual brain with a highly developed facility to handle 'photographic memories'. Some children can recall detailed test drawings weeks after they have been exposed to the figures. The ability to recall these 'eidetic' images tends to diminish after the age of eleven, but Ruth remained an 'eidetiker', managing to mobilise and scan perceptual memory traces with great clarity.

The case of Ruth has told us a lot about hallucinations which can masquerade as ghosts but it also had something to say about collective apparitions too. On rare occasions, animals and other people seemed able to share Ruth's hallucinations. Her cocker spaniel became very distressed when an involuntary hallucination appeared in the bathroom: but the animal cannot provide independent verification of this experience and may well have been responding to physical and emotional cues provided by her mistress. The same objections, however, cannot be levelled against the apparition of her husband, created by Ruth and apparently shared with her father.

> My car was down the street, maybe twenty yards away, and was half in shadow from a nearby tree. I made an apparition of Paul sitting behind the steering wheel. He had shadows across his face, but I could see him plainly. I told Daddy, who was standing next to me, to look in the car, because I thought someone was sitting there.
>
> 'Oh yeah,' he said, 'It looks like a ghost sitting in there. Isn't that the damnedest thing? It looks like a man, just like Paul!'

Later, Ruth's father admitted to her that he too could create apparitions, raising the possibility of an underlying genetic component.

An even more convincing shared apparition took place while Ruth was alone with her husband. Ruth was bored and a little anxious about her forthcoming transatlantic flight. While sitting on a chair, she created an apparition of herself on the sofa. While talking to her husband, she also held a mental conversation with her own apparition. It soon became apparent, however, that Paul was also speaking to the hallucination having mistaken it for his wife,

The Sceptical Occultist

When he saw me sitting on the chair near the front door, where I'd been sitting all along, he stopped as if he'd seen a ghost. He said, 'You were just sitting on the sofa. How did you get over to that chair?' ... I said that was an apparition of me you saw on the sofa! Before you started to talk to me, I'd made the apparition and had been talking to it in my mind about whether the plane I'd be on to England would crash. It was still there while you and I were talking. Paul nearly went up the wall. He said, 'I'm catching this business of seeing apparitions from you. It's rubbing off on me.'

Telepathy seems a good candidate to explain collective apparitions.[8] In some instances, like those described by Ruth, the telepathic impulse comes from a living person. The problem with the telepathy hypothesis is that collective apparitions have, in the past, been held as evidence *against* the idea of telepathy. Surely, it has been argued, if telepathy was involved, all the participants would receive the same telepathic impulse and see exactly the same thing. But that is not what happens, as different participants appear to see the apparition from their own perspective. If a person is standing behind the apparition, they see the back of the figure or if they are standing to one side, they appear to see the figure in profile. And these different views are maintained as the figure walks across the room. How could this degree of co-ordination possibly result from a single telepathic idea pattern?

In fact, it has been argued that this is not an insurmountable problem. A telepathic message in the form of an hallucinatory telegram – an apparition – requires a brain to process it and project it out on to a visual field. In other words, it is a hybrid construction formed by both telepathy and a brain. Different participants within the immediate area of the drama will organise the message within the constraints of their own visual fields. The 'organiser' in each person's subconscious ensures that the resulting drama is well co-ordinated and believable. It is known that such co-ordination is possible. When people such as Ruth experience an hallucination arising from their own subconscious, and a figure is seen reflected in a mirror, the apparition and its mirror-image are perfectly co-ordinated.

But there are other problems with the telepathy hypothesis.

How are telepathic messages 'addressed' so that they reach the right person? How does the agent know where to send the message? Long before Jan Ehrenwald postulated the mother-child link as the cradle of telepathy, investigators had noted that those apparitions which occurred after the death of the person recognised, seemed to indicate a strong emotional link between the 'sender' and 'receiver' in that the participants in these dramas were often family members or close friends. Does this emotional link in some way determine the 'address' and the specificity of the telepathic impulse? Certainly, not everyone would appear to be able to receive telepathic messages. We have already considered Mr Z.'s account of the apparition in his house; and throughout his entire investigation, Morton Schatzman was never able to share any of Ruth's hallucinations. On the other hand, there is some evidence that telepathy is not always specific but can be picked up by bystanders within the immediate location. In the following case, Mrs Clerke was unable to perceive the apparition which was seen by her servant.[9]

In August 1864, about 3 or 4 o'clock in the afternoon, I was sitting reading in the verandah of our house in Barbados. My black nurse was driving my little girl in her perambulator in the garden. I got up after some time to go into the house, not having noticed anything at all, when this black woman said to me, 'Missis, who was that gentleman that was talking to you just now?' 'There was nobody talking to me,' I said. 'Oh yes, dere was, Missis – a very pale gentleman, very tall, and he talked to you, and you was very rude, for you never answered him.' I repeated there was no one and got rather cross with the woman, and she begged me to write down the day, for she knew she had seen someone. I did, and in a few days I heard of the death of my brother in Tobago. Now, the curious part is this, that *I* did not see him, but she – a stranger to him – did; and she said that he seemed very anxious for me to notice him.

We are finally in a position to assess the evidence for ghosts. Edmund Gurney and F. W. H. Myers believed that only a handful of cases arising from testimony were of sufficient character to offer evidence in this respect,

There remain three, and I think only three, conditions which might establish a presumption that an apparition or other immediate manifestation of a dead person is something more than a mere subjective hallucination of the percipient's senses. Either 1) more persons than one might be independently affected by the phenomenon; or 2) the phantasm might convey information, afterwards to be discovered to be true, of something which the participant had never known; or 3) the appearance might be that of a person whom the participant himself had never seen, and of whose aspect he was ignorant, and yet his description of it might be sufficiently definite for identification.

With the case of Ruth, and the growing suspicion that some collective apparitions are just hallucinations shared by way of telepathy, it is clear that Gurney's and Myers's first condition is no longer strong enough. But a case would be more impressive if one of the parties was a spectator with little or no attachment to the person recognised in the apparition. The following case was printed in the magazine of 'The Orphanage and Home, Aberlour, Craigellachie' and was verified by the Warden and participant, the Reverend Charles Jupp,[10]

In 1875, a man died leaving a widow and six orphan children. The three eldest were admitted into the Orphanage. Three years afterwards the widow died, and the friends succeeded in getting funds to send the rest here, the youngest being about four years of age. At this time the Orphanage contained nearly 30 inmates, for the smaller ones of whom the Warden did everything that was required. There was not a spare room in the house, and visitors to the Orphanage had to be lodged in the parsonage. About six months after the arrival of the younger children referred to above, two visitors arrived unexpectedly late in the evening – too late to get a bed aired at the parsonage; it was therefore arranged that they should have the Warden's room, he agreeing to take a bed in the little ones' dormitory, which contained ten beds, nine occupied. No other change except this was made in the usual order of things.

In the morning, at breakfast, the Warden made the following statement: 'As near as I can tell I fell asleep about 11 o'clock, and slept very soundly for some time. I suddenly woke without any apparent reason, and felt an impulse to turn around, my face being towards the wall, from the children. Before turning, I looked up and saw a soft light in the room. The gas was burning low in the hall, and the dormitory door being open, I thought it probable that the light came from that source. It was soon evident, however, that such was not the case. I turned round, and then a wonderful vision met my gaze. Over the second bed from mine, and on the same side of the room, there was floating a small cloud of light, forming a halo of the brightness of the moon on an ordinary moonlight night.

'I sat upright in bed, looked at this strange appearance, took up my watch and found the hands pointing to five minutes to one. Everything was quiet and the children sleeping soundly. In the bed, over which the light seemed to float, slept the youngest of the six children mentioned above.

'I asked myself, "Am I dreaming?" No! I was wide awake. I was seized with a strong impulse to rise and touch the substance, or whatever it might be (for it was about five foot high), and was getting up when something seemed to hold me back. I am certain I heard nothing, yet I *felt* and perfectly understood the words – "No, lie down, it won't hurt you." I *at once* did what I felt I was told to do. I fell asleep shortly afterwards and rose at half-past five, that being my usual time.

'At 6 o'clock I began dressing the children, beginning at the bed furthest from the one in which I slept. Presently I came over to the bed over which I had seen the light hovering. I took the little boy out, placed him on my knee, and put on some of his clothes. The child was talking with the others, suddenly he was silent. And then, looking me hard in the face with an extraordinary expression, he said "Oh Mr Jupp, my mother came to me last night. Did you see her?" For a moment I could not answer the child. I then thought it better to pass it off, and said, "Come, we must make haste, or we shall be late for breakfast."'

The child never afterwards referred to the matter, we are told, nor has it since ever been mentioned to him. The Warden says it is a mystery to him; he states the facts and there leaves the matter, being perfectly satisfied that he was mistaken in no one particular.

In 1883, Edmund Gurney wrote to the Reverend Jupp asking for further verification, the Warden replied,

Dear Sir, – I fear that anything the little boy might say now would be unreliable, or I would at once question him. Although the matter was fully discussed at the time, it was never mentioned in the hearing of the child, and yet, when at the request of friends, the account was published in our little magazine, and the child read it, his countenance changed, and looking up he said 'Mr Jupp, that is me.' I said 'Yes, that is what we saw.' He said 'Yes', and then seemed to fall into deep thought, evidently with pleasant remembrances, for he smiled so sweetly to himself, and seemed to forget I was present.

I much regret now that I did not learn something from the child at the time.

(signed) CHAS. JUPP.

This story has the ring of truth and it would be difficult to account for this case on the basis of fraud, mistaken identity or exaggeration. An illusion is an unlikely explanation as one of the participants, the child, was asleep. It might be argued that the Warden experienced a vivid waking dream, but what of the child's testimony? It could be ascribed to chance, but in that case it is a double coincidence as not only did the Warden and the child have an unusual experience on the same night but, of the ten beds over which the light in a dream might have been seen to hover, it chose the bed of the only child to later report an unusual occurrence.

Mrs Sidgwick believed that this case would *not* stand as evidence for the possibility of communication with the dead as she preferred to ascribe it to an hallucination created by the sleeping child and transferred to the Warden. However, unlike the case of Mr and Mrs P. and the ghost of the naval officer, there is no additional evidence to prefer this explanation. More importantly, if Mrs Sidgwick was right, then it is the case that sleeping and dying children create hallucinations which are transferred to onlookers, as this case is representative of a whole class of collective apparitions.

A similar anecdotal case was collected by Professor Camile Flammarion after two French journals, the *Petit Marseillais* and the *Revue des Revues*, conducted surveys of paranormal experiences. In a letter, a woman explained that she was called away from home and left her child with her mother. While she was away, she dreamt that her daughter had become ill. This turned out to be the case and the girl died about ten days later.

I had a daughter of 15. She was my joy and my pride. Once, when I had to go away from home for a few days, I left her with my mother. Two days before my child died I was lying in bed with my eyes closed, though I was not asleep. My daughter was asleep in the next room with the nurse watching her. Suddenly, a penetrating brightness filled the room. I called the nurse, but it was a few seconds before she answered. I jumped out of bed and hurried to my daughter's bedside. Then the light faded and the room was only lit by the night-lamp. The nurse was quivering with fear, and I tried in vain to discover what had frightened her. . . . The next morning she related how she had seen my husband, who had died six months before, at the foot of my child's bed.[11]

A third case was brought to the attention of the SPR by the Reverend Alfred Holborn. A written statement was provided by one of the participants and signed by both.[12]

Dec. 9th, 1903

At Mr Holborn's request I enclose an account of our experience last June. I have consulted the father and [sister] of the boy mentioned, and they would much rather the names should *not* be mentioned if you think fit to use it in any way. I may say that Mrs G. [assumed initial] and I were as close friends as it is possible to be. She often remarked, 'We really think aloud when together.'

Many times I went to her when she needed me without knowing why I did so, and she also came to me. We worked together eighteen years at a Mothers' Meeting, taking the lessons alternatively. Often when I had thought of a prayer suitable to the women's needs, when it was her turn to speak, I suddenly changed the thoughts, and took up the line she was thinking of, quite ignorantly of it, so you will understand how natural it seemed to see her that evening . . . The sister referred to in the account cannot write about it but she will give her signature as to its correctness.

. . . A little friend of ours, H.G., had been ill a long time. His mother, who was my greatest friend, had nursed her boy with infinite care, and during her short last illness was full of solicitude for him. After her death he seemed to become stronger for a time, but again grew very ill, and needed the most constant care, his eldest sister watching over him as the mother had done. As I was on the most intimate terms with the family, I saw a great deal of the invalid.

On Sunday evening, June 28th, 1903, about 9 o'clock, I and the sister were standing at the foot of the bed, watching the sick one, who was unconscious, when suddenly I saw the mother distinctly. She was in her ordinary dress as when with us, nothing supernatural in her appearance. She was bending over the boy with a look of infinite love and longing and did not seem to notice us. After a minute or two she quietly and suddenly *was not there*. I was so struck that I turned to speak to the sister, but she seemed so engrossed that I did not think it wise to say anything.

The little patient grew gradually worse, until on Tuesday evening, June 30th, I was summoned to go at once. When I arrived at the house he had passed away. After rendering the last offices of love to the dear little body, the sister and I again stood, as on the Sunday, when I said, 'M— —, I had a strange experience on Sunday evening here.' She quickly replied, 'Yes, mother was here; I saw her.' The young girl is not given to fancies at all, and must have been impressed as I was.

In this case, the correspondent infers a degree of telepathy between herself and the deceased woman but this may just be chance-coincidence or imagination and, anyway, there is other evidence that bystanders without any particular 'gifts' can become party to collective apparitions. There is also the possibility that one of the women, caught up by the pathos of the situation, consciously or subconsciously created a vision of the child's mother.

The same criticisms cannot be levelled at our next case of this type. Here a vision of the recently dead mother is seen by all in the room.[13]

March 1889

My mother died on the 24th of June 1874, at a house called The Hunter's Palace, Silima, Malta, where we were then residing for her health. She had always a great fear of being buried alive, and extracted a promise from my father that wherever she died he should not allow her to be buried for a week, and I remember we had to get special permission, as it was the custom to bury within three days in a hot climate. The third day after death was the last time I saw her, and I then went into the room with my father, and we cut off all her hair, which was very long and curly. I have no remembrance of being at all nervous or in the least frightened. On the seventh day after death she was buried, and it was on that night she appeared to me. I slept in a little dressing-room opening out of

Ghosts

the larger nursery, which, like many old houses, had two steps leading to it. The smoking-room where my father generally spent his evenings, was across the hall, and my little room also had a door opening on to the hall, so that it was not necessary for me to go through the nursery, where my two little brothers slept, to get out.

On this particular evening the weather was stifling hot, and intensely still. I had been put to bed earlier than usual, and had no light in the room; the Venetian shutters were open as far as they could go, and the night was so beautiful that the room was quite light. The door to the nursery was only partially closed, and I could see the nurse's shadow as she leaned over her work, and I gazed at the shadow of her hand moving up and down with an irritating regularity until I fell asleep. I seemed to have been sleeping some time when I woke, and turning over on the other side towards the window saw my mother standing by my bedside crying and wringing her hands. I had not been awake long enough to remember that she was dead and exclaimed quite naturally (for she often came in when I was asleep) 'Why dear, what's the matter?' and then suddenly remembering I screamed. The nurse sprang up from the next room but on the top step flung herself on her knees, and began to tell her beads [say the Rosary] and cry. My father at the same moment arrived at the opposite door, and I heard his sudden exclamation of 'Julia, darling!' My mother turned towards him, and then to me, and wringing her hands again retreated towards the nursery and was lost. The nurse afterwards declared that she distinctly felt something pass her, but she was in such a state of abject terror that her testimony is quite worthless. My father then ordered her out of the room, and telling me that I had only been dreaming stayed until I fell asleep. The next day, however, he told me that he too had seen the vision, and that he hoped to again, and that if ever she came to see me again I was not to be frightened, but to tell her that 'papa wanted to speak to her,' which I faithfully promised to do, but I need scarcely say that she never appeared again.

What has struck me as curious since then is that I saw her as she usually came to see me the last thing at night, dressed in a white flannel dressing-gown trimmed with a band of scarlet braid and her long hair loose and flowing. She *was* not buried in that dressing-gown, and we had cut-off all her hair. Years afterwards, when we were speaking of it, my father told me that she had promised to come back after death if such a thing was possible. That being the case it is curious that she should have appeared to me. The nurse from that time forward refused to sit alone in the nursery, and predicted no end of dreadful things as likely to happen, but when a few weeks afterwards I sickened for a long and serious illness she was quite satisfied. She was Maltese and when we left the island we quite lost sight of her. My father died just three years ago, so that I am now the only eye-witness left. My father's second wife has, however, heard the story from him and will sign this.

L.H.
M.S.H.

Some of the details of this case hint that the eight-year-old girl, who was the main participant in this account, may have been responsible for the apparition of her mother. It may be significant that the apparition occurred on the evening after the mother's burial. It is also interesting that the figure was observed in her normal dress, with long flowing hair and that the child, upon awakening, had forgotten her loss and had mistaken the apparition for her mother. However, in a following letter she claimed that she had had no other hallucinatory experiences and the apparition did seem life-like and responsive to the presence of both the girl and her father.

A more recent and intriguing collective apparition was first described by Hilary Evans at a recent meeting of the SPR[14]. Taken from the pages of a journal of psychiatry, it provides an analysis of how the medical profession views the experiences of a patient who claims to have seen an apparition.

Mr B. was a thirty-two-year-old clerk who lived with his elderly mother and his sister J.B., also single, who was employed as a shorthand typist. A third sister V.B. was married with two children and lived in the same street. Mr B's mother died in January 1957 at the age of seventy-two. For some time she had suffered from senile dementia and an inoperable cancer of the stomach. In her last months of life the patient was nursed by her daughter J.B. and by the married sister V., who would often call in to 'give a hand'.

After his mother's death, Mr B. collapsed, suffering from fatigue, a 'swimming head' and severe agoraphobia or a fear of meeting people. An exacerbation of a duodenal ulcer resulted in him being admitted to hospital in February 1957 when surgeons were forced to remove part of his stomach. For the next thirteen months, Mr B. did not work but continued to suffer from an anxious depression and frequently entertained thoughts of suicide. In March 1958, he was admitted to a psychiatric ward at Barrow Hospital under Dr N. Lukianowicz. Much of the resulting clinical report centred on a most extraordinary story which he and his sisters related to the doctor.

At the request of his doctor, Mr B. wrote an account of his experiences which he entitled a 'History of My Life and My Visions'. Mr B. was a shy, nervous man. A timid child, he had been something of a scholar until a prolapse of the retina, at the age of eleven, had resulted in the 'complete loss of sight in the left eye', and the development of a 'severe inferiority complex'. He found it difficult to form an attachment to girls and described himself as 'nervous, panicky, self-conscious and wanting in confidence'. His hobbies were passive: record playing and photography. He did not smoke and drank sparingly. He had certainly been a child who was prone to 'seeing things', relating that he was persecuted by 'evil and frightening faces in the dark. I would see them mostly when just falling asleep. Often I was so frightened that I lay awake for hours, with my eyes open, seeing these red and yellow faces lurking in all corners. I was too afraid to call out.'

As a child, Mr B. admitted to several 'psychic' experiences. During the German air-raids of the Second World War he admitted to two precognitive experiences, both of which were confirmed by his two sisters. In one, he correctly anticipated a direct hit on the family's air-raid shelter in their back garden. The other was more striking. During a flying bomb raid, he and his mother took refuge in a public shelter. 'At first I stood with a group of people in the centre of the shelter, when, again, something told me to get away from this place. I did, and moved to the entrance of the shelter. I asked the others to follow me; but they only laughed and nobody moved but my mother. After a few seconds a bomb hit the centre of the shelter, and only I and mother, and a few people who stayed near the entrance, remained alive.'

I have related Mr B.'s personal and medical history in some

detail as the prosecution would insist that Mr B. was the sort of person most likely to experience hallucinations. After his mother's death, Mr B. felt himself persecuted by her apparition, 'Since my mother died, her apparition comes twice a week through the closed door of my bedroom and stops at the foot of my bed. She stands there for a while and stares at me. I always have the impression that she wants to tell me something but can't. Her dress is colourless and indescribable.'

Mr B. was so afraid of the apparition of his mother that he would hide his head under the pillow or blanket until the experience had ended. Mr B. was a nervous man who was still prone to 'seeing things'. The defence would argue that none of this is of any real consequence as the most extraordinary aspect of Mr B.'s testimony, and the primary cause of his breakdown, was also experienced by his two sisters. His sister, J.B., who slept in the next room (previously the mother's bedroom), was also troubled by apparitions of her mother. When interviewed by her brother's doctor, J. told him,

> I have never at any time, seen my mother during the daytime. But I have *heard* her footsteps and *felt* that she was near. At night I have seen her in my room standing near my bed, or near the fireplace. She has also appeared to walk through the locked door. Sometimes she was crying, sometimes *calling* my name ... Except on one occasion, she was dressed in a long white gown, as I saw her after death ... These visions have occurred before sleep.... I would say a short time *before sleep*, perhaps ten minutes. I cannot say exactly; I only know that I have felt drowsy.... *Upon waking I have seen her*, standing by my bed, just looking at me. Always I have tried to keep her out of my room, trying to push her away. But I have not felt anything to touch.... I have awakened and *felt her gripping my arm*; and though I could not see her, I felt her presence.... The last time I saw her, she was dressed in a red dress, which she often wore in life. I still did not see her feet. She looked happy, and I spoke to her. I asked her where she was, and if she was happy. She assured me that she was very happy, nodding her head, and saying 'yes'. This time I was not afraid, and I tried to keep her with me. But she disappeared through the window ... Since then I have not seen her. It was on the night before my brother went to the hospital. But I still hear her calling to me. Also, I feel at times she is in my room. But I never see her now.

The evidence so far might be interpreted as the brother and sister experiencing separate post-bereavement hallucinations. And yet their testimonies contain some curious synchronised aspects. While alive, their mother was in the habit of getting out of bed in the morning, going to the landing, and calling to one or other of her children. After the mother's death, and while Mr B. and his sister were at breakfast, they would hear 'her' leave her room and call out from the landing, but each heard their own name being called. But the most astonishing aspect of this case was that, totally unbeknown to B. and his sister J., their married sister was also experiencing apparitions of her mother. This was only revealed when Mrs V.B. was interviewed by Dr Lukianowicz.

> It's funny you should have asked me this question. In fact, I have seen my mother very often, but I wouldn't tell anyone but my husband. But he just laughed and said 'Rubbish'. But I saw her many times, usually just *when I was falling asleep*. She would come in, right through the panels in the door, and then would stop at my bed and gaze. I got frightened, and had hid my head under the pillow, and kept it there till she went ... And do you know, what's the funniest part of it? That *I could see her with my eyes closed*. Twice I waked up my husband, but he is no use. He never could see her, though she was there, just at the foot of the bed staring at me. Then Frank [her husband] said that I was as mad as my poor mother was, and the next minute he snored again ... And you say they [her brother and sister] had seen her, too? Funny thing, they never mentioned. I think they were afraid. I don't blame them. I was afraid too. And the funniest thing is that it all should have stopped so suddenly, once my brother went to hospital. ... I have never seen her since. ... Yes, I have *also heard her* sometimes, *calling me from upstairs*, when there was no one there. ...

Perhaps, not surprisingly, Dr Lukianowicz concluded that Mr B. and his two sisters had experienced subjective hallucinations of their mother. This is the explanation that science affords to these sorts of experiences, but is it the right one? From the very beginning, Dr Lukianowicz is forced to blur the distinction between scientific fact and his own beliefs. He entitled his paper 'Hallucinations à Troix' which is an allusion to 'folie à deux', a term coined by Dr Jack Oatman writing in the *American Journal of Psychiatry* in 1942. In his classic paper, Oatman described two patients who seemed to be speaking the same words in a simultaneous synchronised manner. In fact, with careful measurements Oatman was able to show that one patient was speaking a fraction of a second ahead of the other, who then only repeated what he had heard. But is 'folie à deux' applicable to the present case, where Mr B. and Miss J.B. were experiencing apparitions of their mother in the family home, while 300 yards down the street the married sister was also experiencing an almost identical apparition at the same time and yet neither of the two parties knew of the experiences of the other!

Lukianowicz concluded that the guilt which each individual experienced, as the result of nursing their mentally ill mother, was sufficient cause for each of the children to have experienced persecutory hallucinations of their mother after her death. However, most of us experience guilt at the loss of a loved one. Many of us may find ourselves plagued by incessant questions. Could we have done more? Should we have wished for the 'happy release', only to ease our own burden? And, yet, how many of us experience hallucinations of the deceased in such a striking manner after their death?

Lukianowicz mentioned and then rejected the parapsychological literature on apparitions, commenting that these ideas would not have led to a better understanding of what was happening here. Nevertheless, a purely scientific appraisal leaves one glaring observation unexplained. Why did the visual apparition experienced by the two sisters cease abruptly after their brother had been admitted to hospital? Is it possible that this nervous man, who was prone to hallucinations, created an apparition of his mother which was then transmitted to his sisters?

Lukianowicz correctly labelled many of the apparitions as hypnagogic and hypnopompic imagery. He drew attention to this by emphasising the relevant areas of the two sisters' statements (which appear in italics). Commonly many hallucinations do occur just before sleep (hypnagogic imagery) or upon awaking from sleep (hypnopompic imagery). But is there another explanation for this observation? If telepathy was involved, is it likely that Mr B's sisters were in a more receptive state, immediately before sleep or on just awakening, when they were conscious but in a very relaxed state of mind?

Dr Lukianowicz also emphasised those areas of the sisters' statements where one or other remarked that they continued to see their mother even with their eyes closed or with their heads under the blankets. This he takes as further evidence for the hallucinatory nature of these experiences. After all, while it is clear that Dr Lukianowicz did not countenance such things, the traditional idea of a ghost is that it is a real object standing 'out there'. But as we have seen, ghosts are not real objects, they are experienced internally, which is why it is so difficult to separate ghosts from hallucinations.

Was there a ghost in this case? It can only be said that we cannot exclude the possibility. The apparition had a certain independence of the three observers. Certainly, the unmarried sister continued to 'sense' her mother's presence after her brother had been admitted to hospital. If the mother's spirit was responsible for these manifestations, why did the visual apparitions cease after the brother was admitted to Barrow Hospital? Is it possible that Mr B., a man with alleged 'psychic' abilities, acted as a sort of 'repeater station', amplifying the telepathic message from his mother and unconsciously relaying it to his two sisters? Or might it have been the case that the mother's spirit, having driven her son to a nervous breakdown, ceased her manifestations? Some of these latter questions may appall the reader schooled in the classical sciences but is it not better to consider all the possibilities, rather than labelling such experiences 'Hallucinations à Troix' in the mistaken belief that this constitutes a full explanation?

There is yet stronger evidence for ghosts in the other two categories of phantasms: those conveying correct information that might not otherwise have been known and the appearance of a figure the participant has never seen, but whose identity is later discovered and verified. A case of each type should suffice.

In the first, involving a priest, any explanation centring around a subjective hallucination would also be forced to account for the additional element of clairvoyance. The following written account was given by the Reverend Father C.,

The Sceptical Occultist

a well-known Catholic priest to Sir Ernest Bennett, on 10th February 1935.[15]

On the 3rd December 1908 I was living with the R. C. Bishop of Southwark at his house in St George's Road, London, S.E.1. One other priest lived in the house, but at this date was away from home, so that the bishop and I were alone except for the servants, whose quarters were in the semi-basement.

This being the bishop's official residence a number of people came and went in the daytime, and occasional visitors came and stayed. On the evening of the 2nd the bishop and I dined together alone, and after dinner he went to his room and I to mine on the third floor.

At about 6.30 a.m. on the 3rd December I got up and proceeded downstairs to the bathroom. As I turned the corner of the stairs from my room on the third floor and was proceeding down a flight of steps which led to the landing on the second floor, I saw an elderly man standing at the foot of the stairs. He was a stranger to me and wore a cassock and white cotta or short surplice. This man, who had grey hair and a very long upper lip, stood with his hands joined and his head on one side looking up at me in an enquiring sort of way. I thought that he was some priest who had come on after dinner overnight and that he was looking for the Bishop's oratory, and was just about to speak to him, when he vanished completely. I still thought he had gone into one or other of the passages and looked for him in both. Till I failed to find him I had no idea but that he was a living man. I then went upstairs again a couple of times and came down in the same way as I had done at first to satisfy myself that it was not some trick of the light shining in from the street, but nothing more happened and I saw no more of the figure.

At breakfast later I asked the bishop if anybody had stayed in the house overnight and he said, No.

I then went about my usual work and at luncheon, the bishop told me that he had had a telegram to say that a Father F. of Bromley, Kent had died that morning at 6.30 a.m.

As I did not know Father F. even by sight this information did not affect me at all.

About five or six weeks later I was appointed to take the place of Father F. at Bromley. When I got settled in and began to visit my parishioners I went into a house and in the 'parlour' I saw a large framed photograph of an elderly priest, without a shadow of a doubt the man I had seen on the stairs on December the 3rd. When the owner of the house came in I asked, 'Whose portrait is that?' She replied, 'Why, don't you know, that was dear Father F.'

The above is as plain a narrative of what happened as I can write. There are one or two points to be noticed. 1. The apparition was straight in front of me. 2. The subject of the apparition was entirely unknown to me. 3. At the relevant date there was no thought of my being appointed to a parish. 4. Although the only light was through the windows from the street lamps, I saw every detail of the apparition quite clearly. 5. At this time I was in my thirty-eighth year and had not had any previous occult experience.

The reader must decide from this testimony what they think is more likely to have occurred. Did Father F.'s concern for his parish drive him to seek out his successor at the moment of death? But is the better explanation that Father C. experienced a random hallucination on the stairs, coincident with Father F.'s demise, and later mistook the portrait of the old priest for that of the apparition? Perhaps Father C. subconsciously chose to identify the hallucination as Father F. in order to invest the experience with a spiritual content? Certainly, the sceptic's argument against all such cases is one of mistaken identity.

Our last case is probably the most famous ghost story on record.[16] The incident became part of the legal record of the state of North Carolina and ultimately resulted in the Superior Court accepting a son's account of his father's apparition, and the information it provided, which resulted in the discovery of a more recent Will. The story is to be found in all good textbooks of parapsychology and continues to be featured in professional papers whenever parapsychologists argue for the reality of apparitions of the dead.

A newspaper account of the case was read by a Canadian member of the British SPR, who then hired Mr J. M. N. Johnson, Attorney-at-Law, of Aberdeen, North Carolina, to examine the matter on his behalf. The resulting investigation was very thorough and included the court records and sworn statements from two of the principle witnesses.

The facts of the case are these: James L. Chaffin, the Testator and a farmer in Davie County, N.C., was survived by his

The Sceptical Occultist

wife and four sons, John, James, Marshall and Abner. His first Will, and that on record, was made on 16 November, 1905 and attested by two witnesses. It bequeathed the farm to the third son, Marshall, who was also appointed sole executor. On 7 September, 1921, James Chaffin died as the result of an accident and Marshall Chaffin obtained Probate on the Will on 24 September of the same year. Four years passed and events now centred on James Pinkney Chaffin, the Testator's second son, as seen through his sworn statement to Mr Johnson on 21 April, 1927,

> In all my life I never heard my father mention having made a later will than the one dated in 1905. I think it was in June of 1925 that I began to have very vivid dreams that my father appeared to me at my bedside but made no verbal communication. Some time later, I think it was the latter part of June, 1925, he appeared at my bedside again, dressed as I had often seen him dressed in life, wearing a black overcoat which I knew to be his own coat. This time my father's spirit spoke to me, he took hold of his overcoat this way and pulled it back and said, 'You will find my will in my overcoat pocket,' and then disappeared.
>
> The next morning I arose fully convinced that my father's spirit had visited me for the purpose of explaining some mistake. I went to mother's and sought for the overcoat but found it was gone. Mother stated that she had given the overcoat to my brother John who lives in Yadkin County about twenty miles north-west of my home. I think it was on the 6th of July, which was on Monday following the events stated in the last paragraph, I went to my brother's home in Yadkin County and found the coat. On examination of the inside pocket I found that the lining had been sewd together. I immediately cut the stitches and found a little roll of paper tied with a string which was in my father's handwriting and contained only the following words: 'Read the 27th chapter of Genesis in my daddie's old Bible.'
>
> At this point I was so convinced that the mystery was to be cleared up I was unwilling to go to mother's home to examine the old Bible without the presence of a witness and I induced a neighbour, Mr Thos. Blackwelder to accompany me, also my daughter and Mr Blackwelder's daughter were present. Arriving at mother's home we had a considerable search before we found the old Bible. At last we did find it in the top bureau

Ghosts

drawer in an upstairs room. The book was so dilapidated that when we took it out it fell into three pieces. Mr Blackwelder picked up the portion containing the Book of Genesis and there we found two leaves folded together, the left hand page forming a pocket and in this pocket Mr Blackwelder found the will which has been probated.

The second Will which was probated in December 1925, read,

After reading the 27th chapter of Genesis, I James L. Chaffin, do make my last will and testament and here it is. I want, after giving my body a decent burial, my little property to be equally divided between my four children, if they are living at my death, both personal and real estate divided equal, if not living, give share to their children. And if she is living, you must all take care of your mammy. Now this is my last will and testament. Witness my hand and seal.

James L. Chaffin,
This January 16, 1919.

James Pinkney Chaffin's statement continues:

During the month of December, 1925, my father again appeared to me about a week before the trial of the case of Chaffin vs Chaffin and said 'Where is my old will', and showed considerable temper. I believed from this that I would win the lawsuit as I did. I told my lawyer about this visitation the next morning.

Many of my friends do not believe it is possible for the living to hold communication with the dead but I am convinced that my father actually appeared to me on several occasions and I shall believe it to the day of my death.

The second Will, although unattested, was valid under state law if the document could be shown to have been written entirely in the Testator's hand. The jury decided that this was the case. By the time of the trial, Marshall A. Chaffin had died, leaving his widow and son to contest the second Will but they withdrew their suit after they were shown the Will in the Testator's handwriting and were told that ten witnesses were prepared to give evidence that it was indeed his handwriting.

Parapsychologists have been divided over the interpretation

The Sceptical Occultist

that has been given to these events. Some, such as Professor Ian Stevenson, believe that the case offers good evidence for survival and the fact that the dead can communicate with the living through apparitions. The other camp, adherents of the 'supernature' worldview, prefer the 'lesser miracle' that James Pinkney Chaffin became clairvoyantly aware of the existence of his father's second Will and that this information was presented to his consciousness in striking and highly dramatised form. In other words, it is a case of ESP and not a communication from beyond the grave.

There is, of course, the third and obvious hypothesis that no miracle was involved and the second Will was a fake, but this is usually summarily dismissed on the basis of the document being in the Testator's handwriting.

Let us pause briefly to look at this story again. The Chaffins were a divided family. The first Will made no provision for the widow or the other three children and the estate was left not to the eldest son but to one of the younger children. We are now told that, two years before his fatal accident, the father experienced a marked change of heart (after reading the story of Jacob and Esau in the 27th Chapter of Genesis) and made a second Will, providing for a more just distribution of his wealth, with some provision for his wife. And yet, he failed to have the second Will witnessed; neither did he tell his family, or leave it in a place where it would be accessible after his death. But now comes the strangest part of this story; the father leaves a clue to the Will's whereabouts concealed in the lining of the inside pocket of his overcoat. Was James L. Chaffin's religious faith so secure, we might ask, that he was certain he could appear from the grave, to set in place a paper-trail to tantalise the family after his death?

The reader may agree that the message in the lining of the overcoat is a red-herring: a piece of the jigsaw that really does not fit. Surely it could not have been sewn into the coat by the father as an *aide memoire*, because if he could forget that the second Will was in his father's Bible, clearly he could forget that the clue was sewn into the lining of his overcoat! What was the purpose of this message?

In James Pinkney Chaffin's statement we are told that the

apparition of his father said to him in the dream 'You will find my *will* in my overcoat pocket,' and yet when the son goes to look for the overcoat he does not ask for witnesses to accompany him. He is clearly fully aware of the legal position, because when he goes in search of the Bible he takes three witnesses and allows his neighbour, Thomas Blackwelder, to conduct the search and actually discover the second Will. *Does this suggest that James Pinkney knew all along that he would not discover the Will in the overcoat but simply a clue directing him to its actual hiding place in the Bible?* The coat had been discarded and given to another brother, which appears to add credence to the story but, even if it had been lost, it would not have mattered as the Will was safely tucked away in a Bible in the widow's possession. Might we not suggest that the message in the overcoat was placed there by the living to further dramatise these events and support a ghost story that provided the means of introducing a second Will?

The other members of the family clearly had both motive and opportunity. As for the handwriting, James L. Chaffin's script was distinctive and possibly easy to counterfeit and there were four years in which this might have been done. It may be significant that the 'apparition' only appeared after the death of Marshall Chaffin, the sole beneficiary of the first Will. This is not to suggest that the second Will *was* a fake but rather that the reader may feel that this account introduces an element of doubt which detracts from the efficacy of the evidence.

The reader need only find a single case proven, to establish the reality of ghosts and all that that entails. The sceptical position has been to attack each case on the basis of hallucinations, mistaken identity, illusions, exaggeration and fraud, but is the element of doubt sufficient to demolish each and every case?

The sceptic raises two general objections to the type of evidence detailed in this chapter and these need to be answered. The first is that these accounts collected by the early investigators are not seen today and thus by inference, they merely represent the Victorians' preoccupation with death. During the two years in which I researched this book, I was

The Sceptical Occultist

struck by the number of early cases that came to the attention of the Society for Psychical Research by way of the leading members' extensive professional and social contacts or from interested third parties who supported their brave new investigation into the unknown. Other cases were windfalls, but more still, like the Chaffin Will Case, were collected by ordinary members, at considerable cost to themselves in terms of time and money.

Parapsychology was once a gentleman's game but society has changed. The leading members of today's SPR are drawn from the same professional backgrounds but they lack the extensive personal contacts prevalent in Victorian high-society. Furthermore, the groundswell of enthusiasm amongst the ordinary membership has declined and many would-be interested parties are no longer even aware that the American and British Societies still exist.

Whilst listening to investigators and while interviewing and corresponding with many others, it became clear that apparitions, poltergeists and other strange happenings are just as common today as in the past. As a result of the generosity of John Stiles, the Spontaneous Cases Officer, and other members, I was able to join teams investigating cases. I have interviewed people who have experienced collective apparitions and hauntings, but their accounts lack the impact of some of the older, well-researched cases in this chapter and I chose not to include them. Whatever interpretation we may choose to put on these experiences, the paranormal is with us still and thus would seem more than Victorian foolishness.

The other argument levelled against the evidence in this chapter is that human testimony will always fall short of scientific proof; but surely the testimony in this chapter is exactly the sort of evidence which underpins the two other sources of knowledge about the world – history and journalism. What would a professional historian, particularly one who has specialised in assessing evidence, think of the case reports in this chapter? Happily, one of the most pre-eminent historians of our day has addressed himself to this very question.

George Kitson Clark was a Reader in Constitutional History at Cambridge University and a Fellow of Trinity College. In his famous work, *The Critical Historian*, Clark assessed the types of evidence and methods of proof available to the historian and compared them to those available to the lawyer. The problem for the historian is that often he is forced to work with hearsay evidence. Without corroboration or balance, the historian is left to question the evidence in the light of his own motives and experiences, or of that which he has observed in other people, in order to arrive at a probable account of what really happened. But to apply this test is usually to dismiss the unusual and, in respect of miracles, to reject most of parapsychology out of hand. Clark continues,

> This is, after all, the argument that people normally use against there being any possible truth in the stories of ghosts, or the supernatural, or paranormal. It is true that ghost stories often contain physical impossibilities, figures suddenly appearing in locked bedrooms or walking through brick walls; but given the premise on which ghost stories rest these things are not impossible. Many people, however, see no reason to accept that premise. They argue that there do not appear to be a sufficient number of adequately authenticated cases even of such paranormal events as cases of telepathy or phantasms of the living to force belief in events which are so different from the ordinary experience of life. ... For leaving on one side the more melodramatic old-fashioned ghost stories, and possibly, in general, stories of phantasms of the dead, the amount of carefully checked evidence in favour of phenomena, which are to say the least of it paranormal – phantasms of the living, telepathy, clairvoyance and even possibly pre-cognition – which has been laboriously collected by the appropriate societies is impressive. If those who deny its authenticity had considered and rejected this evidence their position would be defensible; but in fact many have not looked at it, and have no intention of doing so.

Dead men tell no tales and at death the majority of us disappear into oblivion. But then, is it not strange that so many people experience apparitions in such curious circumstances as to suggest that they are more than hallucinations? At the end of Morton Schatzman's investigation of his patient Ruth, he observed a single event which he found difficult to explain.

On a Sunday evening before Ruth was due to fly home to see her maternal grandmother, who was very ill, they tried one last experiment. Ruth was anxious about her grandmother, who had been the sole source of comfort and strength during her childhood, and, for this reason, Ruth had a marked reluctance to create apparitions of the old lady. With the tape-recorder running, Ruth began to conjure an apparition for the experiment but it was the form of her grandmother which appeared in the chair opposite her. As usual Morton Schatzman saw only the empty chair.

> She said, 'Cheepy, you already know I need you. I'm waiting for you. And I want to know when you're coming.'
>
> ... I asked, 'Will I ever see you? Will you be dead when I get home?'
>
> She replied, 'I'll only be as dead as you'll let me be. Hold your head up, you're as good as the best and better than the rest.' Grandma had tears running down her face, and she was smiling. That was all.

On Monday morning Ruth was telephoned by her mother to say that her grandmother had died at 5 p.m. Sunday afternoon (11 p.m. London time). Towards the end she had entered a coma and had hallucinated a great deal before she finally passed away. Morton Schatzman was left wondering what interpretation to put on these events,

> I was left to puzzle over what had just happened. The visit of the grandmother's apparition fascinated me. It had occurred only six and a half hours before the grandmother's death. It had occurred even nearer in time to – and possibly simultaneously with – the grandmother's entry into her final coma.

At the end of his book, Schatzman speculated on the high frequency of post-mortem apparitions and asked, 'Could all the testimony be fraudulent?'

Summary of the Evidence

The simplest explanation of apparitions is that they are purely subjective hallucinations or illusions. However, those apparitions which are collectively perceived are something of an embarrassment for this hypothesis. Hallucinations are private experiences. Consequently, the psychologist must argue that, in the case of collective apparitions, the participants simply do not see the same thing. The problem remains that in the light of the participants' testimony, this explanation is not very convincing.

Telepathy explains collective apparitions without the need to invoke spirits of the dead. One person conjures an apparition which is then shared with the other parties. The account of Ruth suggests that telepathy may be a real possibility. Even in the case of the apparition of the recently deceased woman, who was seen by her daughter, her husband and the Maltese nanny, there is still a nagging doubt that the spectre was just the creation of the daughter's unconscious.

In other cases, where the phantom conveys information or was unknown to the participant, it can be argued that here at least is evidence for phantasms of the dead. But is the evidence really compelling? Can we exclude coincidence, self-delusion, mistaken identity or simple fraud? Hume would argue that we cannot exclude these 'lesser miracles'. I leave the reader to make his own decision.

5

Hauntings

Prosecution's claim is that hauntings arise from a complex interplay of purely physical events, fear, superstition, and hallucination.

Britain's most famous haunting came to the attention of the public in 1892, when a twenty-two page diary was published in the *Proceedings of the Society for Psychical Research*.[1] It is remarkable for several reasons. It was well documented and attested to being seen by approximately seventeen witnesses and heard by more than twenty. Most importantly, it has withstood the test of time and even today there are sightings of the tall lady in black who unaccountably hides her face behind a handkerchief. Unlike many more spectacular cases, it has survived the usual accusations of fraud and attempts to rationalise the events purely in terms of psychological or physical phenomena. It is also a description of a classical haunting, containing all the puzzling elements which defy explanation either in terms of science or the supernatural.

The author was a young medical student, Miss (later Dr) Rosina Despard, who shared the house with her parents, four sisters, two brothers and the usual complement of servants. A sixth married sister, Mrs K., was an occasional visitor to the house. The property was rented from a friend and, fearing that the story would damage its market value, Rosina's father, Captain Despard, insisted on anonymity. Consequently, Rosina used the pseudonym 'Miss R. C. Morton' and for nearly a hundred years the case was known simply as the 'Morton Ghost'. At the time of Rosina's account, the three-storey residence, on the corner of Pittville Circus Road and All Saint's Road, Cheltenham, was called Donore. Since then the house has been renamed St Anne's.

The Despard family moved into the house in March 1882 and Rosina was first visited by the ghostly figure on the night of 31 July. Just after retiring to bed, she heard someone at the door.

> On opening the door, I saw no one; but on going a few steps along the passage, I saw the figure of a tall lady dressed in black, standing at the head of the stairs. After a few minutes she descended the stairs and I followed for a short distance, feeling curious what it could be. I had only a small piece of candle, and it suddenly burnt itself out; and unable to see more, I went back to my room.
>
> The figure was that of a tall lady, dressed in black of a soft woollen material, judging from the slight sound in moving. The face was hidden in a handkerchief held in the right hand. This was all I noticed then; but on further occasions, when I was able to observe her more closely, I saw the upper part of the left side of the forehead, and a little of the hair above. Her left hand was nearly hidden by her sleeve and a fold of her dress. As she held it down a portion of a widow's cuff was visible on both wrists, so that the whole impression was that of a lady in widow's weeds. There was no cap on the head but a general effect of blackness suggests a bonnet, with a long veil or a hood.

It was soon seen by other people. Rosina's eight-year-old brother and his friend were playing on the balcony outside the drawing-room windows when, looking through the glass, they saw 'a tall figure in black, holding a handkerchief to her face with her right hand, seated at the writing-table in the window'. The figure was in full light and appeared to be weeping. The married sister, Mrs K., was coming down the stairs late one afternoon when she saw a tall figure in black cross the hall and enter the drawing-room. From the long veil, Mrs K. thought that the figure was a Sister of Mercy. A dark shadowy figure was then reported by two servants in a basement passage near the servants' hall.

During the next two years the apparition was seen about six times, at shorter and shorter intervals. Soon a pattern became apparent in the apparition's movements. It was seen on the landing on the second floor, from where it would descend the stairs to the ground floor. It then entered the drawing-room, where it might be seen for periods of up to thirty minutes standing by the window. It finally left to follow a passage through the servants' quarters to a garden door where it seemed to disappear. It was also seen in the garden and orchard, sometimes apparently retracing its steps back through the garden door.

Whatever their nature, it has been the role of ghosts in history to terrify the living. Rarely has a phantom found itself pursued and cornered by a nineteen-year-old girl. Was it really a ghost? Rosina asked, stretching thin string across the stairs, fastened at various heights and in such a way as to fall at the slightest touch. Her question was soon answered. 'I have twice at least seen the figure pass through the cords, leaving them intact.' If it was a phantom, did it have some sort of message to impart and, if so, would it speak to her? What would happen if she lay in ambush and attempted to corner the lady inside the drawing-room?

> I opened the drawing-room door softly and went in, standing just by it. She came in past me and walked to the sofa and stood still there, so I went up to her and asked her if I could help her. She moved, and I thought she was going to speak but she only gave a slight gasp and moved towards the door. Just by the door I spoke to her again, but she seemed as if she were quite unable to speak. She walked into the hall, then by the side door she seemed to disappear as before ... I also attempted to touch her, but she always eluded me. It was not that there was nothing to touch, but that she always seemed to be *beyond* me, and if followed into a corner, simply disappeared.

By 1885 the haunting had reached a peak and the figure of the tall lady in black was accompanied by footsteps, bumps against doors and the sound of door-handles turning. The apparition had become common knowledge within the household and the cook, a parlourmaid and gardener had all reported seeing the figure. In its various manifestations it had also been reported by neighbours and visitors to the house. Servants left the Despards' employment and care was taken not to mention the haunting to their replacements, but the footsteps and noises on the upper landings soon announced its presence.

Two years later, the appearances had become less common

and from 1887 to 1889 the figure was seldom seen. The loud noises had generally ceased but the footsteps could still be heard. Lighter footsteps seemed to persist longer but finally even they ceased. At the beginning of Rosina's record, the apparition was solid and life-like; standing in front of the window, it appeared to intercept the light and could be seen through the glass panes. Gradually, it became less distinct and seemed to just fade away.

In respect of the figure and noises and the clearly defined time interval during which these phenomena were experienced, the Morton Ghost is a classical haunting but, as we start to ask questions about these events, the paradoxical nature of all hauntings becomes apparent.

The first explanations to be raised against any haunting are those of fraud or exaggeration but neither seem to find any support in the above narrative. As the main participant, Rosina kept a diary of these extraordinary happenings and related her experiences to a close friend in a series of letters, but this information was not shared with any one in the household until the haunting began to gather momentum and the figure had been seen by other people. On 5 August 1882, Rosina told her father and her story was quickly corroborated by the other witnesses.

A number of physical explanations have been proposed to explain the haunting. Mrs Despard was an invalid, often confined to her bed, and neither Captain Despard nor his wife ever admitted to seeing the figure. It has been suggested that the ghost was in fact Captain Despard's mistress who entered and left the house by the garden door but, for this to be true, the mistress must have been an extraordinary woman or most of the witnesses' statements highly fanciful.

During the years 1884 and 1885 the haunting was most intense in the months of July, August and September and this unusual observation led the investigator G. W. Lambert to suggest that the noises were due to an underground stream.[2] He postulated that the noises created by the subsequent movements of the house then frightened members of the household into seeing a type of figure frequently reported in other hauntings. When accounts of the 'ghost' became common knowledge within the household, the apparition began to take on an agreed appearance as details were added by successive witnesses.

Superficially, there is much to commend this ingenious theory. The positions of pumps and wells in the locality, shown on an Ordnance Survey map of the time, and elevation of the land could be taken as evidence for an underground stream running from the River Chelt downhill in a north north easterly direction to Wyman's Brook. Lambert proposed that the course of such a stream would lie close to the eastern edge of the house. This could explain another puzzling aspect of the Morton Ghost, in that the noises, footsteps and other disturbances centred on four bedrooms on the first and second floors, one pair directly above the other, on the *eastern* side of the house. On the basis of this theory, we might have expected the hauntings to have been more intense in the winter months, when the rains flooded the Chelt and overflowed through the underground stream into Wyman's Brook. In fact, the noises and reported sightings of the apparition were at their worst during the *summer* months. Lambert attempted to rescue his pet theory by demonstrating that the Cotswolds had experienced two wet summers in 1884 and 1885, the two years when the haunting was at its worst.

There is, however, a major flaw in this theory. Lambert notes that the head waters of the River Chelt were dammed to create the Dowdeswell reservoirs, which were opened on 19 October 1886, 'The dam across the valley enabled the head waters of the Chelt to be controlled to a much greater extent than formerly, and that presumably diminished the flooding of the channels by which the storm water broke north from its natural bed.' Lambert assumes that *all* the disturbances gradually diminished after this date, 'In 1886 the disturbances were so few and slight that Captain Despard was much less anxious about the reputation of his house, and in 1887, the Jubilee year with its long-remembered exceptionally fine summer, there appear to have been no incidents between February and November.'

Rosina's account says something quite different,

> During 1887 we had few records; the appearances were less frequent ... During the next two years, 1888 to 1889, the

figure was very seldom seen, though footsteps were heard; the louder noises had gradually ceased ... From 1889 to the present, 1892, as far as I know, the figure has not been seen at all; the lighter footsteps lasted a little longer, but even they have now ceased.

On the basis of the underground stream theory, we might have expected the *noises* to have stopped with the damming of the Chelt in 1886 but it was the apparition which was becoming 'less distinct' and being seen less frequently. The noises, or at least the lighter footsteps, were the last phenomena to disappear.

In linking the noises to the apparition, Lambert proposed that the footsteps, knocks and the door-handles turning were just generalised noises of the 'haunted house variety' – caused by the underground stream – which gave the house an air of mystery and fear which, in turn, prompted people to 'see things' and these 'things' were at best a generalised hallucination which was interpreted variously as a lady in black, a nun or a widow. However, the testimony of witnesses simply does not support this idea. Rosina was concerned more with pursuing her phantom than the attendant noises and, at least at the beginning, the servants were neither mystified nor frightened. Mrs Brown, a parlourmaid, had several experiences and certainly distinguished between those which seemed just unusual and others which filled her with terror.

> I think that the first besides Miss Rose who saw it was Master Willy. He was then about 8 or 9 years old, and was playing in the garden with another young gentlemen, when they both looked in through the drawing-room window, and saw a widow in the room [Not recognising the figure the boys entered the drawing-room to find it empty]. They ran up to their mother's room – she was an invalid and seldom left her bed – and told her what they had seen, but Miss Rose, who was there, laughed it off.
>
> The next time it was seen by Mrs K., the married sister, who used to come and stay a month or so in the house every year. She had been there three days when she said that she had seen a widow in the drawing-room. Then Master Willy called out that that must have been the same woman whom he had seen; and after that Miss Rose told that she had been in the habit of seeing the figure.

The Sceptical Occultist

So all those in the house knew; but when a new servant came we used to take care not to tell her, because it was hard to get a girl to stay.

Some months after the thing became known I was alone in the house one evening with Lizzie, a new cook, and we were standing at the door of the servants' hall, on the basement floor. The passage was lit by gas. Lizzie had heard nothing of the ghost, I am sure. Suddenly we both saw a dark shadowy figure, dressed in black, and making no noise, glide past us along the passage and disappear round a corner. Neither of us spoke as it passed; but directly after we looked at each other, and each saw that the other had seen it, and we mentioned it to each other. We had seen the same thing. I have myself never seen any white about the figure; but I know that others have seen her hold a handkerchief up to her face. The figure has never looked to me quite solid; but it has always vanished too quickly for me to look closely at it.

The next time that I saw it was in the drawing-room, when I went in to light up the gas at dusk on a summer's evening. I saw a dark figure walk round the ottoman and disappear. I was not much frightened. The next time I saw no figure, but I was more frightened than any other time. I was going off on a holiday, and I sat up late in my room with some sewing. My room was between Miss Morton's and the schoolroom on the top floor, where the sounds were apt to be worst. I heard a loud noise and looking up I saw the handle of my door twisted round, as if someone was trying to come in. The door was locked, and this was not a mere slip of the handle. The handle was quite firm and never slipped of itself. I knew that no one was up or about and I was motionless with fear. I could scarcely go to bed. Next morning when I looked at myself in the glass I saw that one side of my face was twisted by a slight stroke.

. . . I saw it twice more, both times in the drawing-room. Once it was as I was lighting the gas, as I had seen it before. The other time was when I had entered the room in the morning and had taken down one shutter. I then saw it close by me, and was frightened and called another servant to come to me. . . . I often heard noises on the attic landing near my room – scuffling and knocking. Sometimes I would hear Miss Rose open her door and go downstairs. I know now that she was following the ghost. But I heard her before I knew about the ghost at all.

Recent evidence from Severn Trent Water suggests that

Lambert's stream never existed. Nevertheless, these ideas serve to demonstrate the problems of superimposing a purely physical explanation on the Morton Ghost. What was it that the women saw? The lady in black does have many of the elusive qualities of an hallucination. The figure was seen most frequently by Rosina but at times only its footsteps and other noises could be heard. Other people saw the apparition but it was heard more often that it was seen. When Rosina attempted to corner the apparition, it simply disappeared; while on other occasions, it managed to keep ahead of her. If the figure was an hallucination fixed into a certain position on her visual field, then no matter how fast she pursued the phantom, it would always remain beyond her grasp. A cold wind was sometimes associated with the footsteps but this too is likely to be hallucinatory as the flames from candles remained still.

And yet, this is no simple hallucination. The two boys both reported seeing a lady at the writing desk and their description was similar to that reported by Rosina and Mrs K. The maid and the cook also seemed to see the same black figure as it slid along the passage in the basement. This presents us with the same problem as collective apparitions although, in the case of hauntings, the figure is seen not once but again and again. Some of Rosina's sightings are also reminiscent of collective apparitions, where one participant sees the whole figure, while a second sees only the top of the body; or the slightly different accounts of the figure crossing Killegar lake in the previous chapter. On one occasion Rosina and her married sister both saw the apparition on the balcony but when it entered the room, only Rosina saw it.

> On the evening of August 11th we were sitting in the drawing-room with the gas lit but the shutters were not shut, the light outside getting dusk, my brothers and a friend having just given up tennis, finding it too dark; my eldest sister, Mrs K., and myself both saw the figure on the balcony outside, looking in at the window. She stood there some minutes, then walked to the end and back again, after which she seemed to disappear. She soon after came into the drawing-room, when I saw her, but my sister did not.

Not only does this strange observation gel with collective

apparitions but it adds credence to Rosina's statement, since a less careful observer might have removed this detail lest it detract from their account.

It we continue to plumb for a commonsense explanation, we have to accept that the two boys, the two sisters and the maid and the cook did not see the same figure but that on each occasion both saw something different, which coincidentally was described in the same way – a long string of double coincidences. Another explanation is that the lady was a collective hallucination, but who then was the agent sending out the telepathic message?

We therefore arrive at the million dollar question, 'Was this a ghost?' only to find ourselves in more trouble. The house was previously occupied by Mr Swinhoe. The first Mrs Swinhoe died and her husband, tortured by grief, began to drink. His second wife, no doubt believing that she could rescue him from the demon, also became an alcoholic and was forced to leave her husband some months before his death. Two years later, she also died from an alcohol-related condition. Rosina believed the lady in black to be the second Mrs Swinhoe, having identified her from a photograph of her sister, whom she was said to resemble. But the second Mrs Swinhoe was not present at her husband's death and there is no evidence that she ever wore black for him. So we have the first Mrs Swinhoe, who was never a widow, and the second who, while she was a widow, never lived in the house. It should be noted here that the apparitions in most hauntings cannot be identified with an historical person.

If we assume, for the sake of argument, that some other departed soul formed an attachment to the house, we still find ourselves wrestling with problems. In collective apparitions, we can understand a concern by the dead for relatives still living, but the emotional link in hauntings is to a house or a specific location. On the basis of any theory of telepathy, the strange repetitive actions of the haunting ghost are less suggestive of a telepathic telegram than of a psychic beacon which intermittently emits this strange message. So, rather than providing evidence for survival, haunting ghosts present a picture of the mere semblance of a human personality. This has led some modern writers to compare them to holograms.

Hauntings

These problems have long been appreciated and several magical explanations have been proposed to account for the facts. One suggestion is that human beings leave a psychic imprint on buildings during their lifetime – shades of sympathetic magic – which produces the ghost that is seen after their death. But surely, investigators have argued, if this was true, the imprint should occasionally be seen *before* the death of the person and establishments with a long history of occupation, such as monasteries, stately homes and public houses, should be populated with ghosts of both the living and the dead!

Another idea expressed by Victoria Branden is that ghosts are concentrations of energy which are 'developed' by changes in the atmosphere. Fully 'developed', the ghost is seen by all, but when only partially 'developed' it is apparent only to those with psychic abilities. There is, however, no evidence that hauntings or apparitions can be correlated with changes in the atmosphere and, while mist and fog may appear as if by magic when air cools to below the dew point, ghosts are reported under all conditions and are not restricted to damp northern climates.

During the Cheltenham haunting, F. W. H. Myers suggested to Rosina that she should try to photograph the ghost.

> I kept a photographic camera constantly ready to try and photograph the figure, but on the few occasions I was able to do so, I got no result; at night, usually only by candle light, a long exposure would be necessary for so dark a figure, and this I could not obtain.

It is not clear from these remarks whether all Rosina's attempts to photograph the ghost were at night but, unlike the fleeting apparition which is usually only seen once or twice, figures seen in hauntings are available to be photographed. There is, however, no good evidence that ghosts are in any sense real objects which can leave an image on photographic film. The Fortean Picture Library holds a range of these anomalous photographs showing ghostly animals, cowled figures and macabre faces. In most instances, the photographer has claimed that the figure was not seen at the time the photograph was taken. One exception shows a baby looking at a cylindrical cloud. From the child's exclamation, 'Nana, Nana', this was taken to be the spirit of his recently deceased grandmother. The photograph appears to indicate that the child *did* see something but again this was not perceived by the photographer. The psychic, Ted Serios, took numerous photographs of phenomena allegedly produced by psychokinesis or will-power, for Dr Jules Eisenbud and other investigators. Eisenbud has given good evidence to support this conclusion. A range of similar photographs, apparently obtained spontaneously by members of the public, is held by Mr Maurice Gross of the Society for Psychical Research. Again, the indications are that they were produced by psychokinesis. In those rare photographs purporting to show ghosts, and leaving aside fraud, we can best assume that the image was produced by psychokinesis in a manner similar to that allegedly employed by Ted Serios. Just who or what produced them remains an open question.

Like most hauntings, the Despards' ghost gradually disappeared. Or was it their sensory capability to detect this strange phenomenon that tailed off? I pose this question because there is good evidence to suggest that the various manifestations of the haunting are still continuing. After the publication of his book, *Hauntings and Apparitions*, Andrew MacKenzie was approached by a retired schoolmaster who, after speaking on the local radio, had been contacted by several members of the public who had some unusual stories to relate.[3]

After the Despards left the house in 1893, it remained empty until it was taken over as a preparatory school for boys. The school closed after nine years, remaining empty until 1910 when it became an Ursuline convent. (It is reputed that the school was so haunted that it had to be closed.) After only two years, the Order of Ursulines also departed and the house became St Anne's Nursery College, a school for training nannies. In 1935, it was purchased by the Diocese of Gloucester to serve as a diocesan house. After its closure in December 1970, it remained vacant until 1973 when it was bought by a housing association and converted into flats.

The Reverend Simon Ward (pseudonym) spent a residential weekend at the house in 1969. He had heard nothing of its reputation. After compline, the other members of the clergy decided to visit the local hotel, but Ward was suffering from a heavy cold so he excused himself and retired to bed early and soon fell asleep.

> I woke to the strange sound and sensation of fingers scratching the eiderdown across the back of my neck and thought it must be a silly practical joke by some other man who had come into the bedroom, leaving the others outside. So I sat up suddenly to catch the man in the act, as it were, only to find no one by the bed. The room felt bitterly cold when to my amazement, the bedclothes, which I had carefully tucked in myself, seemed to be pulled slowly from me on to the floor at the foot of the bed.

The room was quite light and, opening his prayer book, Ward began to intone a prayer from the office of evensong.

> As I said the words, a grey shape took form at the door and came at me slowly, passing over my head and through the wall on my left shoulder. I put on the light and searched the landing staircase and house. I was alone.

Ward decided to say nothing of these events but in 1970, after learning of the haunting and meeting another clergyman who had a similar experience at St Anne's, he gave the above statement to Andrew MacKenzie.

Mr Joe Higgs (pseudonym) and his wife were the first couple to occupy the flat which included Rosina's bedroom and the adjoining servant's room. Returning home one Boxing Night, Joe climbed the main staircase at around 10 p.m. and was surprised to see the figure of a woman gliding down the stairs. He described her as being between thirty-five and forty, in a grey dress, with her fair hair, brushed back from her forehead, hanging down her back. The flat was also troubled by poltergeist-type disturbances. Pictures flew off the walls and a shelf in what used to be Rosina's bedroom sprang away from the wall, taking the eight screws and rawlplugs with it. A large houseplant was seen to move through the air as though it was being carried by unseen hands. Objects disappeared, sometimes reappearing in unusual locations. There was also a sense of 'presence'. Mrs Higgs would sometimes feel that someone was watching her, particularly when she was making mince pies, and occasionally she felt a presence which prevented her from leaving her bed.

Mrs Doreen Jackson, an assistant cook, was having a driving lesson in her lunch hour. As she approached the gate of St Anne's, she saw a tall woman in black, with her hand held to her face, step off the pavement into the path of her car. The woman, who wore old-fashioned clothes, seemed unaware of the approaching car. Changing gear, Mrs Jackson braked. 'My instructor asked me what I was doing. I told him there was a woman crossing the road in front of me, and he said "I can see pink elephants too."' At the time Mrs Jackson claimed to have no knowledge of the haunting.

A number of books on hauntings have featured the Cheltenham or 'Morton Ghost' and the story has passed into folklore, introducing the possibility that people only see what they expect to see, given the St Anne's reputation. This said, the ghost appears to have been seen by other residents of Cheltenham. Mr Percy Wilson, writing in *Light*, the magazine of the College of Psychic Studies, reported that his wife's family had seen the ghost many times. Her Uncle George, recalling his boyhood in Cheltenham, said 'We used to go and see the ghost dancing across the lawn on many occasions when I was a boy. It used to be quite a common experience with the boys in the town.'

What is it that is seen in hauntings? An illusion? A collective delusion? Many experts would plump for an hallucination, but then how is it collectively perceived? We can *say* that the individuals did not see the same thing but if we examine the testimonies fairly, this is certainly not what the evidence suggests.

There is another explanation as to what is going on here. As an explanation it is weak, based as it is on a small number of single experiences of apparitions, not hauntings. In these cases, some collectively perceived, it seems as though the individuals concerned were able to step into the past. They were not seeing spirits but a sort of 'film clip' from another time. The most celebrated case broke in 1910, when Charlotte Moberly, Principal of St Hugh's College, Oxford and her colleague, Eleanor Jourdain, published *An Adventure*, sparking a controversy which has continued to this day. The book gives an account of their visit to the gardens of Versailles, where they were suddenly confronted with scenes from the French court of 1789, appearing to walk amongst gardeners, courtiers and a woman who resembled the French Queen Marie Antoinette.

Sir Ernest Bennett collected other cases of this type, including a statement from a Mr Tom Horner of Ripon, who, while motoring across Marston Moor (an English Civil War battlefield) at night, was forced to swerve and brake for three figures resembling Royalist soldiers. The figures were also seen by his companion in the car. In Bennett's Case 66, two sisters and their maid were returning from an evening service at their village church on a foggy evening. The three women heard footsteps and a man passed them whistling but a second man was not seen by the younger sister and, as the elder sister tried to attract her attention and pull her out of his path, he collided with her and simply disappeared into the folds of her dress.

> As I spoke, the man disappeared – it seemed, into C.'s dress; neither C. nor the maid had seen him, and he made no sound. In another moment we were all bewildered at the sight around us; men, women, children and dogs, all were moving briskly about, some singly, others in groups, all without a sound; they appeared mist-like ... We three were never mistaken as to the identity of the different shapes; if one saw a man, all saw a man; if one saw a woman; all saw a woman and so on. Overhead it was perfectly free of them; they were all walking on the ground as we ourselves were.

The last case, investigated by the famous researcher, Gardner Murphy and his colleague, Herbert Klemme, is the least ambiguous and best researched of this type.[4] On 3 October, 1963, Mrs Buterbaugh, the secretary to the Dean of Wesleyan University, Nebraska, was asked to deliver a message to another professor who had an office in the C.C. White Building on the campus. She entered the building and walked past the music room, from which she could hear the sound of students and a marimba playing. As she entered the professor's room everything became deathly quiet. She stopped, realising that something was wrong. She was repelled by a strange musty odour and was struck by the sense of somebody else being in the room. Looking up, she saw the figure of a tall, black-haired woman dressed in early twentieth-century period clothes.

> She had her back to me, reaching up into one of the shelves of the [music] cabinet with her right hand, and standing perfectly still. She wasn't at all aware of my presence. While I was watching her she never moved. She was not transparent and yet I knew she wasn't real. While I looked at her she just faded away – not parts of her body one at a time, but her whole body all at once.
>
> Up until the time she faded away I was not aware of anyone else being in the suite of rooms, but just about the time of her fading out I felt as though I was still not alone. To my left was a desk and I had a feeling there was a man sitting at that desk. I turned around and saw no one, but I still felt his presence. When that feeling of his presence left I have no idea, because it was then, when I looked out of the window behind that desk, that I got frightened and left the room. I am not sure whether I ran or walked out of the room. Dr Murphy, when I looked out that window there wasn't one modern thing out there. The street (Madison Street) which is less than half a block away from the building, was not even there and neither was the new Willard House. That was when I *realised that these people were not in my time, but I was back in their time* [Murphy and Klemme's italics].

The detailed descriptions of the apparition fitted an old photograph which was discovered later, of Miss Mills, a music teacher, who had died suddenly in the building in 1936. Furthermore, a 1915 photograph of the campus showed a scene very similar to that seen through the window by Mrs Buterbaugh. Murphy and Klemme stated that it was very unlikely that she had seen the photographs. A psychologist might describe Mrs Buterbaugh's experience as a metachoric waking dream – one where the whole visual field is transformed. Set against this, Murphy and Klemme point to a disturbing series of coincidences.

1. The incident occurred at 9.00 a.m., the same time as Miss Mills's sudden death.

2. Mrs Buterbaugh's task that morning was to complete some arrangements concerned with choral singing. Miss Mills had been concerned with choral music.
3. On the shelves on which the apparition had been extending its right arm, was found a series of items on choral singing by well-known composers.
4. The office's new occupant was a visiting scholar, Professor Martin, who was a distinguished specialist in choral music and who had come to the Wesleyan University to study the same.

Murphy and Klemme considered all possibilities and ended their paper with these remarks,

> The case may be viewed as relatively 'normal' or relatively 'pathological' as far as the neurological record is concerned [Mrs B. admitted to several experiences of *déjà vu* and exhibited one slight abnormality in an electrocephalogram trace characteristic of predormital sleep paralysis; a not uncommon complaint where the sleeping individual is unable to move a muscle]. It may also be regarded as presenting a 'good' line of evidence for paranormal contact with the past, or this evidence may be regarded as unconvincing. Our purpose is not to plead, but to lay bare for consideration what seems to be rich psychical research material and some rich neurological material which interdigitate and give meaning one to the other. For us, then, the case as a whole, and not only its parts, remains 'unfinished business'.

Summary of the Evidence

At the end of her famous paper *Phantasms of the Dead*, Eleanor Sidgwick, a hard-headed academic who tended to rationalise these sorts of experiences in terms of hallucinations, wrote 'I must confess myself quite unable to form any satisfactory theory – any theory which makes us feel that if it is true, the phenomena are just what we would expect. I have doubted even whether it is yet of any use attempting to theorise . . .' Almost one hundred and ten years later, our understanding of hauntings has not moved forward a single inch.

The first and obvious explanation is that hauntings are complex psychological phenomena. Mysterious noises of a purely natural origin impel one person to experience a purely

The Sceptical Occultist

subjective hallucination which arises out of their own subconscious. This creates a 'ghost culture' within the household and an air of unconscious expectancy which prompts others, by way of illusion or imagination, to 'see' the same sort of figure. There is also some evidence – from those instances where two or more people simultaneously see the apparition – to suggest that, like Ruth in the last chapter, one person produces an infectious hallucination which is seen by others. The problem with this hypothesis is that one would expect the haunting to be restricted to the household and to terminate abruptly when the family leaves the house. We might also expect the 'ghost' to follow the family rather than remain fixed in the house, but, in these strange phenomena, it is the locations and not the people which appear to be haunted. A purely physical explanation also forces us to ignore a long list of improbabilities and coincidences.

The more popular view, and the one which has earned millions for the directors of horror films, is that there is a disembodied intelligence within the house. If this is true, it does not appear to share the same sense of reality as the living people and furnishings. Nor does this explanation account for the ghost's strange repetitive actions and its gradual fading away at the end of the haunting, or for the fact that it is seen by some, but not all, of those present.

The next hypothesis suggests that the ghost is not in our world but communicates mind to mind with the living. But, unlike simple apparitions, the emotional link here is to a location rather than another mind. The living appear to be casual observers who find themselves in a situation akin to living in a foreign film without the subtitles.

An alternative explanation is that the building itself causes the hallucinations in some way. But when we start to ask why it should produce similar recurrent hallucinations in different people, we find ourselves being pushed towards the magical explanation that human beings leave a psychic imprint on brick and mortar, for which there is no evidence.

The last explanation also suggests that hauntings have nothing to do with spirits but are clairvoyant in nature, allowing us to obtain glimpses of the past. This hypothesis does account for cases where, for example, the ghost is seen wearing clothes of an earlier period or where phantoms appear to walk on a level below that of the existing floor. But it does not explain the unusual noises associated with some hauntings, or why that particular location should be favoured with the power of retrocognition.

There are no good theories of hauntings, only the evidence which has been reported for hundreds of years in many different cultures. I leave the reader to consider his verdict on the prosecution's claim.

6

The Marian Apparitions

Prosecution's claim is that the Marian apparitions are no more than a generalised hallucination of a 'white lady' which seers interpret as the Virgin Mary in the light of religious and personal preconceptions. Occasionally, complex apparitions also involve illusion and mass delusion which provide a miraculous gloss to these experiences.

The cases in the next four chapters of this book are some of the most complex mysteries ever to have taxed the human mind. We have moved away from science and the parapsychologist's 'supernature' worldview, crossing that ill-defined border between parapsychology and religion. What is at stake here and what the reader must decide – on the basis of the evidence and not a particular religious belief – is whether there is a supernatural intelligence under-pinning an alternative reality; an Intelligence which the Marian apparitions would suggest occasionally intervenes in the affairs of Man. In order to dispel some misconceptions and prepare the reader for the strange testimonies he is about to read, let us first state the facts on which the defence and prosecution both agree.

Apparitions of the Virgin Mary are often collectively perceived, once again raising all the problems associated with collective apparitions. They are rarely single experiences. They can occur at regular intervals over long periods of time and so we are also faced with some of those problems related to hauntings. From written records of the last 600 years, we also see that these visions always contain the same strange aspects. In essence, they represent a meeting of two intermediaries: one, the 'Mother of God', mediates for her son Jesus Christ, the other, a child or adult seer, is coerced by the

The Marian Apparitions

vision into serving as a go-between who will carry the vision's messages to the local community.

It is difficult to reject the Marian apparitions as Catholic propaganda, for the simple reason that they do not serve the interests of the decision makers within the Church. They are grass-roots phenomena which are not welcomed by Mother Church, since they present complex problems in theology and logic, with the ever present threat that the laity will take one view and the theologians the other. Nor does Mary confine her appearances to Catholics as both Coptic Christians and Moslems have been graced with apparitions.

In the 1960s, the Second Vatican Council declined to discuss the Virgin Mary or her alleged apparitions in a separate document setting limits on the degree to which the Mother of God could be aggrandised. Otherwise, some of the cardinals feared, 'Marian maximalism would find no checks in its extravagant flights.'

In its wisdom, the Church has placed belief in these wonders outside the canons of faith, leaving their interpretation to the individual conscience. Nevertheless, the sites of alleged visitations have provided beacons of faith and every year two million pilgrims visit Fatima, four and a half million make the trip to Lourdes, twelve million visit the Basilica of Our Lady of Guadalupe and just over one million make a pilgrimage to the various sites in Belgium.

Another important point is that the woman described by the seers in these apparitions does not, in any sense, resemble the historical Mary. She is often seen as a fair child, or a young Caucasian woman or she bears a striking resemblance to the figure depicted in religious paintings or statues. This has prompted psychologists and sociologists to argue that the apparition is just an hallucinatory projection of these conventional religious figures. People in other cultures also report seeing a 'white lady' and the Chinese, for example, associate this vision with a goddess.

Mythologists and psychoanalysts have long been drawn to the similarities in the rich folklore of different cultures. Carl Jung, one of the pioneers of psychoanalysis, was struck by the fact that many societies throughout the world share similar symbols and legends. The bird was often used as a symbol for the human soul, darkness was associated with evil and light with good, and the different cultural heroes – mythologist Joseph Campbell's 'hero with a thousand faces' – would act out Man's higher self. Jung finally decided that human beings, no matter when or where they live, seem to share an unconscious language. He called the shared symbols in this language 'archetypes' and considered them to have been genetically inherited from the beginnings of mankind. Deep within our unconscious, Jung believed that we can meet these archetypes in our dreams and occasionally as waking hallucinations. One archetype recognised by Jung was the 'white lady'.

However, there is another quite different interpretation of the woman seen by the seers. The Revelations of St John the Divine (xii, 1–5) describing the Apocalypse tell of a powerful woman,

> And there appeared a great wonder in heaven; a woman clothed with the sun, and the moon under her feet, and upon her head a crown of twelve stars.
> And she being with child cried, travailing in birth, and pained to be delivered.
> ... and the dragon stood before the woman which was ready to devour her child as soon as it was born.
> And she brought forth a man child, who was to rule all nations with a rod of iron: and her child was caught up unto God, and to his throne.

After the twelfth century, theologians came to identify this wondrous lady with the Mother of God. Seemingly, evidence for this belief was soon provided by ordinary people who reported religious experiences. When seers began to describe their visions as a lady 'clothed in light' or 'brighter than the sun', she became identified with the Virgin Mary.

The Marian apparitions occur when the community is under an external threat or when Mary's role within the church is being re-evaluated or when a community is preoccupied with her cult. For example, the early Spanish apparitions often occurred against a background of epidemic and famine. The apparition at Guadalupe in Mexico was seen at a time when the Indian Catholics were being oppressed by their Spanish masters. Bernadette Soubirous experienced her visions of the Virgin Mary just after a long debate within the Catholic Church as to whether Mary had been born without the stain of Original Sin (the 'Immaculate Conception'). The apparition at Fatima occurred during the First World War and at a time when Portugal was governed by a virulently anti-Catholic Republican administration. Many other little-known apparitions occurred during the height of the Cold War and the visions' statements were often concerned with a final apocalyptic war in Europe between Soviet-Bloc and NATO forces.

One of the strange characteristics of these apparitions is that the vision is reluctant to identify itself and when it does it often makes only oblique references to its identity:

'I am the Virgin Mary', Cubas, 1449.
Reference to 'My son' [God?], Lleida, 1458.
'Virgin Mary', El Torn, 1483.
'Saint Mary of the Cross', Escalona, 1490.
No reference, Pinos, 1507.
'Do not fear for I am Our Lady', Quintanar de la Orden, 1523.
'I am the Blessed Virgin Mary', Guadalupe, Mexico, 1531.
Reference to 'My son', La Salette, 1846.
'I am the Immaculate Conception', Lourdes, 1858.
'I am Our Lady of the Rhine', Alsace, 1873.
'I am she who was immaculately conceived', Marpingen, 1876.
'I am Our Lady of the Rosary', Fatima, 1917.
'I am the Virgin of the Poor', Banneux, 1933.
'I am the Sign of the Living God', Marienfried, 1946.
'I am Co-Redemptrix, Mediatrix, and Advocate', Amsterdam, 1945–1959.
'I am the Mediatrix of All Graces', Balestrino, 1960.
'Our Lady of Mount Carmel', Garabandal, 1961–63.
'I am the Mother of Consolation and the Afflicted', San Damiano, 1964–81.

This problem with the identity of the vision has led psychologists to argue that it is the seers themselves who unconsciously project an identity on to the apparition, either alone, or in conjunction with other members of the community. This is to say that, if a child from a devout Roman Catholic community experiences a vision of a lady in white, it is likely to be

The Sceptical Occultist

identified as the Virgin Mary and, in later visions, this purely subjective hallucination, arising from the child's own mind, will appear to adopt this identity.

Finally, we have the problem of the messages and instructions that the apparition imparts to the seers. Some are just devotional messages to consecrate chapels or images which are to serve as special sources of grace or religious energy. Sometimes the vision provides messages of consolation to communities, or advises that prayer can ameliorate the effects of social disasters such as war or famine. Frequently, the apparition warns of a coming apocalyptic war. It has been suggested that the vision simply mirrors the community's preoccupations, reflecting their deepest fears and proving a focus for action in the guise of a supernatural being.

In Catholic countries such as Spain, we recognise two great periods of Marian apparitions. From 1400–1525, appearances of the Virgin Mary began to replace the orthodox visions of the saints. The seers were usually drawn from those living on the outskirts of the community, such as shepherds or animal herders. They were usually poor but not destitute. In the beginning, most records speak of male seers. Women were distrusted in religious matters and their accounts were not always recorded. They were thought 'sin laden' (sexually active), foolish and hysterical. But, in time, the seers came to be drawn increasingly from young children, particularly prepubescent girls. The bloody work of the Inquisition put an end to the first era of apparitions but much of this strange pattern continued into the second great period, which began in the mid-nineteenth century and has continued to the present day.

Our cases begin with that of a 12-year-old-girl, Ines Martinez.[1]. The year is 1449 and the place, Cubas, in what is now Madrid, Spain. A devoutly religious girl, she was herding her father's pigs on the hills outside the town when a beautiful lady, dressed in gold garments, asked her 'What are you doing here, little face?' Ines replied, 'I am watching these pigs.' The lady then asked her why she fasted on the days of Saint Mary (Virgin Mary) and the child replied that she was following her parents' instructions. On hearing this, the vision praised her and promised that anyone who fasted on those days would earn an indulgence of eighty thousand years. The figure then told Ines to tell the people to put their souls right as a great epidemic of 'pain in the side' was coming. When Ines asked, quite naturally, if her mother and father would die, the vision replied that it would be as God willed.

Not surprisingly, Ines dared tell no one about this strange experience. The lady appeared again, this time ordering Ines to take her message to the people. When the child asked whose message she would be carrying, the lady refused to identify herself. Ines did, however, pluck up the courage to tell her family and a few of their friends. Unable to fully carry out its task, Ines now found herself pursued by the apparition. She was lying down on the hillside, watching her animals in the valley below, when the lady appeared for the third time. 'Get up daughter. Do not fear.' Ines startled, again asked the apparition its name. 'I am the Virgin Mary,' it replied and took Ines' right hand, pressing her fingers into the form of a cross. 'Now,' the apparition told her, 'go with this sign and they will believe you.'

The townspeople did believe her and when a procession arrived at the spot where Ines had seen the last apparition, the vision once again appeared, but it could be seen only by the child. The lady issued more instructions and she demanded that two masses should be said in the town and a further two at the church of Lady Saint Mary of Guadalupe. Then, the lady promised, when Ines returned to this spot, her paralysed hand would be released.

The 'sign' was, in fact, 'undone' during the second mass at Guadalupe, a point not lost on the devout who began to question the authenticity of the vision. When Ines arrived back in the valley and the apparition appeared again, she questioned it as to why the 'miracle' had not happened as the lady said. 'You do not understand because of your haste to question me. That is why I sent you to my House in Guadalupe, so that when you went there it would be undone.' Not impressed with this evasion, Ines asked for another sign because, she explained, there were many who did not wish to believe. Hearing this, the Virgin Mary replied, 'This I can well believe. But do not worry, daughter, for I will give them such a sign, that even if they wanted to they will not be able to believe, for blessed are those who saw it and believed it.' Upon saying this, the lady at once disappeared.

Ines later told a commission established to investigate the apparition, that she had not been afraid until she saw the apparition vanish. She went on to say that 'Mary' was a small woman and that when she knelt in front of the rough cross, which Ines carried in the procession, she left small footprints in the sand. The footprints, confirmed by other witnesses, were, Ines estimated, like those of an eight-year-old child.

There is much in this account which would be familiar to the psychiatrist. Otherwise normal children do experience hallucinations and the apparition's messages reflect one of medieval man's greatest preoccupations. To die without being in a state of grace was to court eternal damnation in hell or many thousands of years in the cleansing fires of purgatory. Regularly partaking of the sacraments of Confession and Communion guaranteed a state of grace, but this could be upset by sudden death. And one form of death could be very sudden indeed. Between 1347 and 1350, one third of Europe's population was wiped out by the bubonic plague or the 'Black Death'. Professor William Christian, a historian specialising in medieval and renaissance Spain, believes that the vision's prophecy of an epidemic of 'pain in the side' could be a reference to the swollen lymph nodes or buboes in the armpits of those with bubonic plague.

The epidemic burnt itself out in Castille in 1349 but continued to smoulder on in many of the towns throughout Europe. The townspeople were only too aware that a whole family could become sick and die long before a priest arrived to give absolution. The vision suggests strict religious observance (frequently she demands more churches and thus more priests) to counter this disaster and, for those facing purgatory, she offers an indulgence of eighty thousand years.

Not for the last time, we see a 'miracle' devalued by a flawed prophecy which, in this case, wrongly predicts the time at which the child's hand would be released from its paralytic contortion. This surely must raise the possibility that the

The Marian Apparitions

'sign' was simply the result of hysteria. Finally, we have that point in the child's testimony where she describes 'Mary' as small, leaving the footprints of an eight-year-old child. What are we to make of this? Everything, a psychologist might reply, pointing out that diminutive figures or 'Lilliputianism' is a common feature of hypnagogic hallucinations and a common characteristic of visions of saints. In Lleida, Spain, nine years after these events, two children, Jaume and Celedoni Cirosa, reported an apparition of a young girl with long blonde hair in a red cape carrying a cross. Asked how he could identify the cross, Jaume replied, '. . . it seemed to him like one that is on the altar of Saint Sabastian of Riner', raising the possibility that these figures are no more than stored memories of religious icons. In five other Spanish apparitions the figure also appeared as a small child clothed in white, red or gold.

However, what is missing from this analysis is the sheer majesty of these experiences, where an uneducated child comes face to face with a 'force' (be it a subjective hallucination or a supernatural being) which it neither controls nor understands. Again and again we will see the seers gently coerced into obeying the apparition and serving as an often frightened and sometimes unwilling go-between. What sows the seed of doubt in these cases is the context of the apparition; the way these experiences begin and end and the way the lady manages to control events, manipulating whole communities and even authorities within the Church into following her instructions.

Ten years after Cortes' invasion of Mexico and the destruction of the Aztec empire, the Indian population was brought to the brink of insurrection. Many of the Spanish settlers, greedy for the promised riches, wanted to enslave the defeated Indian population. This powerful faction was headed by the leader of the civil administration, Nuno de Guzan, whose cruel taxes had already forced Indian families to sell their children into slavery. They were opposed by Father Juan de Zumarraga, Bishop of Mexico and a stout supporter of Indian rights and social justice. Most of his flock were Indians who had converted to Catholicism, taking Spanish names and adopting the culture of their masters.

The Sceptical Occultist

One young convert, Juan Diego, was so enthusiastic about his new religion that every morning he would walk from his village of Quahutitlan, near present-day Mexico city, to Tlatilolco where he could hear mass. His route passed a little hill called Tepeyacac. On the morning of 8 December, 1531, he was enchanted to hear a beautiful chorus of bird song coming from the summit. Suddenly, this strange music ceased and he heard a soft feminine voice call his name. On climbing the hill, he was confronted by a wondrous vision of a radiant Indian woman who spoke in Juan's native Nahuatl dialect, identifying herself as the Virgin Mary. She explained that she had a mission for Juan: he was to go to the bishop's palace and tell him to build a church on Tepeyacac in her honour.

The bishop, preoccupied with the gathering political storm inside Mexico, heard Juan politely but suggested that they should discuss his experience at a later date. Obediently, the bemused Indian returned to the hill and was promptly sent back to speak again with the bishop. This time Juan literally had to force his way into Zumarraga's apartments. The bishop was impressed with Juan's fervour and suggested that he should ask his apparition for a sign. Juan again returned to the hill, where the apparition agreed to provide a sign on the morning of the next day. But during the night, Juan's uncle, Juan Bernardino, who lived in the same house, became dangerously ill. In the morning, Juan set out to find a priest and, passing the hill on his way to Tlatilolco, was confronted by the apparition who chided him for his lack of faith. After promising that his uncle would recover, the figure took him to the top of the hill, where the cactus and scrub had been miraculously transformed into a wonderful garden. Gathering a bouquet of Castilian Roses and other southern European flowers, the apparition placed the blooms in Juan's cactus-fibre cloak. The apparition then warned the hapless Indian that on no account was he to open his cloak for anyone but the bishop.

When Juan eventually opened his cloak in front of the bishop, a more wondrous sight met the onlooker's gaze than a bouquet of flowers. The full length of the Indian's cloak was impressed with the image of a dark-skinned, brown-haired

The Marian Apparitions

Virgin Mary with her hands in prayer, standing on a crescent moon supported by an angel. Upon seeing this wonder, Zumarraga fell to his knees and begged forgiveness for having doubted the authenticity of the apparition.

Just a touching religious fable? Well, no, there is a little more to it than that. The church was eventually built and today stands as the Basilica of Our Lady of Guadalupe at Villa Madero, a few miles north of Mexico City.[2] Zumarraga wrote an account of the apparition and between 1531 and 1638 another thirty-three documents relating to the miracle were placed on record. The Vatican at first was very suspicious of an alleged miracle in the New World but in 1666 the documents were collected and a commission gave its tacit approval to the apparition. As recently as 1946, Father Jose Bravo Ugarte, an expert on Mexican history, stated in his *Cuestiones historicas guadalupanas* that there could be no doubt that the story of the Guadalupe apparition rested on historical fact.

The cactus-fibre cloak is still venerated at the Basilica of Our Lady of Guadalupe. In February 1979, the Image of Guadalupe Research Project arranged for Dr Philip Callahan, a University of Florida biophysicist and an affiliate of the US Department of Agriculture, to investigate the cloak. After analysing the image with infrared photography, he reported that the resulting prints showed no brush strokes or underlying blue-print. The image was still in full colour and, surprisingly, the heat from the many hundreds of thousands of candles which had been lit under the icon over the centuries had not caused any cracking or fading of the image. One part of the image was shown to be fake. No doubt, hoping to improve on the handiwork of the apparition, religious artists had added a sunburst and fixed stars around the figure and trimmed the edges of the cloak with a golden border. All of these areas revealed brush strokes and all had faded. Some scientists have estimated that the plant fibre should have started to disintegrate after twenty years.

The 'miracle' became a beacon of faith within Mexico and resulted in mass conversions amongst the Indians. The impetus for an insurrection waned and eventually Nuno de Guzan was replaced with a more liberal governor and returned home to Spain in disgrace. Our Lady of Guadalupe is

The Sceptical Occultist

an impressive case but it cannot on its own offer conclusive evidence for the Marian apparitions, particularly with the current, understandable reservations about religious relics.

One major problem in assessing these experiences is that the Marian apparitions do *not* offer a consistent pattern of evidence. Even in modern times, between the period 1928–1975, there were 232 *uninvestigated* apparitions of the Virgin Mary reported throughout the world. While some may be 'real' apparitions of the Virgin Mary, others are more like persecutory hallucinations.[3] In the 1950s thousands of Catholics flocked to Necedah, Wisconsin, to hear the messages of Mary Ann Van Hoof, who claimed to have enjoyed apparitions of the Virgin Mary over several years, but the 'Virgins's' later messages were decidedly coloured by White supremacist doctrines. Veronica Lueken from Bayside, New York, claimed to have had visions of the Virgin Mary since the early 1970s. The 'Virgin's' later messages showed an increasing obsession with the former Soviet nuclear submarine fleet. At that time there was widespread concern that Russian submarines could launch a successful pre-emptive nuclear strike from America's eastern seaboard.

There is another problem. Some apparitions which do superficially appear to have the hallmarks of a spiritual experience are later flawed by the secrets given to the seers by their vision. Between 1949 and 1952, two 11-year-old girls in the West German town of Heroldsbach-Thurn reported seeing the Virgin Mary on a daily basis. The apparition spoke of a coming apocalypse and gave the children personal messages swearing them to secrecy. The children wrote down the messages and sealed them in envelopes before handing them to a lawyer. After several other seers experienced apocalyptic visions in which Germany was destroyed, the envelopes were opened and the Virgin's promise made public, 'When the Russians come I will protect Heroldsbach and Thurn. Even when the houses shake when the bombs fall. But I will protect Heroldsbach and Thurn.' This is surely just a reflection of the fears that were current in Europe during the Cold War. Many psychologists would argue that this is just what they would have expected.

The Marian Apparitions

This throws us back to Professor Flew's question of how we can know which apparitions – if any – are authentic and which are just subjective hallucinations. While researching this book, I put this question to a senior spiritual adviser within the Catholic Church, who quoted the advice attributed to Christ on the subject of false prophets: 'By their fruits you shall know them.' But this offers cold comfort when we are confronted by a really complex apparition, as we shall see when we consider the next case, which continues to trouble many within the Church. It was the first apparition of modern times to take place outside religious cloisters and the first contemporary collective apparition to be recognised by the Church.

La Salette is a little village near Grenoble in the French Alps. On 19 September, 1846, two children were watching their animals on Mount Planteau, just outside the village. One was Melanie Mathieu, the 14-year-old daughter of a day labourer. The fourth of ten children, Melanie had been sent to work in the local farms as a shepherdess. She spoke the local dialect but had only an imperfect understanding of French and could neither read nor write. Rejected by her mother and shut out of her home, Melanie was an emotionally isolated child. Her companion was Pierre-Maximin Giraud, the fourth son of a wheelwright. At eleven years of age, Pierre could not read and his only religious education had been the slow, painful memorisation of two simple prayers. He did, however, speak both the local dialect and French. Like Melanie, Pierre-Maximin had been rejected and had experienced a long history of cruelty at the hands of his step-mother. The two children had known each other for two days when they had the single experience that made them famous.

The afternoon began like any other. They had eaten lunch with the other shepherds on Mount Planteau but then had fallen asleep in the sunshine. They awoke to find their cattle had strayed. While looking for the beasts the children came upon a whirling light within which they could see the oval features of a face. The light finally materialised into the form of a seated woman. The figure was so bright that it hurt the children's eyes but they noticed that she was wearing white shoes, a cape encircled by roses and a crucifix around her neck. The children later gave an account of the subsequent extraordinary events to Abbé Francois Lagier, the Curé of Saint-Pierre-de-Cherennes.

The apparition beckoned them forward saying, 'Come near, my children, don't be afraid! I am here to tell you great news.' The lady then spoke at length in French about coming chastisements from her son, the importance of hearing mass on Sunday and a terrible impending famine which would take the lives of many children under the age of seven. As this monologue progressed, it became clear that Melanie was having trouble understanding the lady's French. Melanie turned to Pierre-Maximin and asked him to explain the meaning of pommes-de-terre (the French for potatoes) and at this the apparition interjected 'You do not understand, my children; I will say it in a different way,' and continued in the local dialect. Explaining the message again, the apparition reminded the children of certain childhood memories to emphasise her points. She then spoke about the importance of prayer, before telling the youngsters 'Now my children, make this known to my people.' She then rose into the air and disappeared.

Walking back down Mount Planteau with their cattle, the children were still confused and frightened. Melanie remarked to Maximin, 'If I hadn't seen her rise up into the air I would have believed it was some woman who wanted to kill her children.' Pierre-Maximin had thought of a woman 'whose son had beaten her and left'.

It was left to others to identify the vision as the Mother of God. Later it was claimed that a spring appeared at the site of the apparition but there is evidence of an old spring in that area and we can dismiss this detail. There is little convincing evidence of fraud. The story only came out because Pierre got into trouble with his employer over his late arrival back at the farm. Did he then invent this story as an excuse for his tardiness? If he did, this uneducated child managed to tailor his story to fit almost exactly into the tradition of the Marian apparitions. The children never varied their statements despite extensive interrogation.

The Marian Apparitions

The children came from violent, emotionally impoverished backgrounds and the lady's message can be interpreted as referring to situations of family violence. Psychologists would argue that these two factors neatly dovetail if we assume that this was just an hallucination created by the children's attempts to come to terms with their pasts. Catholic commentators have also dismissed the apparition at La Salette, but for different reasons. Subsequently, as was expected of seers, both children entered the Church but their lives were unhappy and largely unproductive. This prompted the Jesuit scholar, Father Thurston, to express doubts about the validity of their experiences. But it would seem that Thurston wanted *two* miracles. Firstly, an apparition of the Virgin Mary on Mount Planteau and secondly, that two uneducated, emotionally-isolated children should, on the basis of a single spiritual experience, be able to overcome their handicaps and integrate into essentially middle-class professions!

All of this is irrelevant to the paradox which La Salette presents to us. On the one hand, are we to believe that a supernatural being, the Mother of God, did not know that Melanie spoke French imperfectly and was unlikely to understand her message? On the other hand, if this was an hallucination, how did both children come to experience it? We might argue that it was a product of Pierre's mind; after all, it was the boy who had a good command of French. However, if we adopt this hypothesis we are forced to accept four facts:

1. That Pierre-Maximin created the hallucination of the lady.
2. The hallucination was also seen by Melanie.
3. The boy's brain not only coped with projecting an hallucinatory fragment of his unconscious but also allowed him the stream of consciousness necessary to conduct a conversation with Melanie.
4. The resulting hallucination was a marvel which was not only seen by both children but appeared to interact with them as well.

Leaving aside the identity of the apparition, the reader may decide that there were three people present on the slopes of Mount Planteau.

What of the vision's warnings? The apparition referred to a famine and the blight of the potato crop. In the previous year, the great potato famine had started in Ireland where, over the next six years, it would be responsible for 800,000 deaths, forcing roughly the same number to emigrate. By 1846, the year of the apparition, the blight had spread to the continent where it also caused widespread hunger. France's wheat harvest also failed and a virulent fungus decimated much of the grape crop. Some parts of France experienced severe famine, others were spared but nowhere did it reach the same proportions as Ireland. Of the thousand or so recorded deaths, most were infants which recalls the apparition's warning. There is, however, a more terrible menace implicit here, one designed to manipulate the community. Catholic children attain the age of reason at seven, becoming morally responsible for their actions. Below this age, they are innocents and arguably the most precious commodity of a simple rural community. This threat must have had considerable impact on those who might otherwise have been tempted to reject the apparition's warnings.

La Salette was also the beginning of the tradition of 'secrets' which so mark the modern apparitions. Both children were given messages and sworn to secrecy. In 1851, Pope Pius IX personally ordered Church officials in La Salette to obtain statements from the children about the secrets they had been given by the vision. The seers only agreed on the condition that the messages were placed in sealed envelopes and delivered personally to the Pope. These secrets were finally made public, some years later. Melanie published hers, with the permission of the Bishop of Lecce, in the form of a pamphlet in 1879. Versions of Pierre-Maximin's secrets were released in 1878 and 1915. Both were cryptic and seemed to mirror the writings of St John the Divine, foretelling an apocalyptic war in Europe and the rise of the Anti-Christ.

Many interpretations have been placed on these secrets but, more to the point, the reader may find himself in sympathy with the Abbé Henri Souillet, who was in charge of a

The Marian Apparitions

parish near I'le Bouchard, France, when four children reported an apparition of the Virgin in December 1947. Writing to a friend, the Abbé remarked that it was a mystery to him why God, who would surely not speak without good reason, would choose to reveal messages to seers who were then instructed not to divulge them. He suggested that there was 'something bizarre here which called for the greatest caution'.

On Thursday 11 February, 1858, just twelve years after the vision at La Salette, a 14-year-old peasant girl was collecting bones near the River Grave with other children, when she noticed 'something white' in the thick scrub at the foot of a cliff known as Massabeille. As Bernadette Soubirous watched, she saw the form of a young girl who smiled at her and disappeared. Later, in a statement to the Lourdes police commissioner, Bernadette referred to the vision as 'Aquero' (which translates as 'that one') suggesting that sightings of unidentified beings were not uncommon among the locals. Certainly, the consensus amongst her friends was that it was possibly an evil spirit – when Bernadette returned in the company of other girls on the Sunday after mass, they armed themselves with a bottle of holy water. At a grotto in the cliff, however, they knelt down and said the Rosary, suggesting that another speculation was that the vision had been the Virgin Mary. As the children were praying, the apparition briefly appeared to Bernadette again.

The news undoubtedly caused some excitement amongst Bernadette's immediate circle because, on the Tuesday, the child was persuaded to return in the company of several women. The apparition appeared to Bernadette but remained silent. The apparition appeared to Bernadette again on Thursday, 18 February, and this time it asked her to have the grace to return every day for the next fifteen days. From 18 February to 4 March, the vision appeared to the child on all but three days. Very soon the news had spread through the district and Bernadette's experiences were watched by a growing crowd of onlookers. During the apparition on 25 February, Bernadette was seen to crawl into the back of the cave and dig in the ground until she uncovered a pool of muddy water which would become the famous Lourdes' spring. Public speculation was further excited by the alleged cure of Eugenie Troy, a child who had been born partially blind. Other cures were soon being ascribed to these healing waters.

On 2 March, the apparition instructed Bernadette to go to the local priests with a message demanding various religious works and a chapel to be built in honour of the Virgin Mary. The child's reception at the presbytery was frosty. Father Dominique Peyramale, the Curé of the parish, asked Bernadette if she had the money for a new chapel and when the child said she did not, he said that he did not either and told her to ask the lady to give it to her. Other priests jokingly asked for a miracle. Matters were made worse by the apparition's persistent refusal to identify itself. When questioned by the priests, Bernadette had to admit that 'I do not know that it is she' (the Virgin Mary) only describing her vision as 'une petite demoiselle' (a small lady) and, on another occasion, 'une fille blanche, pas plus grand que moi' (a girl in white, no taller than myself).

It is fair to say that when the apparition did finally offer an identity, it had more impact on the clergy than on the child. For many hundreds of years the Church had been involved in a theological debate as to whether Christ's mother had been born without the stain of Original Sin. In its wisdom, the Church finally decided in 1854 that from the moment of conception in the womb of her mother Anne, the Virgin had never been stained by Original Sin. The apparition's strange utterance, 'I am the Immaculate Conception,' four years after the Church's proclamation was taken by many as supernatural confirmation of Rome's decision. As for the seer, Bernadette walked home constantly repeating this strange phrase lest she forget it.

The chapel was finally built and the curative properties ascribed to its spring resulted in Lourdes becoming the pre-eminent Catholic shrine. Bernadette also received secrets from the apparition, the 'public' messages being concerned about Marian devotions. The Jesuit scholar, Herbert Thurston, rejected many alleged Marian apparitions and considered others uncertain but never entertained doubts about

The Marian Apparitions

the authenticity of the events at Lourdes.[4] However, being the private experiences of a single individual, it lacks the same evidential value as later apparitions. The miracles associated with the spring are discussed in the next chapter. Certainly there have been 'cures' reported from Lourdes but the reader will be asked to decide for himself as to whether they can really be described as 'miracles'.

News of a more spectacular apparition began to trickle out of Portugal in the autumn of 1917.[5] Three children working as shepherds on the hills outside Fatima reported seeing angels and a beautiful lady. Our accounts of this series of visions come mainly from the autobiography of Lucia de Santos, the youngest daughter of poor landowners and the only seer to survive to adulthood. The other two children who shared these experiences were her cousins, Francisco and Jacinta Marto.

Close friends, the three children were very devout and had previously shared other mystical experiences. In the spring of 1916, while the three friends were playing at the Cova de Iria, a hollow outside the town, where the children often took their sheep to graze, an apparition of a boy materialised on the hill and exhorted them to pray. The 'angel' appeared twice more, once at the hollow and then at Lucia's house. The children were told that the angelic visitations were a prelude to an appearance by the Virgin Mary and, from the very beginning, they marked Lucia as the chief seer.

The first of the six appearances of the 'Virgin' took place on Sunday 13 May, 1917. The children were again playing in the hollow, when a bright flash of light heralded the materialisation of a beautiful woman standing within the foliage of an oak tree. The children later described her as a small woman, about eighteen years old, wearing a white veil bordered with gold and surrounded by a dazzling light. The two girls both saw the figure but only Lucia ventured to speak. The boy, Francisco, saw and heard nothing. When Lucia asked the apparition why Francisco could not see her, it replied that the boy would have to say many Rosaries. Under Lucia's instruction the child did recite the Rosary and in time he could see the figure but was never able to hear it speak. Keeping to the tradition of these apparitions, the 'Virgin' asked the children to return to the Cova on the thirteenth day of the next month. The figure then glided to the east and disappeared.

On the basis of the evidence so far, many would interpret the 'vision' as a purely subjective hallucination arising from the unconscious of a devout child brought up on Marian devotion and accounts of the angels heralding Christ's birth (the Annunciation). Even the request to return on a fixed day of the next month appears to be an imitation of the apparition at Lourdes. The other two children might have deluded themselves that they shared Lucia's experience or they may have imperfectly shared in it by means of telepathy. Any indications of wholesale fraud are ruled out by the subsequent events.

The children pledged themselves to secrecy about their experiences of the beautiful lady but Jacinta let the story slip out that they had seen the Virgin Mary. The parish priest was far from pleased at the story of this marvel now sweeping through the village. He questioned Lucia but she could only reply that she was not sure that the 'pretty little woman' was really the Virgin. The priest gave his consent for the children to go to the Cova on the 13 June but told Lucia's mother that if the apparition was seen again, the children were not to be allowed to return there.

The seers' families now found themselves on the 'wrong side' of the parish priest and they were ridiculed by many in the village. In turn, considerable pressure was exerted on the children to admit that the beautiful lady was just a figment of their imaginations. The day of the second apparition fell on the Feast of St Anthony and a large, curious crowd gathered at the Cova. Many in the crowd had come from neighbouring villages. Some were merely curious but others were ill or handicapped and had been drawn to the apparition site in the hope of a cure. Many had arrived early and were eating their lunch when the three seers arrived at around eleven o'clock, accompanied by friends and family members. A child from Boleiros had started to lead the crowd in a litany when Lucia stopped her, saying that there would not be time. She then called to Jacinta, telling her that the Virgin was coming, remarking 'there's the lightning'. The three children ran to the oak tree where the apparition again appeared in the upper branches.

Lifting her hands in prayer, Lucia asked 'You have asked me to come here; please tell me what you want.' The apparition replied, 'I want you to come here on the thirteenth of the next month. Say the Rosary, inserting between the mysteries the following ejaculation "O my Jesus, forgive us our sins. Save us from the fires of hell. Lead all souls to Heaven, especially those who have most need of Thy mercy." I want you to learn to read and write and later I will tell you what else I want.'

As the date of the third apparition approached, the village found itself divided. The priest believed that the apparitions were the work of the devil, a belief shared by Lucia's mother. The civil administration and the republican press viewed events at Fatima as superstition woven into Catholic propaganda. Portugal's last king had been deposed in 1910 by a revolutionary government very hostile to religion in general and the Catholic Church in particular. Diplomatic relations between Portugal and the Vatican had been severed in 1913. Church property and lands had been confiscated, anti-Catholic propaganda was rife and members of the clergy found themselves second class citizens. The Church, hoping to survive this turbulent period by maintaining a low profile, was simply embarrassed by events at Fatima.

When the apparition appeared once again on 13 July, the Cova was ringed by a crowd of four or five thousand spectators. On this occasion the apparition told Lucia, 'I want you to come here on the thirteenth of next month and to continue to pray the Rosary every day in honour of Our Lady of the Rosary, in order to obtain peace for the world and the end of the war, for she alone can help. Continue to come here every month. In October, I will tell you who I am and what I want. And I will perform a miracle so that everyone may see and believe.'

Amongst the crowd were Jacinta and Francisco's father, Manuel, who was to report a 'little greyish cloud' over the top of the oak tree and a 'delicious fresh breeze' which suddenly sprang up as the Virgin appeared to the children. Like many in the crowds, he claimed to hear the Virgin's 'tiny voice' which sounded like 'a mosquito in an empty bottle', and which others described as the 'buzzing of bees'. At the end of the apparition, Manuel heard a clap of thunder as Lucia rose to her feet and, pointing at the sky, cried 'There she goes! There she goes!' Manuel and many others left the Cova convinced of the authenticity of the apparition.

Now faced with the possibility of a religious revival on 13 October, the Portuguese Government decided to act. Arthur d'Oliveria Santos, the subprefect of Ourem, was dispatched to Fatima to discredit the apparitions by forcing confessions from the children. Unable to elicit a retraction during extensive interviews on 11 August, Santos had the children abducted on the day the apparition was due to appear. Still the crowds at the Cova reported hearing thunder and seeing lightning and an unusual rainbow covering the apparition site. Held in solitary confinement, the children were brutally interrogated and threatened with execution. Finally, when each child had been led to believe that its playmates had been murdered and still no confessions were extracted, Santos could do no more and the children were released. On 19 August, the apparition appeared to the children while they were with their sheep, instructing them to pray for sinners who did not believe, make sacrifices for them and pray for an end to the war in Europe.

On 13 September, some 30,000 pilgrims gathered at the Cova. Illusion, delusion or supernatural intervention, increasing numbers of people were reporting public miracles and not all of these were so easily dismissed. Monsignor John Quareman, the vice-general of Leiria, and a fellow priest went to Fatima incognito. Joining the throng, they heard a loud sigh go up from the crowd.

> To my surprise, I saw clearly and distinctly a globe of light advancing from east to west, gliding slowly and majestically through the air ... My friend looked also, and he had the good fortune to see the same unexpected vision. Suddenly the globe with the wonderful light dropped from sight.

The children saw the globe come to rest in the branches of the oak tree. Suddenly the air was inundated with a rain of

The Marian Apparitions

white petals which disintegrated before hitting the ground. The 'rain of flowers' which was seen by the crowds was photographed by a government official, Antonio Robelo Martins, who in 1919 published the pictures in his book *Fatima; Espérance du Mond*.

By October, Portugal was at fever pitch. On the morning of the thirteenth, a crowd in excess of 70,000 was standing in the pouring rain around the Cova. Some of the women were barefoot, carrying their shoes in bags above their heads; the luckier ones sheltered under umbrellas. Amongst the throng were government officials, senior clerics and representatives from all the major newspapers. In the village, troops moved into position to quell the expected riot.

When the children arrived at noon, the crowd was reciting the Rosary in a sad chant. Lucia addressed them, asking them to lower their umbrellas and join her in prayer and the crowd immediately complied. When the apparition appeared to the children it identified itself as 'Our Lady of the Rosary' and, speaking directly to Lucia as usual, requested a chapel to be built in her honour in the Cova. The lady then, somewhat prematurely, predicted that the First World War was about to come to an end. At the conclusion of her messages and secrets to the children, the lady spread her arms and showed the children a series of visions. Then, as the apparition ended, the Virgin rose into the air and opened her hands. As Lucia watched, the ascending apparition appeared to project its own light on to the sun. Suddenly, as Lucia cried out, to many onlookers it appeared as if the sun had begun to spin, throwing off coloured lights. People reported this happening twice, the whole experience lasting approximately twelve minutes. Then without warning, the sun seemed to plunge towards the earth. Observers later reported that the heat became intense and only at the last moment, with the crowd panicking, was the 'sun' restored to its place in the sky.

It has been claimed by some that this was only a simple illusion, the sun only appearing to spin and move as the clouds scudded across its face. However, it has been passionately argued by others that, whatever this was, it did not involve the sun, which had been hidden behind a thick bank of clouds all morning and which was in a different part of the sky from the huge 'silver disc' reported by many in the crowds. To add to the mystery, observers in out-lying villages also reported seeing the 'dance of the sun', while some observers actually present at the Cova claimed later to have seen nothing unusual.

In many ways, the apparitions at Fatima ended badly. Lucia's family, still very frightened and feeling isolated within the village, used threats and beatings in a fruitless effort to force a retraction. Neighbours and friends also rejected the children's account and, when Lucia refused to speak about the messages and secrets, the parish priest also rejected it as a divine experience. Feelings ran high when the priest, to all accounts a popular man, left Fatima, telling friends that he did not want to be associated with what was happening there. Lucia's relationship with her family and other members of the community remained uneasy and in 1921 she entered a convent in the city of Porto. Lucia's mother reputedly died of a broken heart. Pressed by her bishop, in 1941 Lucia wrote an account of her conversations with the Virgin Mary.

The apparition's first secret, that Jacinta and Francisco would soon join her in heaven, was seemingly borne out when the boy perished in the great flu epidemic of 1918–19 and Jacinta died after major surgery in February 1920. Other secrets reputedly included a terrifying vision of Hell and the threat of another great war, if Man did not stop offending God. This was to be heralded by 'strange lights in the sky'. Some commentators have linked this with the spectacular and widely reported display of the Aurora Borealis, or Northern Lights, which was seen throughout much of Europe in January 1938 – some eighteen months before Hitler invaded Poland. The Virgin also asked the devout to pray for the conversion of Russia, warning that otherwise the 'error' of Communism would spread throughout the world. The last secret, revealed to Pope Pius XII but never made public, is believed to contain a warning of a third and final apocalyptic war.

La Salette began the tradition of secrets, events at Lourdes added the powerful psychological impact of regular serial apparitions, which were refined at Fatima by the addition of angels and miracles. Finally, at the small Spanish village of

The Marian Apparitions

San Sebastian de Garabandal the miracles would become the prominent feature of the most 'supernatural' Marian apparition of recent times.[6]

San Sebastian de Garabandal was little more than a collection of mud and tile houses, nestled in the mountains of northern Spain. On Sunday, the priest came from nearby Cosio to say mass in the morning and in the evening many of the 100-odd families gathered in the village square to exchange news.

On the evening of Sunday 18 June, 1961, four girls slipped away from the adults to steal apples from the schoolmaster's orchard. Taking a few apples each, they ran off to eat them in the calleja or narrow rocky lane which led to a small stand of pine trees outside the village. Suddenly, there was a loud roll of thunder and an 'angel' materialised in front of the children, who later described it as a boy of about eight years of age with pink wings and dressed in blue robes, a 'very beautiful figure that shone brilliantly but did not hurt my eyes at all' as 12-year-old Maria Concepcion 'Conchita' Gonzalez-Gonzalez later noted in her published *Diary*. It was the first of more than 2,000 alleged apparitions of angels and the Virgin Mary. Most of these were shared with 10-year-old Maria Cruz Gonzalez Barrido and Jacinta Gonzalez-Gonzalez and Maria Dolores Mazon Gonzalez, both of whom were twelve years of age.

Shocked and frightened, the children ran to the church intending to enter and pray, but instead they ran around the back of the church 'to cry'. They related their experience to every child they met and the story quickly spread around the village and reached the ears of the schoolmistress. While others in the village mocked and taunted the girls, the schoolmistress was supportive, encouraging them to pray, and on the next day, when the apparition failed to reappear, she consoled them by suggesting that the angel had not come because it was cloudy. Each child later reported that, in the evening, while preparing for bed, they heard a voice which said 'Do not worry. you will see me again.' On Tuesday 20 June, the children again returned to the calleja but again it seemed that nothing would happen. Then, just as the girls were preparing to leave, they found themselves surrounded by a light so dazzling they were hidden from one another. They began to scream, but the light quickly faded.

A clue to what may have been happening in the village is suggested by events at the third apparition on Wednesday evening. Some of the women wanted to believe that the Virgin Mary had come to their village, while others were very sceptical, but all were curious and a large crowd followed the girls to the apparition site. The children, falling into a state of ecstasy, found themselves in the presence of a shining figure. Some of the women were laughing at the children and they heard Conchita say 'Holy Virgin they do not believe us!' but when the figure smiled and bowed at the mention of the Virgin, the children decided they were in the presence of an angelic messenger. Other women did believe and became quite excited. One of them, Clementina Gonzalez, called to Conchita, *'Call upon Our Lady of Mount Carmel; call upon the Sacred Heart of Jesus; tell Him something! Ask Him what He wants of us.'* On six of the following eight days, the children were graced with a silent vision of an angel. On 1 July, the 'angel' broke his silence to announce that the Virgin Mary would shortly appear to the children as 'Our Lady of Mount Carmel'.

By now the news had filtered out of the village, reaching the ears of parish priest, Father Valentin Marichalar, in Cosio. Disturbed by these stories, Marichalar returned to Garabandal and told the children to demand that the vision reveal its mission. The priest then found lodgings in the village, determined to witness these apparitions for himself. He did not have long to wait. On the Thursday, while at the calleja, the children went into a trance so complete that they were insensible to slaps or pinpricks. When he left the village, the priest was no longer in any doubt that whatever was happening at Garabandal was more than children's games. Conchita later wrote that the priest had been supportive but had been very nervous about their experiences.

On 2 July, the girls reported the first of several thousand apparitions of the Virgin Mary. At around six o'clock, while the children were walking towards the lane intending to say

The Marian Apparitions

the Rosary, they were met by an apparition of the Virgin Mary flanked by two identical angels. To the Virgin's right side they saw a large, unblinking eye. Conchita, puzzled by this, said later that it seemed to be the 'eye of God'. Arcane theology suggests another interpretation, one with which a twelve year-old child is not likely to be acquainted.

Our knowledge of angels comes from early Middle Eastern civilisations and the Old Testament. For example, the prophet Enoch was allowed a revelation of the angel hierarchies but much of this early work, collected together by St Jerome, did not meet with the approval of the early church fathers and was relegated to the Apocrypha or 'hidden writings': fourteen books sometimes included as an appendix to the Old Testament. Later, in his *Summa theologica*, St Thomas Aquinas described the nature of angels, their hierarchies and appearances, while the angelic court was invented in the fourth century by Pseudo-Dionysius out of the writings of Paul (Col i, 16; Eph i, 21). These winged beings were said to be divided into three hierarchies, each having three orders. Those allowed to interact with Man as guardians and messengers, such as the Archangels, Angels, Principals and Powers, were said to materialise in the form of all-seeing eyes. The religious symbolism is striking; or is it just a coincidence?

There was more symbolism in the appearance of the Virgin who was holding a chalice into which blood or tears were falling, a cup which was brimming over. The lady spoke at length about the children's daily lives and smiled at their accounts of their lives in the fields. Finally, she instructed them in the proper recitation of the Rosary.

What makes the apparitions at Garabandal so fascinating are the alleged associated miracles and paranormal activity. The children were never told when to expect the next apparition, the appearance of which was heralded by synchronised 'feelings of joy'. When the Church authorities, recognising Conchita as the primary seer, removed the child to Santander, her apparitions continued to coincide with the ecstatic trances of the other three children. The girls were confined to their homes, watched by the Civil Guard, but still they managed to arrive at the apparition site together. When pilgrims

The Sceptical Occultist

began to flock to the little village, a tradition was started amongst the crowds who gave the children their wedding rings to be kissed by the Virgin. This apparent feat of clairvoyance was put to the test on several occasions. One person would collect up to twenty rings from the crowd and hand them to the children who always returned them to the correct owners.

Another extraordinary event was reported by Sanchez-Ventura y Pascual, a Spanish lawyer and economics professor. On 4 August, a man who had brought a tape-recorder to the apparition pushed his way through the crowds to record the mumblings of the children while they were in their trance. When Maria Mazon and Jacinta came out of their trance, the man showed the children the machine and explained its use. Suddenly, Maria went back into a trance while holding the microphone. Continuing her conversation with the Virgin, the child asked if she would provide a miracle for the crowds by leaving an impression of her voice on the tape. When Maria suddenly awoke from her ecstasy, the onlookers eagerly waited for the tape to be rewound. When it was played back, the crowd heard Maria ask the Virgin to speak and clearly heard a sweet female voice reply 'I shall not speak.' This was heard twice more by the excited bystanders but then the woman's voice vanished from the tape.

Doctors were permitted to examine the children while in ecstasy and they confirmed that the children were in an altered state of consciousness. With their heads tilted back, looking upwards and speaking, their faces remained radiant and composed even when lights were shone in their eyes or their legs were pricked with needles. 'What?' one of the girls exclaimed to the apparition, 'they are pricking us? . . . But we don't feel anything.' While the girls were in this state, 'men of the Spanish countryside' were unable to raise them even a few inches above the ground. One witness to these events, Pepe Diaz, told one of the authors of *Garabandal: The Village Speaks*, that he saw many young men in their twenties and thirties fail in their attempts to lift the girls while they were in trance. One strapping young lad in particular had been unable to lift Jacinta but, after the apparition had ended, was goaded by the other men into trying again. He refused, saying that he was frightened by the whole thing. Finally giving in to their good natured taunts, he grabbed the girl and lifted her above his head 'as if she was a doll'. He then became very upset.

In that first summer a strange event took place which would ultimately ensure that news of the Garabandal apparitions would be carried around the world. Father Luis Maria Andreu and his brother Father Ramon Maria Andreu were asked to relieve temporarily the priests of Cosio. Neither Jesuit gave any credence to the authenticity of the apparitions and turned a cold eye on what appeared to be the cynical manipulation of a community. On Sunday 29 July, after the children received communion at the 11 o'clock mass, they immediately entered a trance and at ten minutes past twelve, Conchita was heard asking for a public miracle. When the children and a crowd of onlookers began to climb the hill to the pine grove, Father Luis followed. Few even noticed the priest until suddenly, as Conchita was asking the apparition for a sign to give the crowds proof, Father Luis pointed at the pine trees and loudly exclaimed four times 'Miracle!' Soon after, the priest described that Sunday as the 'happiest day of his life' and affirmed the apparition to all with whom he came in contact. Then, in the afternoon, while being driven to Reinosa, Father Luis let out a small moan and fell dead.

Events then took a very curious course. After the priest's death, the children started reporting messages, one of which promised that when his body was removed from the grave it would not have decayed. On 6 August the children actually conversed with the priest's apparition, while his brother, Father Ramon Andreu, who was standing in the crowd, listened to the children's side of this conversation. When the apparition had ended, he questioned the children, recalling this conversation in *Our Lady Comes to Garabandal*,

> ... I was truly stupefied, the little girls repeated in my presence the words of their vision and I heard them relate the death of my brother and the description of the funeral. They gave a certain number of very precise details concerning the special rites of the burial of a priest. They even knew that Father Luis's burial had involved a few exceptions regarding the traditional rites for the dressing of the deceased: for example they had not

placed a biretta on my brother's head and the chalice which he should have held in his hands had been replaced with a crucifix. The girls also gave the reasons for these variations.

On another occasion I heard the children say in ecstasy that my brother Luis died without having made his profession [a period of study, followed by an examination, taken by all Jesuits]. They also talked about me and my vows: they knew the precise date, the exact place where they had been pronounced and the name of the Jesuit who had taken them at the same time I did. You will understand my astonishment, my stupefaction in the face of this unchallengable array of rigorously exact detail, when I knew pertinently that the children could not have learned about them through purely human means.

And yet, there is a sting in the tail of this story. Father Luis had been buried at the Jesuit seminary at Ona, where he had been a professor of theology. At the beginning of 1976, Ona was converted into an asylum and the bodies of all those buried there were exhumed and transferred to the Ossuary of the Society of Jesus in Loyola. When Father Luis's grave was opened, the body had been reduced to a skeleton.

Finally, we cannot leave the Garabandal apparition without mention of the 'little miracle' which occurred on 18 July, 1962. When the children suddenly announced that they were going to receive communion from an archangel (St Michael), there was considerable opposition from the clergy, on the grounds that angels could not consecrate hosts! This issue developed into something of a pantomime as the children practised with 'unconsecrated hosts' before finally revealing that the actual communion would be a visible public event. One witness, Pepe Diaz, was determined to remain with Conchita as the time approached for the apparition. Just before noon, the child entered a trance and, leaving her house, knelt down in the street outside. The crowd was in a frenzy but Diaz grimly stood his ground and remained only eighteen inches from the child's face. Finally, when Conchita put out her tongue to receive the host, he was filled with a 'sense of deep foreboding' but, as he watched, he saw a 'neat, precise and well-formed Host' appear on her tongue. The host grew in volume and remained visible for three minutes. Other witnesses saw a 'white shadow' or a 'bright circle the size of a

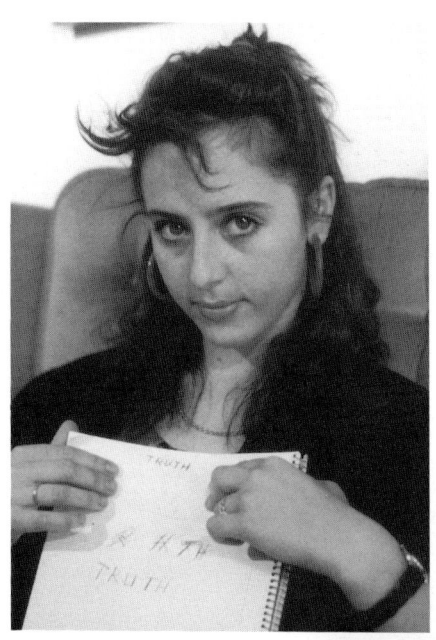

Like the Polish clairvoyant, Stephen Ossowiecki, Monica Nieto Tejada, a 15-year-old Spanish girl, appears to be able to read words hidden inside sealed containers. In this experiment, the target word 'truth' was concealed inside a sealed box. Monica displays the target word and her correct guess. *(Dr Elmar R. Gruber/Fortean Picture Library)*

The child Ilga K., who appeared to enjoy telepathic communication with her mother in Professor von Neureiter's experiments. *(Society for Psychical Research)*

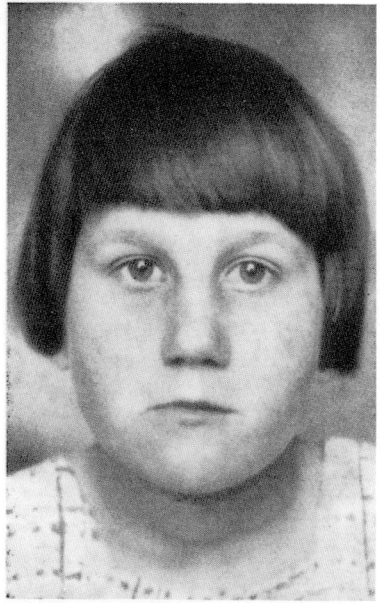

A dramatic poltergeist disturbance at Dodleston, Chester, May 1985, when the kitchen was wrecked, furniture was upended and computer messages were received from an 'entity' which claimed to have been a man who lived in the 16th century. *(Ken Webster/Fortean Picture Library)*

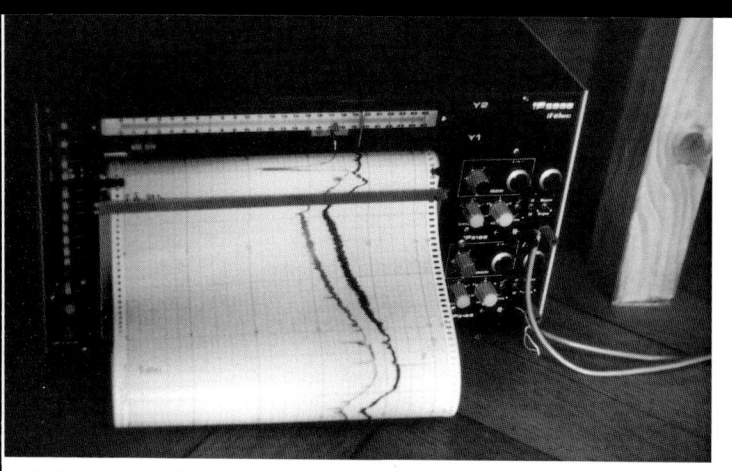

'Cold spots', cold winds and sudden drops in temperature are an often reported feature of poltergeist disturbances and hauntings. Although the phenomenon is frequently rationalised as being purely imaginary or hallucinatory, this continuous temperature recording shows inexplicable temperature fluctuations in a poltergeist-stricken apartment at Mulhouse, France. *(Dr Elmar R. Gruber/Fortean Picture Library)*

This gothic figure of a cowled ghost was taken inside Newby church, near Ripon, North Yorkshire, by the then vicar Reverend K.F. Lord, in the early 1960s. He did not see the figure when taking the photograph; it only showed up when the film was developed. *(Fortean Picture Library)*

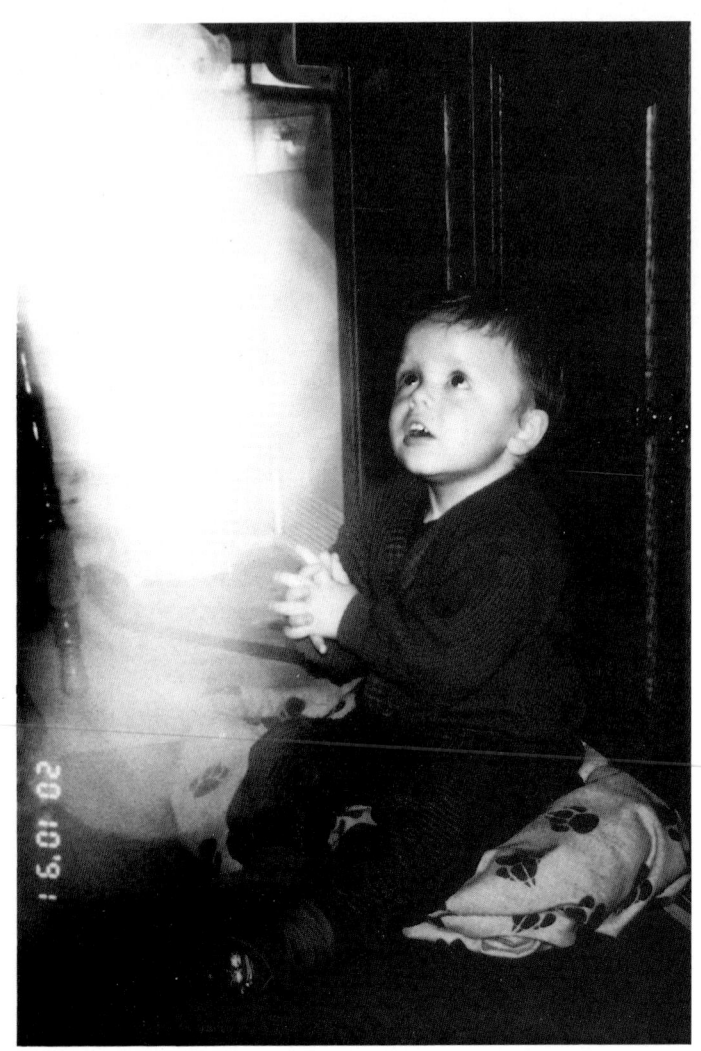

In 1991, two-year-old Greg Sheldon Maxwell began to say 'Old Nanna's here' and point up in the air. When a photograph was taken, this cylinder of light appeared on the developed film. The child's family believe that it represents the ghost of his great-grandmother. It bares a striking resemblance to the five-foot high, 'small cloud of light' which the Reverend Charles Jupp described floating above the bed of a four year-old child at the Orphanage and Home, Aberlour, Craigellachie. *(Marina Jackson/Fortean Picture Library)*

Unlike the fleeting apparition, haunting ghosts are, in principle, available to be photographed. This photograph, taken in 1936, purports to show the Brown Lady of Raynham Hall, Norfolk. *(Fortean Picture Library)*

Lucia de Santos, Francisco Marto and Jacinta Marto, a few days before the final Marian apparition at Fatima on 13 October 1917. *(Fortean Picture Library)*

The crowd at the Cova de Iria, Fatima, witnessing the 'dance of the sun' on 13 October 1917. *(Fortean Picture Library)*

Maria Concepcion 'Conchita' Gonzalez-Gonzalez, Maria Cruz Gonzalez Barrido, Jacinta Gonzalez-Gonzalez and Maria Dolores Mazon Gonzalez in a state of ecstasy at Garabandal, Spain, in the summer of 1961. Each of the seers is looking in a different direction, which is evidence that the apparition of the Blessed Virgin Mary was experienced 'internally'. *(Fortean Picture Library)*

The seers at Garabandal in the summer of 1961. The child in the centre is holding up her scapula to be blessed by the apparition. During their trances, the children were often given wedding rings by onlookers who wanted them to be blessed. Despite various subterfuges, they always managed to return the rings to their correct owners. *(Fortean Picture Library)*

Right: A close up of the apparition of Zeitoun. *(Father Jerome Palmer, O.S.B.)*

Below: The public apparition at Zeitoun, Egypt, seen from the perspective of the crowd around the railings of the church. *(Father Jerome Palmer, O. S. B.)*

The apparition of the Virgin Mary at Zeitoun, showing one of the 'doves of light' above the figure's head. *(Fortean Picture Library)*

Reincarnation is a central pillar of the beliefs of many peoples. In this image by a Canadian Indian artist, the figure of Mother Earth is holding a butterfly which represents the transforming soul or spirit. *(Images Colour Library)*

The American P38 Lightning which routinely attacked the railway system in Upper Burma between 1942 and 1945 and which appeared to feature in the past life memories of Ma Tin Aung Myo. (TRH Pictures)

19th century engraving of a woman possessed by a demon. *(Fortean Picture Library)*

Exorcism from frontispiece of *Kurtze und Wahrhafftige Historia von einer Junckfrawen* by Sabastian Khueller (Munich 1574). *(Fortean Picture Library)*

Demonic being exorcised by San Zeno. Detail from the bronze door on the facade of San Zeno church, Verona (early 12th century). *(Images Colour Library)*

Helmut Schmidt operating an early random-event generator, developed for psychokinesis experiments. *(Fortean Picture Library)*

Random-event generator of the type used to test whether psychokinesis is in accordance with the laws of quantum mechanics. *(Fortean Picture Library)*

five-pesetas coin'. Another said the host looked like a 'snowflake upon which the sun's rays were striking'. Motion pictures were made of this event. A 'white shadow' is a very good description of what is seen on the single frame so often reproduced in devotional literature.

The Catholic Church chose not to recognise the apparition at Garabandal and the children later made retractions, but none of this need concern us for reasons discussed below. In 1961 Bishop Doroteo Fernandez, Apostolic Administrator of the diocese of Santander, set up a commission to investigate the apparition. His appointees included Father Francisco Odriozola, Father Juan del Val Gallo (the present bishop of Santander), a third priest and two doctors, one of whom was a leading psychiatrist, Luis Morales Noriega.

During the four years of apparitions, the board only went to the village on four occasions and refused to hear the statements of many of the witnesses. In addition, supporters of the apparition charged the commission with attempting to remove Father Valentin Marichalar from his parish. Father Marichalar was an enthusiastic supporter of the apparition. Another priest, Father Materne Laffineur, one of the few supporters of the apparition to be interviewed, complained that his testimony was taken in a restaurant by a clerk acting as 'procurator, lawyer and assessor'. Father Laffineur claimed that his answers to questions were interpreted in a way which appeared unfavourable to the apparition. When he refused to sign the statement the clerk had written, the clerk signed for him, writing the priest's name in capital letters. The commission never issued a formal, joint report but Dr Luis Morales Noriega dismissed the apparition as 'child's play', claiming that it had a natural explanation based on psycho-analytical theory.

One problem muddying the waters was that the four seers had made several retractions. The children were under enormous social pressure, both from the clergy and members of the community, to admit that they had been lying about the apparition. Conchita's mother, who was tired of the endless stream of pilgrims who wanted to see her daughter, placed her in the Discalced Carmelite Mission at Pamplona. Even here, Conchita found herself under pressure as her confessor refused to accept the authenticity of the apparition and refused her absolution if she did not publicly issue a retraction. On 30 August, 1966, Conchita was interviewed by the Bishop and several priests, against the wishes of her mother Aniceta. Interviews with the other girls followed. The seers quite naturally had some doubts about their experiences and these were encouraged to the point where the girls signed retractions. As this shabby document was destined for publication, the church officials thought it important that the parents sign also. The mothers of two of the visionaries refused to sign. Jacinta urged her mother to sign the document and her mother agreed on condition that her daughter should immediately fall into the state of ecstasy which had so marked most of the seers' visions, and which had been taken by many as the cardinal sign that the children's experiences were authentic. When Jacinta quietly told her mother that she knew that this was impossible, the woman replied 'Then I do not sign.'

Bishop Fernandez and his immediate successor, Bishop Eugenio Beitia Aldazabel, issued 'Notas' advising the faithful to be cautious about the apparition and prohibiting priests (conducting groups of pilgrims) from visiting the village without permission. None of this curtailed the devotion which grew out of the apparitions or dissuaded the authors of numerous books attesting to its authenticity. Bishop Aldazabel's successor, Bishop Puchol Montis, went further, issuing a statement on 17 March, 1967, which declared that there had been no apparition, no messages and deplored the ill-advised conduct of some of the apparition's supporters.

Retractions were not confined to the seers. On the evening of 30 May, 1983, psychiatrist Luis Morales Noriega, a member of Bishop Fernandez's commission, delivered a key-note address in Santander on the eve of the Catholic Feast of the Visitation in which he surprised his audience with a startling retraction, 'I am here today to speak to you on the apparitions of Our Lady at Garabandal. It is because she herself has worked this change of attitude in me. Moreover, I am speaking with full permission of the ecclesiastical hierarchy . . .' In

The Marian Apparitions

1986, Bishop Juan del Val Gallo lifted the restrictions on worship at Garabandal and appointed a new commission to inquire into the apparition. In 1991, this second commission concluded their investigation and submitted their report to Rome.

Finally, we have come to the most spectacular, public and yet least known of the Marian apparitions.[7] It is also one of the few *recorded* apparitions experienced by non-Catholics. The Coptic Church, or Eastern Church, was centred in Constantinople from where it spread through north Africa and the Middle East. When it finally broke from Rome in 1054 AD, the Church elected its own pope and synod of bishops. The Coptic sect in Egypt is a minority descended from those Christians who refused to convert to Islam after the Arab conquest in the seventh century.

Zeitoun is a suburb of Cairo, populated predominantly by poor Christians and Moslems. It was to Zeitoun, legend has it, that Mary and Joseph fled with the infant Christ when Herod ordered the massacre of the innocents. The site of the apparition was St Mary's Church which stands across the street from a garage. This church is connected with another romantic but somewhat more credible story. The land on which the church was built was donated to the Coptic Church in 1920 by the Khalil Ibrahim family, after one of their number had a dream in which the Virgin Mary urged him to build a church in her honour. When St Mary's was finally built in 1925, the same individual had another dream in which Mary promised to appear over the church in the following year. The promised apparition never materialised but, when they discuss Zeitoun, sociologists point to this 40-year expectancy, which they argue was suddenly catalysed by the social upheavals of 1968. For this was a time when Egypt had been defeated by Israel in the 1967 Six Day War and was losing the War of Attrition. Subject to Israeli air-strikes and commando raids, Egyptian society was under severe stress and was turning some of its frustrations against its religious minorities. Here then, the scientist would argue, are the classical ingredients of the Marian apparition and a complex situation that is alleviated by the mass illusion of a supernatural being.

Two mechanics were leaving their garage around midnight on 2 April, 1968, when one of them looked across the street and noticed 'a figure dressed in white on top of the dome of the Church. I thought she was going to commit suicide and shouted to her to be careful. My friend called the police and I woke up the door-keeper. He comes out and looks and cries "It is the Virgin", and runs to call the priest.'

The news had an electric effect on the neighbourhood. By the time the local police chief arrived on the scene, he was forced to radio for more officers to help control the people. He ordered the crowd to disperse and told them that it was just a reflection from the street lamps. He then ordered his officers to break the lights. Subsequent events were described by one of the crowd, 'The light of the dome remained, and the vision of the Virgin became even clearer. The police chief became frightened and said that he wanted nothing more to do with this; while others came closer to be sure of what they saw.'

The apparition at Zeitoun continued to appear at irregular intervals throughout the next three years and was witnessed by tens of thousands. The appearances were sometimes heralded by 'doves of light' which appeared to fly about the dome and were even reported on the nights when the apparition failed to appear. Others reported flashes of light and meteoric streaks of light from the heavens. The figure would appear in a brilliant flash, which then became a transparent bluish white light, before materialising into a more human form. The apparition was never heard to speak and might disappear and reappear repeatedly throughout the course of the night. Frequently, it would be seen walking around the dome, apparently blessing the crowds. As it disappeared from one side, crowds on the other side of the church would let out a collective gasp and would start to shout that they could see her. Sometimes, it would even materialise above the trees in the surrounding streets.

If it was just an illusion, it was shared by people of all nationalities and social classes. Cynthia Nelson was an American sociologist at Cairo University. Towards the end of April, Nelson went to see for herself and later described her

The Marian Apparitions

experiences in an academic journal. While she waited for the apparition to appear, she chatted to several women in the crowd. One, the daughter of a famous Cairo surgeon, described an earlier experience,

> She was like a statue, hands folded in front, head veiled and bent. She rose up in the sky completely and was illuminated. I first saw the halo, then I saw the Virgin completely. She came down between the palm tree and the dome on this side street here.

Suddenly, a cry went up from the crowd.

> As we were talking, the crowds began pointing to the palm tree and exclaiming 'Its the Virgin – she looks like a nun, and she is swaying to and fro *as if she was blessing us*!' When I looked to where the crowds were pointing I, too, thought I saw a light through the branches of the trees, and as I tried to picture a nunlike figure in those branches, I could trace the outline of a figure. But as I thought to myself that this is just an illusion of the light reflecting through the branches, the image of the nun would leave my field of vision. Still, there was no doubt in my mind that there was a light and that if I looked for the image it would come into focus. I immediately 'explained' this perceptual experience as an illusion caused by reflected light. But the source of the light was a mystery, for all the streetlights had been disconnected all around the church for several days.

Suddenly the Coptic Church found itself with the same difficult decisions which had so often plagued their Catholic counterparts. Bishop Athanasius was sent to Zeitoun to investigate the matter on behalf of Pope Kryllos VI. The details of his report were confidential but he later gave an interview to the Reverend Jerome Palmer, an American priest who wrote up his notes as *Our Lady Returns to Egypt*.

On 6 April, 1968, the bishop arrived at the church just after three o'clock in the morning. He estimated that the crowd numbered around 100,000, many were singing Coptic hymns, some were reciting the Koran and others were praying in a multitude of languages. For the first time in recent history it was possible to sing Coptic hymns in the streets of Egypt, for the first time Christians and Moslems stood shoulder to shoulder, shouting 'Umm el Mokhaless' or 'Mother of the

Saviour'. Athanasius pushed his way to the front of the crowd. The object of their attention was a glowing figure standing some six metres above the dome of the church. It was not rigid like a statue but the body and clothes appeared to move naturally as he watched it slowly circle the dome five or six times. He was then taken to a house south of the church from where he could see the apparition from an upper window. With several other priests, he stood in silence watching the apparition.

> I stood inside for one hour, from four to five o'clock, looking at the figure. It never disappeared. Our Lady looked to the north; she waved her hands; she blessed the people, sometimes in the direction where we stood. Her garments swayed in the wind. She was very quiet, full of glory. It was something really supernatural, very, very heavenly. I saw a large strange pigeon. It came from behind us – I don't know where – proceeded to the church and returned.

Just before five o'clock, he noticed the apparition begin to grow faint. Then gradually it gave way to a glowing cloud which finally disappeared. On 4 May, 1968, the Coptic Patriarchate of Egypt and All Africa issued a statement at a news conference in which he concluded, 'With the facts collected, we have concluded that the apparitions are not false individual visions or mass hallucinations, but are real.'

One year later, during intense fighting between Palestinian guerrillas and the Lebanese Army, a similar vision was reported over a Syrian Orthodox Church in Beirut. This strengthened claims that the Marian apparitions were simply imitative hallucinations. Twelve years later, in June 1981, six children in the former Yugoslav town of Medjugorie began reporting daily apparitions of the Virgin Mary. The seers declared that it was to be the last Marian apparition and that the Virgin Mary was again warning that the twentieth century had been given over to the devil. The apparition gave each child ten secrets and warned of dreadful chastisements inside Yugoslavia and a final apocalyptic war which would engulf the world at the end of the century. Asked by reporters to comment on the similarity between the apparition's messages and the Revelations of St John the Divine, the then archbishop of

Split said that the children did not understand all of what they said and 'that the second coming has always been imminent for prophets.'

Summary of the Evidence

There are basically three hypotheses advanced to account for these enigmatic phenomena. The respectable scientific position is that children experience hallucinations and emotionally-isolated children may experience them more frequently. The apparitions may be no more than the memory of a religious icon but in other cases they seem to be modelled on a living person. Michael P. Carroll, Professor of Sociology at the University of Western Ontario, believes that when the apparition at La Salette spoke of the heavy arm of her Son, this was just Pierre-Maximin creating an hallucination of the step-mother he himself would like to have beaten. At Lourdes, Carroll argues, Bernadette's apparition was modelled on her aunt and godmother, Bernarde Nicoleu, a woman who had two illegitimate children. Did Bernadette, like many people, mistakenly equate the doctrine of the Immaculate Conception with the belief that Mary was still a Virgin when Christ was conceived and associate this with a surrogate mother who had conceived two children without a husband?

The problem with the straight-forward scientific interpretation is that it must ignore the paranormal aspects of the apparition. When faced with the embarrassing evidence that two or more children appear to see the same figure, Carroll tells us '... it seems fairly well established that the occurrence of an apparition to one child can easily provoke similar experiences in other children'. But Carroll's evidence for this extraordinary assertion is drawn from other Marian apparitions. In fact, when scientists discuss collectively-perceived apparitions they are forced to suggest the most unlikely explanations to avoid bringing in telepathy.

The second hypothesis is an attempt to retain the baby, while throwing out the bathwater. It is not an omniscient being at the centre of these wonders but Man's collective unconscious or the combined force of human will or a special type of physical reality underlying the universe and with which we interact. These apparitions are so enigmatic because it is we who create them. The rest of the wonders are just the result of human extra-sensory perception and psychokinesis.

Simple children experience a series of religious visions which end as abruptly as they begin. We see them struggling to understand something which is way beyond their ken. They report arcane symbolism, acquire the gift of clairvoyance and become part of miracles which are even affirmed by Jesuit priests. Surely, a third hypothesis is that some apparitions at least, represent the real presence of the Virgin Mary. But which ones are real and which are false? And how do we reconcile flawed prophecy, cryptic messages and secrets with supernatural omniscience? There is another more puzzling paradox. The woman seemingly created by the writings of St John the Divine still continues to preach these mystical revelations long after their literal interpretation has been rejected even by the clergy.

Do the Marian apparitions only present us with our own riddles? Or are these ideas merely the last gasp of scientific materialism? We will ask how far these theories take us and who the children see, in the last chapter of this book.

7

Miraculous Cures

Prosecution's claim is that miraculous cures all have a poorly understood medical explanation.

Many of the apparitions of the Virgin Mary have been associated with 'miraculous cures' and the public apparition of Zeitoun was no exception. While sociologist Cynthia Nelson was investigating the apparition, a well-known Cairo surgeon wrote to her outlining his experience of such a cure. His letter exemplifies the essential dilemma of a doctor confronted with a miracle.[1]

> A patient of mine upon whom I had operated two years ago for cancer returned to my office three weeks ago for a check-up. Upon examination I discovered that the man had another tumour. I actually felt the tumour during an internal examination and removed a piece of the tissue for biopsy. When the test showed it was malignant I recommended an immediate operation, but the man refused, saying he did not have enough money, and left the office. Two weeks later he returned and asked for another examination. To my astonishment I could not find the tumour, but only some white scar tissue. The man told me he had gone to Zeitoun and prayed to the Virgin for help. I do not believe in such miracles, but I cannot explain the disappearance of the tumour and *it is driving me mad*.

Why do so many doctors and scientists find it difficult to accept that miraculous cures might occur? It is just an inability to think outside the scientific worldview into which they have been educated? Is it the impossibility of accepting the links to a religious faith for which there is so little historical verification? Other sceptics, some of whom, I am sure, would like to believe in the reality of miraculous cures, take Professor Flew's approach and ask if we can really know that miracles have occurred? This was certainly the spirit in which psychiatrist, Professor D. J. West investigated eleven Lourdes miracles.[2]

There were claims of miraculous cures at Lourdes within a few weeks of the first apparition of the Virgin Mary but it was not until 1885 that Dr SaintMaclou set up a medical office to enquire into reported cures. This was reorganised into the Lourdes Medical Bureau in 1947, when Monseigneur Theas was appointed Bishop of Lourdes. Later, an International Medical Commission was created to act as a second tribunal.

When an alleged miraculous healing is reported, doctors at the Medical Bureau study the patient's medical records and try to assess his physical condition before and after the apparent cure. A doctor is then chosen to present the case in front of a full meeting of the Medical Bureau, during which alternative medical explanations for the patient's recovery are discussed. If the case still remains inexplicable, a doctor from the patient's home area is invited to follow up the case, interviewing family members and local physicians who can corroborate the severity of the patient's illness.

A year later, the patient is recalled for a second examination to verify the prolonged nature of his recovery. If the case still seems inexplicable, the Bureau's decision and the relevant files are forwarded to the International Medical Commission in Paris, who appoint their own experts to study the 'miracle'. Only a very few cases survive this selection procedure. In 1946, the Commission rejected thirty-two of the thirty-six cases forwarded by the Lourdes Medical Bureau; sixty-nine of seventy-five cases were rejected in 1947 and seventy-four of eighty-three cases in 1948. When a case is passed by the Commission it faces a further stringent examination at the hands of a Canonical Commission appointed by the patient's archbishop. Only if the cure meets the Catholic Church's own criteria is it declared a miracle. Can all of these experts be wrong?

Professor West believes that even those few cases accepted by the Church are flawed by a lack of scientific evidence. Madame Martin was forty-four years of age when doctors diagnosed adenocarcinoma of the uterus. A radical hysterectomy was performed and the diagnosis was confirmed by a

Miraculous Cures

pathologist who examined sections of the tumour under a microscope. The woman's recovery was complicated by a re-opening of the abdominal incision and hernia formation. Six months later, on 25 April 1947, she returned to her doctor complaining of pain and a fetid discharge from the vagina. The doctor was able to palpate a swelling in her rectum and concluded that the cancer had spread to her bowel. Madame Martin spent the next two months confined to her bed and so heavily sedated with morphine that she developed an addiction. The tumour appeared to be blocking the bowel as the unfortunate woman could only defaecate with the help of an enema. Finally, on 30 June, she was taken to Lourdes in an 'alarming and wasted condition'. Unable to walk, she was lowered into a pool fed by the waters of the famous Lourdes spring. Initially, she continued to decline but, after her third immersion in the waters, she surprised the nuns and attendants by leaving the pool on her own and walking to the toilet. From that day, the vaginal discharge ceased and she returned home feeling perfectly well. Nine months later, a physical examination and X-rays could find no trace of the tumour. Madame Martin's cure was subsequently declared a miracle.

But was this case really inexplicable? Professor West remarks that it is well known that morphine produces constipation, which raises the possibility that the 'second tumour' was no more than impacted faeces. Alternatively, it might have been an abscess or a fibrous mass, conditions which commonly complicate an abdominal operation. What is lacking, he argues, is definitive proof that there really was a second tumour,

> The patient's general condition being very bad does favour the diagnosis of secondary cancer . . . which is hard and nodular, should have been recognisable to the experienced surgeon who examined her. Unfortunately, he gives no description and what is more he places the tumour at the recto-sigmoid junction, a situation normally out of reach to the examining finger.

Overall, West notes that there have been no 'self-evident miracles' such as the regrowth of severed limbs or sight restored to the totally blind. More than 50 per cent of the miracles documented by doctors at Lourdes up to 1910, involved the remission of pulmonary tuberculosis, a lethal disease but one known to be affected by changes in the patient's immune, nervous and hormonal systems. Many of these cases were determined purely on the basis of clinical presentation and unsupported by chest X-rays, or microscopic or microbiological examinations. All of the eleven miracles which West scrutinised appeared to fall through this gap between medicine, the art, and medicine, the science.

It is beyond argument that doctors are the best people to rule on cases of miraculous cures but the uncertainty inherent in medical diagnosis may always prevent us from obtaining that final proof. A famous medical rhyme begins and ends 'The dermatologist sees everything and knows nothing. . . . The pathologist knows everything but a day too late.' In a recent survey, the medical records of 1,000 cases reaching postmortem were compared to the subsequent pathologist's report.[3] It was discovered that in 390 cases, the medical diagnosis was not confirmed at post-mortem while more than 600 cases showed discrepancies in the clinical diagnosis. Even in those cases where the doctor had been confident of his diagnosis, one in four post-mortems revealed disagreements between the diagnosis and the pathology report.

The other factor complicating the investigation of supposedly miraculous cures is the phenomenal power of the mind over the body. Stephen Black was probably the most famous psychiatrist to offer solid evidence for the healing powers of the mind.[4] Seventeen years after the Second World War, Black was asked to treat a former service-woman who had served with a top secret unit of the Royal Air Force under American command. The lady suffered from chronic asthma, diabetes mellitus and severe nightmares. She could remember nothing of her war service but, under hypnosis, she recounted an unusual story. Only a few Women's Auxiliary Air Force support staff survived the war and all of the aircrew involved with the secret unit had been killed. This was a double blow to the woman as she said that the RAF cell had objected to their mission on 'moral grounds'. The patient broke down and was treated by a United States Air Force doctor under the watchful gaze of security officers. In fact she was not treated at all but under hypnosis had been told to 'forget the

Miraculous Cures

whole thing'. Within six weeks of the forced repression of these painful memories, the woman developed severe incapacitating asthma. After Black had been able to confirm most of the details of this story from her service record, he was able to remove the hypnotic suggestion block placed in her mind and bring the patient to terms with her painful memories. The asthma attacks ceased.

Black believed that it was the mind's power over the body which underpinned many of the miraculous cures he had seen worked by witch-doctors in Africa. In a famous series of experiments, Black screened 300 volunteers to select deep and medium trance subjects who also showed common allergies. The psychiatrist demonstrated that his volunteers were indeed hypnotised by their degree of dissociation, their willingness to obey his commands and their inability under suggestion to feel pain when pricked by a needle. All of his seven deep trance subjects and eleven medium trance subjects also showed the angry, red 'wheal and flare' when a small amount of material to which they were allergic was introduced into the skin of their arms. This skin test, diagnostic for one type of allergy, produced a small blister surrounded by an area of red skin, which appeared immediately and increased in intensity over the next twenty minutes.

The volunteers were then divided into two groups. One group was placed in an hypnotic trance before being 'challenged' with the allergen and all showed the characteristic skin lesion. When the second group were in trance, Black told them that they would not show a response to an injection of the allergenic substance. This group was duly injected but no skin response appeared. Biopsies taken from the injection site showed that the chemicals responsible for producing the lesion had been blocked. Black, using only hypnotic suggestion, had been able to obstruct one of the major biochemical pathways responsible for the symptoms of hay-fever and childhood asthma. His work, published in a top medical journal, *The Lancet*, provided evidence that a patient's mind might exert a powerful influence over their disease, for good or for ill.

Having said this, surely, there must be one miracle which

The Sceptical Occultist

can stand as a test-case? A cure so thoroughly investigated by surgeons and pathologists as to leave no doubt to the diagnosis. A recovery from a disease so dreadful with a prognosis so certain as to exclude any possibility of psychosomatic influences. There is such a case. It might be described as the greatest miraculous cure of the twentieth century. A cure so profound, that the Catholic Church not only declared it to be a miracle but accepted it as sufficient evidence to canonise a little-known Scottish martyr. For some parapsychologists it not only represents proof of the reality of miraculous cures but modern-day evidence that refutes the arguments of David Hume. Here then is a miracle 'attested by a sufficient number of men, of unquestioned good sense, education and learning'.[5]

John Connolly Fagan was born on 16 May, 1914 to a Catholic working-class family in the city of Glasgow. As a child he witnessed the human misery which accompanied the First World War and the economic decline of the late 1920s and thirties. He had seen the little miracle of the city's slum clearances when, at the age of twelve, his family was moved from their tenement in Anderston to a council house in Hamiltonhill, where John marvelled at his first glimpse of an inside toilet and bathroom. In his twenties, John left the city for the first time to fight in the Second World War. Five years later he returned to raise a family and, like so many of the city's young men, turned to the hard but regular employment to be found manhandling cargo at the many docks along the River Clyde.

At fifty-one years of age, he was still a very fit man, often rising before dawn for the long journey across the city to a distant dock, only to return home late in the evening. During the winter months of 1965, he began to experience increasing tiredness and would complain of stomach pains but he dismissed his symptoms as indigestion due to encroaching age. Then in the early morning of 22 April, 1965, he woke in the small hours vomiting blood. The long nightmare had begun.

At the Glasgow Royal Infirmary, John was admitted to a surgical ward while the doctors carried out tests to determine whether the vomited blood was the result of a stomach ulcer or something worse. When John was well enough he was asked to drink a grey mixture with the taste and consistency of wet concrete. The radio-opaque fluid highlighted the stomach for a series of X-rays which revealed the unmistakable white shadow of a large tumour infiltrating the stomach wall. Nine days later, on 14 May, John was re-admitted for surgery.

It was a long operation. The tumour had destroyed much of the architecture of the stomach and perforated the stomach lining, before spreading along the digestive tract to the transverse colon. As the surgeons worked to excise the affected areas of the stomach and bowel, a histopathologist worked alongside. A small piece of tumour was frozen, cut into ultra-thin sections and stained before being examined under the microscope. The pathologist agreed with the surgeon, it was cancer: an aggressive adenocarcinoma of the stomach. More biopsies were taken at regular intervals to be studied at leisure. When the surgeons had finished, they repaired the colon, bringing the end out as a temporary opening or colostomy to empty into a bag on John's side.

The prognosis was grim and the pathology report only added to the gloom – there were cancer cells all the way up to the line of resection, strongly suggesting that some of the primary tumour still remained. Worse, the cancer had spread to the local lymph nodes, suggesting that there had been ample time for malignant cells to enter the blood stream and be carried to distant organs where they would grow into secondary tumour deposits. It was left to the surgeon to give Mary Fagan the bad news that her husband had only six to twelve months to live.

Towards the end of June, John's bowel had healed sufficiently for the colostomy to be closed. The family's doctor, Archibald MacDonald, allowed him to return to work in August, where he was given light duties as a 'checker'. To make up the family income, John's wife was forced to take a job in a local factory but, that aside, the family routine returned to normal. The next fourteen months were uneventful. As John was not told he had cancer, he was blissfully unaware that he had outlived his tentative death sentence, but the surgeon's time-frame had only been a guess based on his experience of similar cases.

In late 1966, Fagan became ill again. Following a bout of pleurisy in November, the stomach pain returned and he started vomiting again. During a physical examination, John's family doctor remarked in his notes that he could palpate a mass in the upper abdomen. On December 21, 1966, Fagan was re-admitted to the Infirmary for further X-rays which appeared to show that the tumour had re-established itself in what was left of John's stomach. Deciding that it would be pointless to attempt to intervene further, the surgeon prescribed painkilling medication.

Two months later, bed-ridden and in constant pain, John guessed that he was dying and begged his Mary to allow him to die at home. In fact, Fagan's condition was so weak that, when his brother Jim arrived from Ireland, he was surprised to find him alive. In a Catholic family, when the doctors can do no more, it is left to the parish priest to ask for divine intervention while preparing the patient for the good death. So it was that Father John Fitzgibbon, the assistant parish priest at the Church of Blessed John Ogilvie, came to see John at the beginning of March. John was mentioned every morning at mass and prayers were offered for his recovery but, as the days progressed and Fagan became weaker, the priest was summoned to administer the last rites. As a parting gesture, Father Fitzgibbon pinned a devotional medal of Blessed John Ogilvie to the patient's bedclothes and a small group of parishioners began praying to the martyr on John Fagan's behalf.

John Ogilvie was a Scottish Calvinist who converted to Catholicism while completing his studies in Europe as a young man. In Scotland anti-Catholic sentiment had grown since Henry VIII had abolished the authority of the Church. Under Queen Elizabeth I the old religion was banned and after the Gunpowder plot of 1605, James I introduced new laws which fined practising Catholics and barred them from public office and the professions. If taken, Catholic priests were offered the choice between an oath of allegiance to the English monarch or death for treason. In this climate of fear,

Miraculous Cures

Catholics were forced to hear mass in secret, while their priests were thrown into the life-style of secret agents, sheltered by Catholic families and moving between safe-houses. As a young priest, Ogilvie returned to his homeland in 1613 and immediately established a network of houses in Glasgow where mass could be said in secret. He lasted a year, until betrayed by an informer. He was arrested and tried for treason in 1614. The outcome was never in doubt and, when Ogilvie consistently refused to admit that James I had religious authority over the Pope, he was executed in Glasgow. The young priest's heroism was rewarded by his beatification in 1886 – his canonisation as a saint required evidence of miracles worked in his name as an outward sign of his holiness. In 1965, John Ogilvie was still on the first rung to sainthood but there were some in the parish who thought that a case such as John Fagan's might provide that necessary outward sign of grace.

At the beginning of March 1967, all those concerned who called at the Fagan household were forced to admit that John was in his last days. It had been seven weeks since he had taken his last solid meal and now he was even refusing liquids. On Saturday 4 March, Archibald MacDonald arrived on his regular house-call to the Fagans'. On entering the sick-room, he was appalled to see what he believed to be parts of John's stomach wall together with congealed blood ('solid black tar') in the sick-bucket beside the patient's bed, which filled the room with a terrible smell of putrefaction. The doctor gently broke the news to Mary that her husband's death was very close and promised to return early on the Monday morning to sign the death certificate. Heavily medicated, John slipped into a long sleep with his wife watching by his bed, occasionally wetting her husband's parched lips with moist cottonwool.

On Sunday morning, members of the Legion of Mary arrived to pray around his bed, beseeching John Ogilvie to intercede on the dying man's behalf. Otherwise the day was uneventful; John remained asleep and his Mary kept the death-watch, occasionally slumbering on a chair by his bedside. In the first few minutes of Monday, John experienced a crisis apparition and awoke to tell his wife that he had seen his dead aunt Annie in a dream. 'Are you coming John?' she had asked. In the pale light of the new day, Mary awoke to find the room still. The little fire had gone out and her husband's breathing had apparently ceased. She listened to his chest for the sound of a heartbeat but could hear nothing. She noted the time on the clock above the mantelpiece, it was just after six. Later, she could not recall how long she had sat on the chair weeping, but in her grief she seemed to hear a tiny voice in her head, and suddenly realised that it was John. 'Mary, I am hungry,' he said sitting up in bed. While John sat eating a boiled egg, Mary phoned Dr MacDonald to impart the news that the doctor could hardly bring himself to believe.

The recovery of John Fagan became the most thoroughly investigated miracle of the twentieth century. In October 1967, several priests under the direction of parish priest, Father Thomas Reilly, took statements from Archibald MacDonald and the Fagan family. After reading these statements, the Archbishop of Glasgow, Monsignor James Scanlen, gave his permission for a panel of doctors to be appointed to examine the cure. This consisted of Dr Andrew Curran, Lecturer in Medicine at Glasgow University, Dr Aloysius Dunne, a consultant in geriatrics, and Dr John Fitzsimmons, another Glasgow general practitioner. The panel met for two years, examining Fagan's medical record, taking statements from his doctors and eliciting opinions from experts in the fields of gastroenterology and cancer, before concluding that no medical explanation could be found for John's cure. There was, however, one dissenter, Dr Crean, a consultant in gastroenterology at the Southern General Hospital, believed that Fagan's condition could have resulted from an intraperitoneal abscess – a hypothesis we shall return to later.

Miracles are treated with caution by the modern Catholic Church and it was not until 1971 that Dr Livio Capocaccia, Professor of Gastroenterology at the University of Rome, arrived in Scotland at the request of the Vatican. The professor insisted on starting again at the beginning to examine whether Fagan's recovery might have been due to other straightforward medical conditions.

Surely it was possible, Capocaccia argued, that the operation had removed most of the primary tumour and any secondaries were cured by the patient's immune system. But this explanation failed to account for John's subsequent decline and sudden recovery.

Was the primary tumour a Carcinoid or low-grade malignancy of the argentaffin cells of the intestine which had spread to the stomach? The chemicals produced by these tumours can result in intestinal and other disturbances ('Carcinoid Syndrome'). The sections taken from John's tumour said otherwise, exhibiting the characteristics of a high-grade malignant adenocarcinoma. In addition, it was difficult to explain why the disturbances continued when the tumour had been excised and Carcinoids of the gut are not believed to secrete the chemical messengers responsible for Carcinoid Syndrome. Neither was there any evidence that John had ever shown the 'carcinoid flush' or paroxysmal flushing of the skin of the face, neck and upper body associated with the syndrome.

Perhaps, Capocaccia and the panel reasoned, the primary tumour had been removed, secondaries eliminated by the immune system and John's subsequent condition had resulted from post-operative adhesions. But again it was difficult to explain why such chronic inflammatory structures had only made themselves felt some twenty months after the operation and then disappeared so abruptly.

The panel also considered whether the 'cure' arose as the result of a spontaneous remission – where the tumour dies or is killed by the patient's immune system – but spontaneous remissions almost never occur at the eleventh hour or operate on such an advanced tumour.

So it was that the other medical explanations were rejected by the panel, who came to entitle their report, 'The medically inexplicable cure of a gastric carcinoma, partly differentiated and invasive of the lymphatic glands and colon'. In May 1971, John Fagan was asked to submit to another prolonged investigation at the Western General Hospital in Edinburgh. The results of these tests corroborated the panel's main conclusion that John's subsequent relapse was 'entirely consistent with the natural history of a patient with recurrent gastric carcinoma', adding that there was 'no satisfactory explanation'

The Sceptical Occultist

for his recovery. Professor Capocaccia reported to the Vatican that the healing was miraculous.

With Monsignor James Scanlen in poor health, the next stage of the process fell to his delegate Bishop, Thomas Winning, who was appointed *Judex Natus* (judge) of the Diocesan Tribunal appointed by the Sacred Congregation for the Causes of the Saints in Rome. Under his direction, a list of questions compiled by experts in the Vatican were put to witnesses under oath (the *Interrogatories*). Throughout, the Tribunal record or 'Proceedings' were compiled in English and Italian to avoid errors in translation. Finally, the 'Judgement' of the Tribunal was placed under seal and taken to Rome by John's parish priest Father Reilly.

At the Sacred Congregation for the Causes of the Saints, these documents were incorporated into a 350-page *Summarium* and bound in a leather tooled cover together with a complete medical history, showing medical reports, pathology tests and charts. At the same time, a separate document (the *Fattispecie Cronologica*), containing a chronological summary of the material in the *Summarium*, was prepared and bound. The work was finished in September 1974 and the two documents were then submitted to two independent medical experts who were given eight weeks to render their judgement. The decision of these two experts is absolute and can only be challenged on the grounds that one or both of the *Periti* is guilty of a serious error of judgement. Appeals are almost always rejected.

Concurring with the Glasgow panel, both experts concluded that John Fagan's cure was without a satisfactory medical explanation and the process entered its final stage. The written judgements were submitted to the Vatican's Consulta Medica (Medical Board) where they were rewritten in simple concise language (as the *Informazio*) for the theological experts in the Sacred Congregation for the Causes of the Saints.

The theologians agreed with the doctors and their judgement was submitted to the Promotor-General of the Faith or the 'Devil's Advocate'. The Glasgow miracle fell to Gaetano Stano, a short, round-faced Dominican friar, well known for his asceticism. In time honoured fashion, Stano prepared his objections which drew on both medicine and theology to argue against Fagan's cure being miraculous. This time the job of framing a rebuttal to Stano's 31-page *Animadversiones* was given to the well-known Jesuit scholar, Father Molinari. The resulting 563-page *Responsio*, containing arguments to counter Stano's objections, and copies of all of the documents generated by the investigation were secretly printed and bound and resubmitted to the Congregation. Ten further judgements (the *Revista*) were then elicited from five officials and five Consultors from the theological section.

All ruled in favour of the miracle and their printed affirmation, or *Positio*, was sent to the Cardinals of the Congregation who met in closed congress in October 1975. Again the response was favourable and the *Positio* was finally passed to Pope Paul VI who was at liberty to refer it to his own experts. On 12 February, 1977, after a period of prayer and consultation, the pontiff issued a decree confirming the intervention of a saint. Five days later, the martyred priest John Ogilvie became a member of the calendar of saints of the Roman Catholic Church.

It would be a rash man who was prepared to contradict so many experts and yet, the claim that a cure is miraculous – that it has resulted from supernatural intervention – is in itself a compelling argument for leaving no stone unturned in the search for a medical explanation. Dr Gerard Crean, the Consultant in Gastroenterology at the Southern General Hospital, believed that he had provided an alternative explanation of what had happened to John Fagan. While Catholic Glasgow rejoiced at the canonisation of their martyr, Gerard Crean played with the idea of publishing his expert opinion in the form of a rebuttal. He decided against the idea and his files remained locked in his desk drawer.

Crean's case was that the surgeons had removed most of John's primary tumour but, as a result of the operation, an infective abscess formed in the body cavity which surrounds the internal organs. Such an intraperitoneal abscess is a recognised complication of gastrectomy and may lie dormant for many months. As John's immune system attempted to fight the infection, dead bacteria and white cells decomposed to form the yellow pus that was growing inside his body. This, in turn, resulted in shock and toxaemia which were the cause of the patient's moribund condition. Finally, the abscess discharged itself through the stomach wall which accounted for the fetid vomit, congealed blood and yellow mucus which Fagan regurgitated seven weeks after his last solid meal. John's medical records make no mention of the fever and chills which would surely accompany this condition, but at no time after his operation was John under constant medical supervision. His wife, Mary, may well have dismissed such symptoms as being part of the process of dying from cancer, just as surely as a general practitioner making morning housecalls can miss a fever which peaks in the afternoon or evening.

The Glasgow panel, and later Professor Livio Capocaccia, all rejected Crean's hypothesis, arguing that an abscess alone could not explain John's greatly weakened state. They felt that an abscess should have progressed down through the patient's body and not discharged itself through the stomach wall. But their main concern was the simple question, *'What happened to the cancer?'* It is a bleak fact that by the time tumours present, they are usually so large as to be beyond the control of the body's immune system. It may well be the case that once the report reached Rome, it was this question which mesmerised the experts.

One answer to this puzzle is that it was the abscess itself which resulted in the destruction of the remaining tumour. As the infection grew inside John's body, his immune cells, engaged in the fruitless task of attempting to control the bacteria, became excited and 'angry' and began to turn their attentions to the cancer cells. At first they just controlled the residual tumour resulting in John outliving his surgeon's 'death sentence'. But as the abscess grew, the destruction of the tumour accelerated, adding to the toxaemia and shock. Finally, in a cataclysmic event, the abscess discharged itself through the stomach, by which time most of the tumour had been destroyed. *Put simply, when John Fagan appeared to be on his death-bed he was in fact closer to a natural cure than at any time during his entire illness.* What evidence do we have for this

Miraculous Cures

extraordinary assertion? The answer may lie in a series of scientific 'miracles'.

It is said that the heroes of science are soon forgotten but their work lives on and this is surely true of William B. Coley. Bill Coley was the Professor of Clinical Surgery, Cornell University Medical School, in the early years of this century. He was also a scientist who noticed and explored the anomalies which he saw in his medical practice but could not explain. Finally, he was a man whose great humanity and compassion shines through his clinical case notes.

In Coley's day, surgery was the only effective treatment for cancer. If the tumour was inoperable, the doctor was forced to watch his patient die. It was in the midst of death that Bill Coley noticed that some of his patients experienced apparently miraculous cures. When he compared their case notes he found that all of these patients had suffered from an acute intercurrent streptococcal infection, with fever, chills and malaise. Consequently, Bill Coley decided to try and improve on nature by injecting his cancer patients with bacterial toxins.[6] Some tumours were unaffected and the patients died; in other patients, however, the cancer shrank and, in a small number, disappeared altogether. But as news of Bill Coley's work spread, he found himself presented with the greatest test of his career. Throughout the east coast of America, Coley became the final hope of patients with terminal disease.

A seventeen-year-old boy arrived in Coley's office with a massive tumour disfiguring his face. 'Inasmuch as the only operation that could be performed with any hope of success would have been removal of almost the entire lower jaw ... it seemed wise to do a partial operation, to be immediately followed by toxins.' On 11 January, 1910, Coley removed as much of the tumour as he dared and submitted samples to Jas Ewing, the Professor of Pathology at Cornell Medical School. The professor's report amounted to a chilling death sentence, 'Giant-celled osteosarcoma. It is not the ordinary encapsulated giant-celled sarcoma of the jaw ... but a tumour infiltrating in all directions, of rapid growth and with a large amount of new bone formation.' Nevertheless, Coley pressed ahead and administered daily injections of toxins over a 28-

day period. The result was stunning, 'After the first three or four injections there was noticed a marked diminution in the size of the growth that had been left behind ... Since then, the remainder of the tumour had nearly disappeared. The tumour tissue which was left behind [from the operation] externally also gradually became absorbed, and there was absolutely no deformity remaining.'

As a surgeon, Bill Coley had seen many inoperable cancers but even he was occasionally appalled at some of the cases that were referred to him. J. N., a two-month-old infant had an inoperable osteosarcoma of the scapula which had appeared two weeks after birth. When in June, 1910, Coley saw the purplish-white mass which involved the entire left shoulder blade, he was so shocked and so sure of the hopeless prognosis, that he forgot to complete his tests. The infant was treated for six weeks in hospital and then further regular injections were continued for another five months by the family doctor. 'The improvement evident at the end of the first two weeks of treatment steadily continued ... and in December it had practically entirely disappeared. The child is in perfect health at present and I think no trace of the original growth can be detected.'

C. W. was a 56-year-old man with cancer in the right tonsil which, in the course of just two months, had spread to the lymph nodes in the neck to produce a second growth, the size of an 'English Walnut'. A portion of the tonsil was removed for tests and proved to be a malignant round-cell sarcoma. During the six-week course of injections, the patient became so ill that Coley thought he would lose him, but the treatment had the desired effect. 'The tumour in the neck first became softer and then more movable; at the end of a week it began to decrease in size with final disappearance under four weeks of further treatment. The tumour of the tonsil diminished more slowly but at the end of two to three months, this, too, entirely disappeared.' Eleven months later, Dr Skeels of St Albans, Vermont, the patient's physician, wrote to Coley, 'He is at present perfectly well; there is absolutely no sign of the growth in his tonsil; his recovery here is considered as almost miraculous.'

When reports of this revolutionary therapy appeared in the medical journals, other doctors started using 'Coley's toxins'. At a meeting of the American Cancer Research Society in Buffalo, New York, on 12 April, 1911, William Coley presented eighteen of his own cases and a further thirty-one reports which had come to him from other doctors using his technique. It heralded the beginning of cancer immunotherapy. From 1892–1945, doctors documented more than 600 successful clinical interventions with bacterial extracts and a further sixty-five case histories where tumours had regressed after an incidental intercurrent infection.

Summary of the Evidence

The prosecution's case and the 'lesser miracle' is that John Fagan's tumour was eliminated as the result of an intercurrent infection in the form of a post-operative abscess. We simply invoke 'miraculous cures' when we lack all the pieces of the medical 'jigsaw puzzle'. More importantly, the prosecution would argue that even if there were such things as miraculous cures, we could never arrive at a final incontestable proof.

The reader may want to accept the miracle but not the supernatural connotations. This implies that miracles, in a way in which we do not yet understand, are the product of individual or collective 'psychic' abilities.

However, the reader may be impressed by the fact that many miracles do seem to occur in association with other 'supernatural' events such as Marian apparitions or religious devotions to saints. Is there sufficient evidence to support the assertion that supernatural entities can and do intervene in the affairs of Man? Do prayer and devotion, quite literally, move mountains?

8

Returning from the Abyss? Reincarnation

Prosecution's claim is that reincarnation-type cases are impressive and complex phenomena but they are not reincarnation. Fraud, cryptomnesia, coincidence and childish fantasy may all intermingle with permissive cultural and religious beliefs.

The idea of reincarnation seems strange to many in the west, but even in America and Britain there are those rare children who remember past lives. Christianity, Islam and Judaism all peddle their, not altogether, consistent beliefs about what happens to us after death but to the vast majority of the world's population, we are already staring a form of immortality in the face. Upon hearing the evidence for reincarnation drawn from other cultures, many ask why do we not see more evidence of reincarnation in the west. In fact, it is surprising that we see any at all! Our populations are highly mobile and a man, dying say, in Bradford and being reborn in London, Exeter or even New York will find little to support his memories. Parents, doctors, priests, teachers and most other cultural leaders will tend to dismiss the child's stories as fantasies. The evidence shows that many parents become frightened and hostile when their child talks of 'other parents' and 'other families'. When the child's memories are consistently dismissed as fantasies, the child too will eventually dismiss them.

It may be a strange quirk of population biology that, after major conflicts, proportionately more boys than girls are born in the countries affected by the fighting. This was reported after the American Civil War; in Germany after the Austro-Prussian War (1866) and the Franco-Prussian War (1870–

Returning from the Abyss? Reincarnation

71); in England after the First World War and in a number of Allied countries following the Second World War. In Burma just after the Second World War, a surprisingly large number of children were born who claimed to remember fighting and dying as British, American or Japanese servicemen.

Ma Tin Aung Myo was one such child.[1] She was born in Na-Thul village in Upper Burma, on December 26, 1953 to U Aye Maung, a railway porter, and his wife Daw Aye Tin. Ma Tin Aung Myo was the youngest of four sisters, who were joined some years later by a younger brother. The first strange aspect of this case occurred while Daw Aye Tin was two months pregnant with her fourth daughter. She later told psychiatrist, Professor Ian Stevenson, and his co-investigators that she had dreamt of a stocky Japanese soldier. He wore short pants but no shirt and in her dreams he followed her, declaring that he would come and stay with them. She was afraid of the soldier and told him not to follow her. The dream occurred three times at intervals of about one week.

This was an 'announcing dream' in which the deceased appears to the dreamer, usually the pregnant mother, and announces his intention to be reborn into their family. Announcing dreams, heralding the birth of a child who claims to remember a previous existence, have been reported in a number of cultures but are particularly associated with cases from Burma and Thailand and from amongst the Tlingit Indians of Alaska.

Ma Tin Aung Myo began to speak sometime between two and three years of age but, unlike children in other alleged cases of reincarnation, she did not spontaneously begin to relate details of another life. Ma Tin Aung Myo's reminiscences were suddenly catalysed by an incident, at the age of four, when out walking with her father. Suddenly an aircraft flew overhead and the little girl became very frightened and began to cry. 'I want to go home. I want to go home,' she told her father. What was it that so alarmed her about the aircraft? he enquired. 'It will shoot me,' she replied. He patiently explained that this had happened during the war but would not happen now. This incident was the beginning of a phobia of aircraft which continued into adult life. It also appeared to catalyse memories of a past life.

A little later, Ma Tin Aung Myo was found weeping in the family house. 'What is wrong?' she was asked. The child replied 'I am pining for Japan.' Then gradually she began to tell how she remembered being a Japanese soldier. She had been born in the northern part of Japan and had been married with five children, the eldest being a boy. She remembered running a small shop before joining the army as a cook. At the time of his death, the Japanese soldier she claimed to have been was about to cook a meal near a pile of firewood under an acacia tree, some two hundred feet from the house in Na-Thul where Ma Tin Aung Myo's family lived. He had taken off his shirt and was wearing shorts and a big belt, which he believed was necessary to protect the stomach against the cold. Suddenly, an Allied aircraft appeared overhead and began strafing the village. As the soldier ran around the woodpile to seek cover, the aircraft dived at him, spraying the area with machine-gun or cannon fire. A bullet hit him in the groin and he died instantly. She was not sure whether the aircraft was British or American but remembered that it had 'two tails'.

This important point in Ma Tin Aung Myo's alleged memories can be submitted to historical analysis. During Stevenson's visit to the area in 1974, the people told him that their village was the object of frequent, sometimes twice daily, Allied air-strikes. The significance of the area, Stevenson was told, was the vitally important railway station at Puang, close to Na-Thul. Consequently, while doing research for this chapter, I found myself trying to identify an allied aircraft with 'two tails' which would have taken part in daily air-strikes against the railway in Upper Burma between 1942 and early 1945. As a writer I had some knowledge of the ground war in Burma but knew little of the design and role of Second World War aircraft, so I sought advice from the aviation specialists in the Exhibits' Section of the Imperial War Museum in London.

The railways were an important means of communication for the Japanese 15th Army in Burma. Then, as now, two major railway lines leave Rangoon and run north. One terminates at Prome, close to the foothills of the Arakan mountains in the east of the country. The other runs through the central plains to Mandalay, where it divides into two branches which service the upper Shan highlands and the Kachin Hills on the borders of China and India.

I was told that the Americans launched regular air-strikes against the railways in an attempt to dislocate the Japanese lines of communication. Two aircraft regularly took part in these strikes and both were American. Mitchell bombers were used to bomb the railway junctions and would sometimes fly at tree-top level strafing targets on the ground. A photograph of the Mitchell showed a medium bomber with two large tail-fins but the child's story suggested a more manoeuvrable aircraft, one which could dive on to a target; something like the Tempest and Mosquito fighter-bombers. The other aircraft which regularly took part in these raids was the American P38 Lightning, drawn from the 25th, 449th, 459th, 58th, 59th and 60th squadrons. I enquired rather lamely whether it had 'two tails'? My informant paused for a moment trying to assimilate my question and its lack of technical expertise. 'It did have twin booms,' he replied. A photograph of the Lightning showed that the engines on the wings of the aircraft were connected to the tail by two long cylinders or booms. The P38 Lightning could be described as having two tails. Indeed, the Germans called it *Der Gabelschwanz Teufel* or 'fork-tailed devil'. It was also a very highly manoeuvrable ground-attack aircraft.

This, of course, does not exclude the possibility that Ma Tin Aung Myo had heard descriptions of the P38 Lightning from her father or other villagers who had seen these air-attacks and had then woven their memories into her own. Nevertheless, the child's alleged memories seem to describe an aircraft which was regularly used on air-strikes against the railway in Upper Burma. It had the manoeuvrability to dive on a single Japanese soldier and, almost uniquely amongst World War Two combat aircraft, it had a twin-boom design giving the appearance of two tails. The impact of a single shell from its 20mm cannon anywhere on the human body would have caused devastating injuries.

Ma Tin Aung Myo's memories continued to taunt and dislocate her life. Her phobia of aircraft continued and on one occasion when one flew over the village, she cowered, crying, in the family house. When ridiculed by other members of the family, she retorted acidly, 'What do you know? I was shot and killed.'

She did not enjoy the hot humid climate of Burma or its spicy foods. Her mother prepared separate meals for her daughter using blander foods such as eggs. Any skills that the girl might have had as the result of her previous life as a cook were met by a family prohibition on her cooking for them on the grounds that she omitted the spices and chillies. In his paper, Stevenson notes, 'She had, and stated, an equally low opinion of the competence at cooking of others in the family.'

Ma Tin Aung Myo continued to express a longing for her life in Japan and the children she had left behind. She said she would go there when she was grown up. Sometimes she lay for hours on her stomach crying from home-sickness. As a young child she had talked to herself and the other children using a language that nobody in the family understood but there was no attempt to determine whether it was Japanese or just childish gibberish.

The major problem in Ma Tin Aung Myo's life was her insistence on living, thinking and dressing like a man. During Stevenson's 1974 visit, she boasted to the psychiatrist that she did not own a single item of Burmese women's clothing. Like Burmese men, she wore her hair short and adopted a man's shirt and longyi (an ankle-length skirt, tied at the waist) of check patterns which she wrapped with a knot in the front. Burmese women wear longyis with either a floral design or solid colours and secure them at the waist by tucking the upper edge of the longyi into itself at the left side with a knot. She told Ian Stevenson that she would have preferred Japanese dress.

As a child, unlike her sisters or younger brother, Ma Tin Aung Myo liked to play at being a soldier with toy guns. She also stated that she wanted to be a soldier. Every time her father went to Mandalay, she asked him to buy her a toy gun. She also played at the male sports of football and cane ball with the other boys. Daw Aye Tin spent most of her daughter's childhood insisting that she wear female dress, but her husband was more indulgent and allowed Ma Tin Aung Myo to crop her hair and wear boy's clothes. When eleven or twelve years of age, the school authorities began to insist that Ma Tin Aung Myo come to school dressed as a girl. She refused and was forced to leave the school. After puberty, she began to enjoy the company of the village girls, who addressed her using the male honorific 'Ko' because of her masculine characteristics.

Ma Tin Aung Myo eventually lost her desire to go to Japan. In 1975, at the time of Stevenson's last contact with the girl, she had also lost her phobia of aircraft and had become adapted to the spicy Burmese food. Her memories of her 'previous life' also faded, although at that time she could still remember many of the essential details. One aspect of her personality did not change. She told Stevenson and his co-investigator, U Win Maung, that they could kill her by any method they chose providing that they could guarantee that she would be reborn as a boy.

When U Win Maung visited the village in 1977, Ma Tin Aung Myo was 'going steady' with several girl friends. At the time of his visit, she was on a 'courting trip' to another village. She had told her mother not to worry about her fate after she died and Daw Aye Tin had accepted her daughter's decision to remain single.

It is frequently argued that 'reincarnation-type' cases are simply created and moulded by the cultures in which they occur and that the children are encouraged to invent evidence of a previous life, to fit in with prevailing religious beliefs and to provide status for an otherwise poor, low-ranking family. But this simple interpretation often falls far short of an explanation for many of the children who appear to remember past lives. In his paper detailing the case of Ma Tin Aung Myo for fellow psychiatrists, Stevenson had this to say:

> Some critics of these cases believe that cultural influences suffice to account for all of their aspects. I do not agree and have described in reports of cases published elsewhere evidence that at least some of the subjects of these cases possessed a mass of information about deceased persons they were talking about, which in my opinion, they had not acquired by normal means of communication. The present case does not belong to

this group, but it presents another question not easily resolved by attribution to cultural pressures. If Ma Tin Aung Myo wished, for needs of her own that we cannot perceive, to identify herself with a deceased person, why did she select a Japanese soldier? The Burmese, for the most part, did not come to hate the Japanese as did many Americans during the Second World War; but the Japanese were nevertheless unpopular or detested in Burma, and the personation by a Burmese girl of a Japanese soldier certainly gained her no credit in her family or village. The simplest explanation sometimes *is* the best one ...

Ian Stevenson is the Carlson Professor of Psychiatry, within the Division of Personality Studies, Department of Behavioural Medicine and Psychiatry, University of Virginia. In the late 1950s he began investigating cases in which children seemingly remembered past lives. His work in India, Brazil, Ceylon and Alaska later resulted in his best known work, *Twenty Cases Suggestive of Reincarnation*. While his papers have convinced some of his colleagues that there is a strong case for reincarnation, others remain unconvinced. The scientific, philosophical and religious traditions in the west simply do not permit the possibility of reincarnation. It is a hard fact that some children do have these memories but is the simplest explanation really the best one?

Cases such as that of Ma Tin Aung Myo are termed 'unsolved' as the child's alleged memories provide insufficient information to identify the person whom the child claims to have been in a previous life. Stevenson's department has more than 2,500 cases on record and when researchers compared the details of 850 'solved' and 'unsolved' cases, drawn from six cultures, they came up with some interesting results.[2]

In both types of cases the children began to recount their memories at about three years of age. The memories were most lucid and detailed at between three and five years of age, after which the child no longer felt compelled to talk about them and, in many cases, the memories began to fade. Again, in both types of cases, many children seemed to remember violent, certainly premature, deaths and the mode of death was sometimes reflected in current phobias.[3] For example, Ma Tin Aung Myo had a fear of aeroplanes; children who

Returning from the Abyss? Reincarnation

claimed to have drowned, feared being immersed in water; some of those who claimed to have been stabbed to death, showed a fear of bladed weapons and so on. The alleged fatal wound was sometimes associated with strange birth marks which resembled bullet entry wounds or stab wounds. 'Unsolved' cases were associated with a much higher incidence of memories of a violent death.

Whether the case is ultimately solved or unsolved depends in part upon how quickly investigators come to learn of it. Sometimes no historical person is identified with the child's memories. Frequently, by the time the investigators arrive on the scene, the child has identified the person he claims to have been in a previous life and the two families have met. Sometimes investigators arrive before this happens, finding themselves in an excellent position to check the validity of the child's memories. Occasionally, it is the investigation team itself which locates the previous family.

The nuts and bolts of the subsequent enquiry are always the same. Attempts are made to verify the oral testimony of the child and his family with statements from the family related to the previous personality. This information is supplemented by written records and documents such as birth and death certificates, hospital and legal records and diaries that have to be located and copied. Investigators continue to observe and talk to the child at regular intervals until his memories fade. As the old proverb goes 'talk is cheap' and these periods of observation allow the investigators to watch the unusual ways in which the child is consistently disposed to behave as a result of their alleged memories.

Reena Kulshreshtha was the youngest of six children born to Mr and Mrs Kripa Shanker Kulshreshtha, on 13 September, 1976.[4] The Kulshreshthas were members of the businessman's caste of the Hindu caste system and, from her delivery at the family home, the child found herself in a comfortable, caring, middle-class environment. Her father worked for the Telecommunications Department in Agra until 1980, when he was promoted and temporarily reassigned to the Lucknow office for eight years.

Reena was nine months old when she began alluding to a

previous husband. She said the word 'groom' several times and then lay down on the bed and mimed dying. She would look through the pages of her parents' magazines and books for several hours each morning. At first, her parents were puzzled by their child's actions but then Reena found a photograph which she thought resembled her 'groom' and became greatly attached to it. Every morning she would sit and stare at the picture. At approximately ten months of age, on a warm humid day when a storm was brewing, Reena told her mother that she had died on a day such as this, from an injection that had covered her body with blisters.

Several months later, she told her mother that her previous husband was called 'Shyam' and pleaded with her to help find him. Reena also insisted on wearing the necklace which, in India, is the mark of a married woman. From the roof of her parent's house she was able to point out the route to her former home but, once on the ground, she became confused in the maze of alleyways and always lost her way.

At the age of two and a half, Reena told her mother that she understood why her mother liked to lie with her father and gave other indications that she had an understanding of sexual relationships between men and women. She played with a favourite doll but referred to it as her 'son'. Still less than three years of age, Reena described details of her cremation and claimed that afterwards she was made to lie down for many days on the floor of a temple. After extensive questioning, her father concluded that this was a description of her state after death.

When Reena was three years old, the family was visited by Shyam Babu Yadev, another employee of the Telecommunications Department but of a lower caste, who supplemented his income by selling dried tea. As he handed over the tea to Reena's mother, Reena became very excited and said to her mother as she closed the door, 'That is my groom. Call him.' Reena's mother complied. After this meeting, Reena insisted that her parents invite her 'husband' to family celebrations. When Shyam Babu arrived at the house, Reena would serve him tea and food and then retire from the room in accordance with the Hindu custom. When Shyam Babu returned home,

Returning from the Abyss? Reincarnation

Reena insisted that they arrange the exchange of presents which was in keeping with the Hindu husband-wife relationship.

It was not the first time that Reena had met Shyam Babu. When the child was fourteen months of age, Shyam Babu had attended the wedding of Reena's eldest sister. Unlike either parent, Reena was of a dark complexion and Mr Kulshreshtha remembered his colleague remarking 'Whose influence is upon this child?' This raised the possibility that Shyam Babu became 'fixed' in the child's mind as the role model for her 'groom'; a term which itself might be seen as having allusions to the wedding. Set against this we have the evidence that Reena had identified a certain 'Shyam' as her groom some seven months earlier. There are other stranger coincidences.

Some nineteen months before Reena was born, Shyam Babu's wife had died after fifteen years of marriage, leaving two daughters and a 12-month-old son. In life, Gompti Devi was said to have shared Reena's dark complexion. She had died at the age of thirty, at the general hospital in Agra, from a severe allergic reaction to an injection. The funeral and cremation were held at the white temple, close to the famous Taj Mahal. Mr Kulshreshtha and Shyam Babu worked in different buildings and enjoyed very little daily contact. Neither of Reena's parents had been to Shyam Babu's house or met Gompti Devi. Mr Kulshreshtha was invited to Gompti Devi's funeral, but he was unable to attend.

It might be argued that, in belonging to a lower caste, Shyam Babu had a lot to gain from encouraging Reena's 'memories', but in fact he found himself in an embarrassing situation. He did believe that the three-year-old child was his wife reborn. However, within three months of Gompti Devi's death, he had taken a second wife without observing the traditional Hindu one-year mourning period. He had adjusted well to Gompti Devi's death but he did not tell the child about his new wife. Some time after Reena had identified Shyam Babu as her 'husband', she successfully led her mother through half a kilometre of lanes and streets to Shyam Babu's house where he had lived with Gompti Devi. Shyam Babu was away and the door was opened by his second wife. This was the first that Reena knew of Shyam Babu's second marriage and she never asked to be taken to the house again. Shyam Babu later told an investigator that he never went to the Kulshreshtha's house in the company of his new wife 'because of how she [Reena] would feel'.

Reena frequently took her mother to the house of a neighbour, Kailash Kumari Yadev, who lived across the street from Shyam Babu and who had acted as surrogate mother-in-law for Gompti Devi. At Kailash Kumari's home Reena was shy and would not eat the food offered her in Kailash Kumari's presence, in the same way that Gompti Devi had not eaten in her presence as a sign of respect for a mother-in-law.

Gompti Devi had spent a large part of her married life at the home of her real mother-in-law, Phoowati Devi, in the village of Tilitila, some ninety miles from Agra. After Gompti Devi's death, it was Phoowati Devi who had raised her children. During one of the mother-in-law's visits to Agra, she was taken by Kailash Kumari to meet Reena, who burst into tears and covered her head with a cloth as Gompti Devi and all Hindu daughters-in-law would do in the presence of their mother-in-law. Reena's mother accepted her daughter's behaviour as evidence of the spontaneous recognition of her former mother-in-law.

Gradually contact with Shyam Babu's family declined, but on several occasions the child showed evidence of the telepathic-link that some psychiatrists and parapsychologists believe operates inside families. When she was about four years of age, Reena said, 'Mother, I don't feel like eating because there is some problem in my house.' Some time later on the same day, she said, 'Shyam Babu has been blessed with a son. Tell my mother-in-law to send *laddu* [an Indian sweet] to distribute. Let us celebrate and distribute sweets.' Reena's mother knew that Shyam Babu's second wife was pregnant, and curious, she went to see Kailash Kumari and asked if it was true that Shyam Babu's second wife had given him a son. Kailash Kumari replied that she did not know as the woman was at her mother-in-law's house in Tilitila. Kailash Kumari asked Shyam Babu when he returned from work but he replied that he had not yet had news of the birth. Some days

Returning from the Abyss? Reincarnation

later, Shyam Babu received a letter informing him of the birth of his son on the day that Reena had announced it. Later, Shyam Babu's wife told him that the delivery had been difficult as the umbilical cord had become wrapped around the baby's neck.

In 1980, Mr Kulshreshtha was promoted and the family moved to Lucknow. Contact with Shyam Babu and his family effectively ceased for eight years. In the same year, Reena's mother took ill and was given injections. It was the first time that the child had seen a hypodermic syringe but Reena became very alarmed and developed a very pronounced phobia of injections. While growing up in Lucknow, Reena also demonstrated several other feats of extra-sensory perception with respect to her previous family, accurately reporting the death of Shyam Babu's eldest brother and an operation which saved Shyam Babu's life. When Reena was seven years old, Shyam Babu withdrew from the Kulshreshtha family and the difficult situation in which he found himself, feeling that any relationship between a married man and a growing girl was unseemly.

The case was investigated by Antonia Mills when Reena was eleven years old. She was told that the child was no longer referring to Shyam Babu as her husband but Reena would only respond to questions put to her by her parents. Her father claimed that she had never been like a child but more like an adult trapped in a child's body. She had demonstrated precocity in the household chores and was shopping for vegetables, cooking, sewing and knitting before she was five years old. Antonia Mills reinvestigated the case when she returned to India one year later.

> When I returned in January 1989, I learned that Reena still related to Shyam Babu as her past-life husband. On December 25th, he was among 400 guests invited to a dinner the Kulshreshthas held in honor of the birth of Mr Kulshreshtha's first grandson. Reena was eating dinner when Shyam Babu arrived, but on seeing him, she stopped and retired, as a proper Hindu wife should do in her husband's presence.

In her paper, Antonia Mills rightly concludes that there is nothing in the case of Reena – or indeed in any other case –

that provides *irrefutable* evidence of reincarnation. Leaving aside the instances of alleged ESP, much of the information about Gompti Devi was known either to Mr and Mrs Kulshreshtha or certainly to other employees at the Agra Telecommunications Department. Probably, no case will be discovered which offers a definitive proof of reincarnation. Stevenson himself once remarked that he could imagine the 'perfect case' but had no 'expectations of finding it'.

It is well known that a person can obtain information from books and magazines or from other people and then, forgetting the source, weave the material into their own memories. Psychologists term this process cryptomnesia or source amnesia.[5] In a famous case of the last century, an illiterate woman, aged twenty-five, presented to a young doctor in a 'nervous fever' during which she incessantly raved in Latin, Greek, Hebrew and a Rabbinical Hebrew dialect. The phrases and sentences were all intelligible but unconnected to each other. On investigation, the physician discovered that, as a child of nine, the woman had been taken into the household of a Protestant minister, who was in the habit of walking along the passage reading aloud from his favourite books. In the man's library, he discovered a collection of Rabbinical writings and works of the early church fathers in Greek and Latin. The doctor managed to identify many of the woman's ravings with passages from the books.

The British historian, Ian Wilson, has provided evidence that cryptomnesia may offer the best explanation for many of the past-life memories elicited under hypnotic regression.[6] But it is an incomplete explanation for those of Stevenson's cases where, say, a child provides a wealth of accurate detail about a previous personality who was totally unknown to the child's own family.

Perhaps the children's memories can arise in other ways. It has been suggested that we can inherit some of the memories of our forebears and children who remember past lives may have inherited a larger package of these memories than most. In fact, the 'genetic memory' or 'race memory' hypothesis never really leaves the 'starting-blocks'. Human memory is extraordinarily stable and has been associated with four key

Returning from the Abyss? Reincarnation

areas in the brain but, beyond that its chemical nature remains a mystery. In order to have 'genetic memory', our experiences would need to be encoded into DNA (the blue-print for life). This process would require a chemical called reverse transcriptase and this chemical has never been shown to be produced by the human body. The encoded memories would then need to cross the blood/brain barrier and find their way specifically to the eggs and sperm. This scenario is extremely unlikely. But leaving the actual mechanism aside, how can 'genetic memory' account for cases such as that of Ma Tin Aung Myo or Reena Kulshreshtha, where the previous personality was totally unrelated to the child?

Once we accept the memories of children who claim to remember past lives, we find ourselves drawn to the conclusion that reincarnation may be a very real possibility. It has been a tradition amongst those sceptical of the paranormal to attack the premises of the argument by suggesting that the investigator is either a fool or a crook. In the case of reincarnation it has been suggested that the children's memories are just the product of collusion between families engaged in fraud or self-delusion and investigators who want to believe their fantasies.

The anthropologist, Dr Antonia Mills, started studying the Indians of British Columbia, Canada in 1964. Twenty years later, she started to use Ian Stevenson's methods to investigate the many reincarnation-type cases which are reported by these tribes. In 1987, she extended this work to India. In July 1988, she was offered the post of Research Assistant Professor at the University of Virginia. It was a joint position with Professor Stevenson's Division of Personality Studies and the Anthropology Department. Stevenson agreed not to look at her notes prior to the publication of 'A Replication Study: Three Cases of Children in Northern India Who Are Said to Remember a Previous Life', which included the case of Reena Kulshreshtha and independently confirmed many of Stevenson's earlier findings. Between 1987 and 1989, Mills embarked on a far more imaginative and ambitious venture, the results of which provide some of the most outstanding evidence to date for the reality of reincarnation.

The Sceptical Occultist

As we shall see shortly, it is beyond argument that culture helps shape both beliefs in reincarnation and the cases themselves. This finding presents us with a 'chicken and egg' situation. Which comes first, actual cases of children remembering past lives which then mould cultural and religious beliefs or the beliefs themselves that, in some strange way, are 'acted out' by members of the community?

In order to attack this problem, Mills investigated cases in the racial flash-points of Uttar Pradesh, Rajasthan, Madhya Pradesh and Kashmir in northern India.[7] Here the Hindu majority live uneasily with their Moslem neighbours and tensions can easily boil over into widespread rioting. For the most part, the Moslems are implacably hostile to the idea of reincarnation, a belief in which is expressly forbidden by the Koran. In contrast, the Hindu population believes in reincarnation but this belief is often suppressed for fear of offering offence to their Moslem neighbours. In these areas, it is very rare for Hindus and Moslems to inter-marry. Mills reasoned that, if reincarnation-type cases are just a cultural artefact, it should be very rare to find a Moslem child who remembered being a Hindu in a previous life or, indeed, a Hindu child who claimed to have been a Moslem.

Antonia Mills investigated twenty-six cases of this type in northern India. In eleven cases a Hindu child remembered being a Moslem in a previous life and in six of these cases a previous personality was identified from the child's statements. The cases came to the attention of Mills or Stevenson when a family member or friend broke the taboo and reported it to the investigators. What had overwhelmed the families in these cases was not simply the children's memories but the way in which those memories had disposed them to behave.

Three quarters of the Hindu children who remembered being Moslems insisted on observing the Moslem religious rite of *namez*, in which the devout face towards Mecca, bow the head to the ground and recite prayers in Arabic. The child Mukul Bhauser was observed performing *namez* before he could even speak. His memories of a past life were studiously ignored by his parents. Archana Shastri was thirty months old

Returning from the Abyss? Reincarnation

when she performed *namez* for her father who was ill. Thereafter, she practised *namez* at 5 a.m. and 9 p.m. every day. Hirdesh Saxena practised *namez* until he was five years old and asked his parents to allow him to attend services at the mosque. Most of these children recited vocal prayers during *namez* but this was never clearly identified as Arabic.

At a very early age, Naresh Kumar would quietly slip away to perform *namez*. He took his parents to the house of his previous personality. The startled Moslem family were so impressed with his ability to identify family members that he was given the deceased's Moslem cap, which he insisted on wearing despite teasing from his playmates. Naresh resisted the vegetarian diet of his parents, preferring semia (a Moslem noodle dish), eggs and tea. Four other children with the past-life memories of a Moslem insisted that their vegetarian parents serve them meat. Giriraj Soni asked for mutton and eggs. Subhash Singhal and Kailash Narain Mishra compromised with their parents' habits but insisted on meat and special dishes on Moslem holidays.

In the remaining fifteen cases, seven Moslem children remembered being Hindus and eight recalled being a Moslem in a previous life. Two of the children who remembered being Hindus resisted the Moslem religion. From an early age, Nasruddin Shah refused to say Moslem prayers or go to the mosque. Initially, he insisted on a vegetarian diet but eventually compromised, refusing to eat beef or fish, but accepting mutton. Mohammed Hanif Khan wanted a Rakhi thread tied on him which celebrates the Hindu brother-sister bond. Noor Bano refused to eat any meat and her mother secretly indulged her in her vegetarian diet. Umar Khan refused to eat meat, insisting that he was a Hindu.

Stevenson has described hundreds of birth marks and birth defects which show a strange correspondence to injuries suffered by the previous personality, many of which were ascribed by the pathologist as being the cause of death. Twelve of the twenty-six children studied by Mills had birth marks or defects of which nine were said to be related to the previous life. Nasruddin Shah had a birth mark which corresponded to a spear wound described in the post-mortem report of his alleged previous personality. The child Umar Khan remembered being shot through the head and had birth marks resembling the entry and exit wounds caused by a bullet. Ali Kathat and his previous personality were both albino.

Writing in the Journal of Anatomy in 1951, Dr Theodore James commented that cases of congenital circumcision or 'aplasia of the male prepuce' were so rare that he could find no reference to it in the literature and that there were insufficient cases to provide an estimate of the frequency of it arising in the population. James had seen only four cases during his medical career[8].

Historically, congenital circumcision has created something of a dilemma for Moslems and Jews who circumcise male children in accordance with religious beliefs. In the Jewish Talmud, in the tractate 'Sabbath', there is reference to a dispute between the school of Shammai and the school of Hillel, concerning a child who was born circumcised, and the time for whose circumcision would have fallen on the Sabbath. The Shi'ite Moslem tradition associates it with sainthood. The Prophet Mohammed was said to have been 'born circumcised and happy' and the twelve Imans are also said to have been born circumcised.

Of the twenty-six children studied by Mills, two were born circumcised. The Hindu child, Mukul Bhauser, remembered a past life as a Moslem. In the other case, the Moslem boy, Jalaluddin Shah, remembered a previous life as a Moslem.

Impressive cases such as these are taxing the minds of psychiatrists and anthropologists. They appear extraordinary but the prosecution will argue that, although something strange and even wonderful is happening here, it is not reincarnation.

If reincarnation is indeed a reality, then surely the process should be 'universal' with, say, cases in America bearing a striking resemblance to cases in Alaska, Brazil, the Middle East, India and South-East Asia. There *are* 'universal' features to these cases, for example children who remember dying violently are 'reincarnated' more quickly than those who experienced 'natural deaths'. These children are often concerned with 'unfinished business', such as their previous life being cut short or dependants such as infants or family members who were 'left behind'. Another common feature is that children appear to be reborn into the area in which they died.

But there are also differences. If a particular culture holds certain beliefs about reincarnation, actual cases within the community seem to be shaped by those beliefs. An American child is likely to be 'reborn' into the same family, remembering being a grandparent or an older brother or sister who died some years before the child was born. In contrast, in many Indian, Middle-Eastern and Asian cases, the previous personality is unrelated to the child's family. Also, the interval between 'rebirths' is much longer in American cases than those drawn from other parts of the world.[9]

Some of the differences are more fundamental. Reincarnation is central to the religious beliefs of the Gitksan and Beaver Indians who live as neighbours in northern British Columbia.[10] The Beaver believe in the possibility of cross-sex reincarnation and, in common with American, Indian and Asian children, some Beaver youngsters do remember past lives as a member of the opposite sex. In stark contrast, the Gitksan Indians do not believe in cross-sex reincarnation and such cases have never been described in the Gitksan community.

On the other hand, the Gitksans believe in multiple reincarnation where a single personality is reborn into a number of children and this is a common facet of Gitksan cases. 'Soul splitting' may appear very strange to us, but it was a belief held by the famous psychoanalyst, Carl Jung, who wrote, 'Our psyche is by no means a unity. It seems to be a collection of inherited units, probably fragments of the past or ancestral lives.'[11] This aside, the belief in multiple reincarnation is not shared by the Beavers and, correspondingly, such cases have never been reported in their community. Many anthropologists would argue that this is simply the result of cultural conditioning and not reincarnation, but the individual cases arising within the Beaver and Gitksan communities are just as striking and impressive as those reported from other parts of the world.

The philosopher Karl Popper pointed to the asymmetry

between verification and falsification. The statement 'All boys have red hair' can never be proved by continuing to collect cases of red-headed boys but a *single* case of a blond, brown or black-haired boy is all that is required to falsify the statement. So let us ask if there are reincarnation-type cases which break the rules. The concept of reincarnation entails person A. dying to be reincarnated as person B. sometime later. The whole idea of reincarnation is therefore logically contradicted by cases where the deceased personality was still alive when the reincarnated personality was born and yet, in several 'anomalous cases', that is exactly what investigators did discover. Stevenson described two such cases (Jasbir and Chaokhun Rajsuthajarn) in his earlier studies in India and Thailand but a more impressive case was described more recently by Antonia Mills.[12]

Toran Singh, alias 'Titu', was born in the village of Bad, near Agra, India. Titu remembered being Suresh Verme, the owner of a radio shop in Agra market and an important smuggler, who was shot through the head while sitting in his car on 28 August, 1983. The date of the murder was confirmed by police and pathology reports. The case was more than impressive, it was extraordinary. Titu not only 'remembered' the name of his shop but recognised many members of Suresh Verme's family, even calling them by their nicknames. He cried and fought with his father to remain with his 'previous family'. Furthermore, the child had a red circular birth mark at the exact spot where a pathologist had described the bullet entering Suresh Verme's right temple. The bullet had tumbled through the brain, creating a gaping exit wound behind the right ear. Behind Titu's right ear was a large bony protuberance of the skull.

Despite the fact that Titu's father, Mahavir Singh, was educated – he taught chemistry at the Hubbulal Inter-College in Agra – both parents were confused about the year of their son's birth. Titu's mother had become ill during the last trimester of her pregnancy with Titu and had entered Agra military hospital using the name of the wife of a military friend, since only service personnel were eligible for treatment there. The only registration of a birth corresponding to the name of this friend gives 11 December, 1982 as the date of birth. This is seemingly confirmed by the parent's statements in mid-1987, when they told Mills that they thought that Titu was four and a half. Parents may forget the date of their child's birth but rarely become confused about the child's age. All of this suggests that Titu was born *eight months and 17 days before Suresh Verme was murdered*.

Mahavir Singh later corrected his son's date of birth to 10 December 1983, thereby placing Titu's birth four months after the death of Suresh. But there was no record of a birth to Titu's mother or the wife of her military friend in 1983. Consequently, we have all the impressive evidence for reincarnation, together with a strong indication that for eight months and 17 days, Titu and Suresh Verme were both alive! Do these anomalous cases tell us that, for reasons we do not yet understand, it is possible to see 'reincarnation-type' cases without the reality of reincarnation?

Professor Stevenson does not accept that these few cases undermine the case for reincarnation.[13]

> . . . These cases suggest possession rather than reincarnation, but they show the difficulty of separating the idea of reincarnation from that of possession with a formula that will fit all cases. There are many other cases in which the presumed previous personality died after the body of the subject was conceived (but not born).

Stevenson thus attempts to save the idea of reincarnation by labelling the anomolous cases: 'possession'. But then how can we know the difference between reincarnation, possession and mental illness? Stevenson believes that the answer lies in the paranormal aspects of a case.

> It is true that some instances of possession or apparent possession may be difficult to distinguish from cases of schizophrenia. It is also true that cases of possession may be regarded as a type of multiple personality. Where there is evidence of a possession by a discarnate personality the case differs from the standard case of multiple personality in the paranormal knowledge that the patient/subject shows. The several cases of xenoglossy that I have reported could be considered instances of temporary possession.

We have come to the nub of the cases for and against reincarnation. Reincarnation-type cases provide a range of remarkable evidence that argues for the reality of reincarnation. Against this, we have the seemingly culture-driven aspects of the phenomena and more importantly, there are those few cases which appear to be reincarnation but are not.

Professor Stevenson rescues his case by arguing that the anomalous cases are really instances of the children being possessed by the spirit of the deceased. Is this just an *ad hoc* hypothesis designed to prevent the case for reincarnation falling to its knees or are there really cases of spirit possession complicating the argument?

Our final case is often described as reincarnation but it could equally be described as possession. It is, itself, something of an anomaly. It was first investigated by Ian Stevenson and then independently by V. V. Akolkar.[14] The reader must decide whether it provides sufficient evidence that Stevenson is right when he claims that there are cases of possession overlaying those of reincarnation and confusing the basic issue.

Miss Uttara Huddar was born on 14 March, 1941, at Nagpur Maternity Hospital, Nagpur, in the central Indian state of Maharashtra. Her father, G. M. Huddar, was an intellectual who had fought with the Republican forces in Spain and who later became active in the Indian nationalist movement during the last years of British rule. The family were highly educated and spoke Marathi, Hindi and English. At school, Uttara studied Sanskrit for three years and passed a special examination in that language. Later, she studied science before taking a double M.A degree in English and Public Administration.

Uttara was the fifth of six children and when her mother was pregnant with Uttara, she suffered from terrifying nightmares in which a snake bit her on the toe. As a child, Uttara had a phobia of snakes, which were a common sight in her village, but otherwise her early life was unremarkable. Unlike children in typical reincarnation cases, she had never alluded to a previous life. The extraordinary changes began in 1973, when Uttara was thirty-two years of age. Disappointed in love

Returning from the Abyss? Reincarnation

and in declining health, Uttara had withdrawn into an ashram, where for three years she studied religious books. While practising meditation with breathing exercises, she managed to induce an altered state of consciousness with very frightening results.

The first indication Uttara had that she was not 'really' herself came when she looked into a mirror and would 'sort of see' another image behind her own. Uttara thought that it was her own image but slightly different. She also saw a slim, tall, fair man on horseback in her dreams and during meditation. She began entering trance-like states until finally a second personality emerged which called herself 'Sharada'.

Sharada dressed and behaved as a shy married Bengali woman. She did not recognise Uttara's family or friends, whom she described as 'these people'. She was unable to speak Uttara's native language, Marathi, but spoke a strange language which was provisionally identified as Bengali. On waking in the morning, she dressed in Bengali style before taking a head bath, leaving her hair loose and putting a vermilion mark in the parting. She did not use undergarments and asked for a plantain leaf and cotton during her periods of menstruation. This was consistent with the behaviour of nineteenth-century Bengali ladies.

At first, she refused to help with the chores and spent all her time in prayer or worshipping the Bengali goddess Durga. Unlike Uttara and her family, Sharada preferred Bengali foods, requesting dishes which were specialities of Bengal. Sharada was shy with men and remained inside the house. She made an exception for one man, Dr Z., in whose ashram Uttara had studied for three years. Sharada claimed that Dr Z. had been her husband in a 'previous life' and that the goddess Durga had brought them together again. At the beginning of these manifestations, Dr Z. had asked Uttara's parents to remove their daughter from the ashram. He did not reciprocate Uttara's feelings and could not remember a past life with or without Sharada.

Sharada was amazed and terrified by various household objects. She appeared to have no knowledge of electricity, radios, fans, tape-recorders (which she referred to as a *dakan* or witch), cameras or motor-vehicles. In her later statements she described a world where people travelled by foot or by horse, bullock cart, boat or palanquin. She was familiar only with cooking utensils made of earthenware and metal and showed no awareness of the modern methods of preserving foods. When one of the investigators, Professor Pal, showed her a glass jar for preserving pickles, she was at once amazed and confused.

Bengali speakers recognised the language which Sharada spoke as an archaic form of Bengali, one which had more Sanskrit words than modern Bengali and was marked by a complete absence of English loan words. Such loan words, which now comprise 20 per cent of modern Bengali, first entered the language during the first third of the nineteenth century. During long, sometimes taped, conversations, with Bengali scholars, such as Professor Pal, Sharada used the correct intonations and pronunciations and never used a single loan word. During his own investigation, V. V. Akolkar noted that Sharada used expressions hardly known to modern Bengalis; she wrote the letters of the alphabet as they appear in old manuscripts and wrote them counter-clockwise as had been the practice in the previous century. Although Sharada's Bengali was not perfect, it was fluent and spoken with the inflections of the Burdwan dialect. In a word-association test, in which Sharada was asked to give her responses to a drawing, she used twenty-five words drawn exclusively from Bengali and Sanskrit.

Sharada said that her father's name was Brajanath Chattopadhaya and her mother's name Renuka Devi. She told investigators that her mother had died when she was just an infant and she had been brought up by her mother's sister, Jagatdhatri. The aunt's husband had been a landlord and the couple had a son and two daughters. Sharada talked about her uncle Devinath, who was particularly fond of her because he had lost his two daughters. She claimed that her uncle had composed *Dashavatara Stotra* and the devotional song *Hey Anadi Bhagawan*, in which he referred to himself as *Devidas*. The song ends with the line 'Devidas says: Who says I am a sinner?' During his research which followed from these conversations, Akolkar noted that the *stotra* which Sharada recited is very different from the one known in modern Bengal. The other composition which ends in Devinath's own name was virtually unknown.

Sharada claimed that her maternal aunt had arranged her marriage at the age of seven and she was married three years later. She would not write the name of her husband but said it was the 'name of the god of Varanashi, that is *vishwanath*. He was Nandikore's son.' Other obtuse statements nevertheless identified her husband as Vishwanath Mukhopadhaya, son of Nand Kismore Mukhopadhaya. Shyness in uttering the name of the husband was and still is, common in India. Her husband was a *Kaviraj*, or Ayurvedic physician, and Sharada recalled him giving gold for blood impurities. She and her husband were married for fourteen years and lived in Shivapur. In describing her life, Sharada correctly identified five obscure villages in Bengal and nearby rivers. She also mentioned five temples which she located correctly and showed a detailed familiarity with the Hansheshwari Temple at Bansberia.

She told investigators that following two miscarriages she became pregnant again. At the age of twenty-four, she was taken to her aunt at Saptagram. While picking flowers in her aunt's garden, she was bitten on the toe by a snake and became unconscious. Sharada never said that she had died but merely that she had lost consciousness.

Two investigators traced a family called Chattopadhaya resident in Bansberia, in that part of West Bengal which appeared in most of Sharada's statements. The present head of the family, Satinath Chattopadhaya, has a genealogy of his family which goes back to the early nineteenth century. The name of Brajanath ('Brojesh') Chattopadhaya appeared in this genealogy for the period 1810–1830. Armed with the genealogy, investigators asked Sharada to identify the relationships she had with other members of her paternal family. Without having seen the lineage, she correctly identified her great-great-grandfather, Ram Narayan; her great-grandfather, Narayan of Kestopar; grandfather, Ramnath (she wrote 'Tharurda Ramnath – Bansberia'); father, Brojesh Chattopadhaya; uncles, Shivnath and Devinath; and stepbrothers, Kailashnath and Srinath. Sharada also identified three female relatives of her father but these could not be verified as Indian genealogies only identify male relatives.

From the statements which Sharada made to investigators, both Stevenson and V. V. Akolkar decided that if Sharada was an historically real person, she must have lived in the early part of the nineteenth century. They concluded that Sharada was unacquainted with the modern artefacts which were developed after the industrial revolution. She claimed to have witnessed a ring-total solar eclipse (14 April, 1828) but had not heard of the heroine Rani Laxmi Bai or the Indian Mutiny of 1857. Neither had she heard of other well-known personages such as Ramakrishna Paramhansa (1836–1886) or Swami Vivekananda (1863–1902). Her husband wore shoes made of cloth but she had not heard of the sewing machines introduced by the Gibson Company into Calcutta in 1825 for stitching military uniforms. Sharada's form of Bengali also dates to the early nineteenth century. She spoke of seeing almanacs which were written by hand. According to Sharada, the black ink used was prepared from bean juice and drumstick leaves, while inauspicious days were written in red, using blood drawn from the finger. Almanacs were originally written in ink by priests and scholars and were only printed in Bengal after 1820. She told the investigators that she had been married at ten, and lived with her husband for fourteen years before being bitten by the snake, all of which infers a lifespan of 24 years. V. V. Akolkar estimated that Sharada had probably lived between late 1807–1831, or late 1805–1829. Stevenson independently estimated the slightly later dates of 1810–1834.

'Sharada' manifested more than twenty-eight times from 31 March, 1974, to August 1981 and these spells varied from short trances of a few minutes to periods of several months. Gradually, the spells grew fewer as Sharada began to fuse with Uttara's own personality. Throughout, Uttara claimed to know nothing of Sharada. During his long interrogations of Sharada, and during psychological tests, Akolkar was not only

Returning from the Abyss? Reincarnation

able to demonstrate that Sharada was aware of ⌣͜ ͜
demonstrated that the two personalities overlapped. He ͜
cluded that Sharada was a deeper level of Uttara's own personality. Stevenson and Akolkar decided that there was no evidence of mental illness or behavioural abnormality and both decided that reincarnation was the best explanation.

Two American psychiatrists who exchanged views on the Sharada case in their journals, decided that it was a case of multiple personality disorder (MPD), although they failed to interview either the patient or the investigators. Indeed, the case has many aspects of MPD, an illness we will consider in more depth in the next chapter. Nevertheless, this convenient label provides no explanation as to why a modern Indian woman should possess such a profound knowledge of life in nineteenth-century Bengal or why she chose to dramatise this knowledge in the form of a believable and coherent nineteenth-century personality: 'Sharada'.

Cryptomnesia could explain some of the facts. Uttara was a clever multilingual university graduate well acquainted with libraries and research sources. She had studied some Bengali and lived in a city with a sizeable Bengali population. Might she not have unconsciously assimilated much of the information which was later dramatised as 'Sharada'? But then how was she able to perfect her rich vocabulary of nineteenth-century Bengali? Even extensive contact with modern Bengalis fails to account for her use of archaic expressions and total avoidance of loan words.

The Chattopadhayas were a famous family and their genealogy was published in 1907 in a Bengali magazine with a local circulation. However, Sharada in describing her relationship to male members of the family, used different titles from those appearing in the family tree. For example, Sharada correctly identified her grandfather as Ramnath but in the genealogy he appears as the 'Father of Brajanath'. From where did Uttara obtain the great wealth of additional information?

An investigator can never conclusively prove that information was not derived from normal channels, but he can try to show that this is unlikely. If the Sharada case was fraudulent, it can only be said that it was so elaborate as to outwit two teams of investigators. The normal sources of a biographer were denied to Uttara. There is no evidence that she ever went to Bengal or contacted the Chattopadhaya family. Working in secret, she must have polished her archaic Bengali while obtaining a wealth of detail, not only about the Chattopadhayas but their life and times in nineteenth-century Bengal. This information must then have been integrated into a highly coherent and polished performance which was intermittently sustained for more than ten years.

Both Stevenson and Akolkar favoured the reincarnation hypothesis over possession. Uttara's previous life as Sharada lay in the deeper reaches of her unconscious, only coming to the surface as the result of several misfortunes and her practice of meditation. But if this is really a case of reincarnation, why do we not see more children who remember a previous life and speak a foreign language? Ma Tin Aung Myo spoke no Japanese and there is no conclusive evidence that the Hindu children who remembered lives as Moslems in northern India ever spoke or prayed in Arabic. In favour of possession we see Uttara's memories seemingly controlling her. For many parapsychologists the case remains an enigma.

Summary of the evidence

Some children do remember past lives and Stevenson, Mills and other investigators have independently provided a great weight of startling evidence for the possibility of reincarnation. The great enigma of the reincarnation debate is that many of the explanations proposed to explain these cases in 'scientific terms' are often less convincing than the simplest explanation, which is that some of us return from death to live again in another body.

Recently, we have witnessed an epidemic of cases in Britain and the United States in which children have alleged sexual abuse and, more surprisingly, ritual abuse as part of occult practices. However, it is clear that in some, if not most, of these cases, the social worker, lawyer or psychologist has employed leading questions which have encouraged the child

Returning from the Abyss? Reincarnation

to create bogus memories which the child then com...
believe. Eventually, the point is reached where neither the
child nor the professional is able to discriminate between fact
and fantasy. Is it possible that children in reincarnation-type
cases have simply woven a fantasy past-life from their parents'
statements and the family's religious and cultural beliefs?

While in some cases this may be true, in many it does not
even begin to provide an explanation. Many of these children
remember their 'past-life' spontaneously, while the parents
are left confused, frightened and sometimes angry. Professional investigators only come to hear of the case after the
child's memories are well established and frequently only
after the previous personality has been identified and the two
families have met – Antonia Mills did not investigate the Kulshreshtha case until Reena was eleven years old. Who then
helps create the children's memories? If they arise spontaneously, in some unknown fashion, should not more children
remember past lives? What of those children who provide a
great wealth of accurate detail about an unrelated personality,
who was totally unknown to the child's family? Where does
the information come from and why is it woven into a coherent biography which is sustained for many years? Clearly it is
also difficult to explain those cases where the previous personality was unrelated to the child, on the basis of cryptomnesia.

The genetic memory hypothesis is like a 'bad penny', constantly turning up in the reincarnation literature. There is not
a single shred of evidence for genetic memory. Even if we
were to accept the possibility, what possible mechanisms
could we advance for its chemical and physiological nature?
And how can we explain cases like that of Ma Tin Aung Myo,
where a Burmese girl, born to Burmese parents, remembers a
previous life as a Japanese soldier, on the basis of *inherited*
memories?

As we run through the list of comfortable scientific and
quasi-scientific explanations for the children's memories, the
'lesser miracles' start to become more substantial. Could ESP
be involved? But why should ESP only centre on events in the
life of one deceased individual? And again, why should the

child identify himself as that particular individual and behave in certain ways which are quite alien to his family?

Perhaps the only thing to survive death is human memory. Is there a vast unseen sea of psychic energy surrounding us, composed of fragmented personalities and human memories? Certainly, this hypothesis has been advanced to explain the strange, shallow, child-like personalities manifesting themselves at seances. Can this explain the reincarnation-type cases? Is it possible that the children have become 'infected' by these memories? But then, why do these children have the memories of only one deceased individual? Might we not expect to see a composite of human memories drawn from many different lives?

The defence would argue that the best explanation is the simplest one: these children are providing us with very good evidence of reincarnation. Surely, if we do live many lives in many bodies, the mechanism which usually erases our memories of previous existences will occasionally fail, and an individual will be born who remembers his previous life.

The prosecution would accept that none of the hypotheses often proposed to account for the children's memories adquately provides convincing explanations for all cases. Nevertheless, the case for reincarnation is flawed by cultural overtones and those anomalous cases where the child was apparently born *before* the death of the alleged previous personality. The anomalous cases in particular appear to refute the idea of reincarnation, as here we see 'reincarnation-type cases' without the reality of reincarnation. If several very impressive cases can be shown to be false, then surely all could be false. Just how or why these children come to possess these memories, we are unable to say.

Professor Stevenson would argue that another phenomenon overlays the reincarnation-type cases and may account for the anomalies. It is possible that, in some instances, what we see is not reincarnation but possession by the spirit of the deceased. As we shall see in the next chapter, many psychiatrists would dismiss cases of possession as 'multiple personality disorder' but there are other psychiatrists, just as experienced in MPD, who would claim that some of the alter-personalities they see in these patients really are spirit entities.

Returning from the Abyss? Reincarnation

The case of Sharada appears to prise open this can of worms. Was the second personality, which emerged in Uttara Huddar's trances, repressed memories of a previous life or was she 'possessed' by 'Sharada' – or was it just a highly unusual case of MPD? Leaving aside these questions, the reader must decide whether the case of Sharada really demonstrates that, in the poorly explored borderland between modern psychiatry and parapsychology, there are no hard and fast rules which cover every case. Can the case for reincarnation be given the benefit of the doubt?

9

Demonic Possession

Prosecution's claim is that 'possession syndrome' is simply a collection of mental illnesses.

Few issues create as much friction between science and religion as demonic possession. Psychiatrists and priests are fiercely divided over the interpretation of cases in which a person appears to be possessed by another personality. In an age where every child has at least a nodding acquaintance with the physical and life sciences, it seems incredible that the idea of possession is still current. Indeed, many Catholic and Anglican priests not only reject the idea that devils can possess human beings, but question the whole concept of personalised evil. Irrelevances serve further to confuse the basic issue. I think it has to be said that no other field of paranormal enquiry has had its waters so muddied by unsubstantiated myths and an almost stubborn refusal to come to terms with the complexities of the argument. And yet, if there is one case that refuses to yield to medical explanations, surely this provides *prima facie* evidence for the existence of a reality beyond that constructed by science?

There is an increasing belief, particularly amongst Christian fundamentalists, that demons are to be found everywhere and are responsible for every human ill. It could be argued that, as the churches empty, the clergy are being thrown back on a more literal interpretation of the scriptures. Their congregations, seeking miracles to bolster faith, have become similarly enamoured with the 'paranormal' aspects of religion. Others are turning away from Christianity to embrace witchcraft, magic and satanic ritual to fill the emptiness in their lives.

Demonic Possession

Like two leviathans locked in each other's embrace, Christian fundamentalism and believers in the occult feed off each other in an obscene and perverse form of symbiosis. In attempting to recreate the atmosphere of the sixteenth- and seventeenth-century witch-hunts, Christian fundamentalists have forged the diverse and fragmented occult community into a 'national liberation front' complete with its own headquarters, fighting-fund and teams of solicitors and barristers.[1]

Could Christian fundamentalism have survived without witches, demons and miracles? Would the pagans, witches, magicians and satanists have experienced such an upturn in recruitment without somebody to feed their institutionalised paranoia? How many occult circles have attracted youngsters because Christians have helped breathe life into their crazy *raison d'être* and helped make them appear suitably clandestine and anti-establishment?

From the perspective of this chapter, it is clear that if a person who believes that he has been manipulating spirits comes to believe that he is possessed by them, and turns for help to a priest, who not only believes this is possible but likely, both the sufferer and the clergyman can become ensnared in their complementary belief-systems. Where then does hysteria and mental illness end and possession begin?

While this book was being researched, a priest in east London was casting out the devils of 'alcoholism' and 'criminality' from his congregation of 'down and outs', while an American fundamentalist preacher was performing 'miraculous' healings by casting out the spirits of 'sickness' before packed audiences at Earls Court. Leaving aside the preacher's very dubious track record in obtaining cures, here is one aspect of this subject which so irritates scientists and doctors.

Many diseases are inherited, others appear to be caused by a small number of other predisposing factors. Cancer-producing genes have been discovered which may be activated by carcinogenic chemicals such as the tar from cigarettes. Other 'promoter' genes enhance the malignant transformation of a single cell and some hormones can enhance the growth of the subsequent tumour. Chemicals produced by the cancer induce blood vessel formation so that the tumour becomes well

The Sceptical Occultist

supplied with oxygen and nutrients. Beyond a certain size, it becomes too large to be destroyed by the patient's immune system. *At what point in this chain of causality do we invoke an evil spirit?*

I put this question to an Anglican priest who reminded me that Jesus cast out the devils of sickness in the New Testament. In Mark ix, 17–27, we read:

> A man from the crowd answered him. 'Teacher, I brought my son to you; he has a dumb spirit, and whenever it seizes him it throws him down, and he foams at the mouth and grinds his teeth. He is wasting away with it; so I told your disciples to cast it out, but they could not.' He answered them, 'O faithless generation, how long must I still be with you? How long have I to bear with you? Bring him to me.' So they brought the boy to him, and when the spirit saw Jesus it at once convulsed the boy; he fell on the ground and rolled about foaming at the mouth. Jesus asked his father, 'How long has he been like this?' 'From childhood,' he said, 'it has thrown him into fire and water many a time to destroy him. If you can do anything, do help us, do have pity on us.' Jesus said to him, 'If you can! Anything can be done for one who believes.' . . . Now as Jesus saw that a crowd was rapidly gathering, he checked the unclean spirit. 'Deaf and dumb spirit,' he said, 'leave him, I command you, and never enter him again.' And it did come out after shrieking aloud and convulsing him violently. The child turned like a corpse, so that most people said, 'he is dead'; but, taking his hands, Jesus raised him and he got up.

The French Catholic psychiatrist, Dr Jean L'Hermitte, would have argued that this is one type of demonic possession, where the demon throws the possessed in a fit; but many other physicians would diagnose this child's condition as epilepsy. But should we even be arguing about the pros and cons of this story? Christ and his disciples did not live in a world of tape-recorders and electronic news-gathering. When the Gospels were finally written, the accounts of Jesus's life were intended as religious instruction, to be interpreted by men and women who believed that the earth was flat and contained within a small universe bounded by a canopy of the sky which served to separate God from his creation.

Much more importantly, the exorcism of the 'demons' of

Demonic Possession

sickness and alcoholism, where the 'possessed' seems lucid and sane, does not even begin to encompass the powerful drama and horror of medieval-type possession. What follows is a description of St Norbert of Magdeburg's confrontation with a possessed adolescent girl.[2]

> At first the devil mocked at him ... 'What wouldst thou then? For thee nor for any other will I come forth to-day. Behold! If only I call, the dark legions come to my aid. Eia, up to the fight! These arches and vaults are about to fall upon you.' At these words the people took to flight, but the priest remained bravely and fearlessly in his place. Then the hand of the possessed seized his stole to strangle him with it. As those standing by rushed to frustrate her, he said: 'Leave her! If God has given her strength she may do according to her will.' At these words, all astonished, she of her own will withdrew her hands.... Meanwhile night had fallen and when Norbert saw that the demon had not yet departed he commanded somewhat sadly that she should be led back to her father. On the following morning she was brought again to the mass. When he took off his alb and other vestments, the demon seeing this clapped his hands and cried out: 'Ah, ah, ah! Now thou doest well! All day thou hast done nothing that has so pleased me. The day has passed undisturbed, and thou hast accomplished nothing.'
>
> Forthwith [on the third day] Norbert ordered two brethren to hold the possessed fast not far from the altar; and when he came to the Gospel she was led to the altar itself and several passages from the Gospels were read over her head. The demon again roared with laughter at this and when the priest afterwards elevated the Host he cried out: 'See how he holds his little god in his hands!' This made the priest of God shudder, and strong in the might of the Spirit he applied himself to attack the demon by prayer and torment him. Then the latter, full of anguish, cried out by the mouth of the girl: 'I burn! I burn!' Again the voice howled: 'I am dying! I am dying!' For the third time it uttered loud cries and repeated many times over: 'I will go forth!' ... Leaving behind him a trail of unspeakably stinking urine he escaped, abandoning the vessel which he possessed. She collapsed, was taken back to her father's house, took food and was soon restored to health.

In medieval Europe a family stricken with a case of possession turned to the Church for help. Today, they are just as likely to be referred to a consultant psychiatrist. Before we ask if doctors recognise anything approaching medieval possession in their case-notes, let us ask what it is that the priest sees.

Christian tradition recognises three escalating stages of diabolical interference with human beings. The first stage, *infestation*, involves many of the same phenomena seen in poltergeist cases: strange scratchings in the wall and floors, rappings, objects moving by themselves, cascades of stones and the disappearance and sudden reappearance of objects. Traditionally, infestation has been countered by the *'Exorcism of Places'*: a rite which includes prayers of exorcism, a blessing and the sprinkling of holy water. The second stage is demonic *obsession* where the devil is believed to be 'hiding' within the possessed's body. In addition to the ongoing poltergeist activity, the possessed may display scratches, cuts and bite-marks on their body for which there appears to be no rational explanation. Observers have watched these stigmata develop and they have even taken the form of a macabre correspondence between the 'demon' and the exorcist, where words and numbers appear as if in response to the exorcist's questions.

The last stage is full-blown *possession* with the emergence of a secondary personality and dissociation. At times the possessed's personality suddenly disappears to be replaced by an alien identity which may recount its own life history as a spirit or as a devil with infernal intentions on the possessed's soul. Then, like a revolving door, the individual's personality reappears. The person may claim to watch the possession as a detached observer or, like a sleep-walker, remember nothing of the 'alien intruder'.

The Catholic Church combats possession with the service of Exorcism from the *Rituale Romanum* published in 1614 under the edict of Pope Paul V (1605–1621). The service of Exorcism contains five repetitions of exorcism and prayer, interrupted by readings from the scripture and sandwiched between long prayers at the beginning and the end. The exorcism takes the form of commands and threats designed to induce the demon to leave the possessed's body. The prayers

Demonic Possession

are intended to help the possessed person, increasing his confidence in God's love and reinforcing his desire to be delivered from the demon.

The Ritual warns the priest that he is dealing with an ancient and astute adversary, strong, cunning and the very embodiment of evil. The exorcist must be physically strong as he is advised to fast and pray throughout the period of exorcism, which can last for weeks, even months. He must be psychologically prepared for the obscene attacks on himself and the Church. He must have a devout and confident faith as the rite of Exorcism is carried out in the name of God and his Son, Jesus.

The Ritual also warns the priest that true possession is accompanied by 'signs' or accompanying paranormal phenomena. The 'devil' will speak through the possessed and answer questions in foreign or ancient languages (xenoglossy) unknown to the possessed. This was not a mere creation of the medieval Church. One of the Dialogues of the writer Lucian (born in 125 AD) inquires:[3]

> I should like to ask you, then, what you think of those who deliver demoniacs from their terrors and who publicly conjure phantoms. I need not recall to you the master of this art, the famous Syrian of Palestine ... When he is with sick persons he asks them how the devil entered into them; the patient remains silent, but the devil replies, in Greek or a barbarian tongue, and says who he is ...

The possessed may exhibit what parapsychologists term Psi phenomena. The most common feature is poltergeist activity, which some parapsychologists have associated with disturbed adolescents, but the possessed may also show evidence of clairvoyance and telepathy. All of these activities may be used to frighten and embarrass the exorcist and his helpers.

In 1949, the exorcism of a 14-year-old boy of Lutheran persuasion, Douglass Deen, was undertaken at the Alexian Brothers Hospital by Jesuit priests attached to St Louis University. The protracted and dramatic exorcism was successful but, to protect the child and his family, the entire affair was subsequently sealed behind a wall of silence. Newspaper stories, several novels, a series of Hollywood films and even gossip from within the Jesuit community flooded into the vacuum to provide fantastic and lurid accounts of these events. Two official copies of the diaries kept by the exorcist, Father William Bowdern were consigned to Catholic archives: one to the Jesuits at St Louis University and the second to the Archdiocese of St Louis. A third diary, originally consigned to the safe-keeping of the rector of the Alexian Brothers Hospital, was eventually rescued by Bowdern's assistant, Father Walter Halloran, who gave it to the writer Thomas Allen. The following extract is from Allen's account of the closing days of the exorcism.[4]

> One report says that the 'diabolical personality' within him sensed the goodness and sins of those who entered the room and 'bellowed and roared' whenever 'a person in the state of grace walked into the room'. When a physician entered the room during one of Robbie's [pseudonym] spells, there was no reaction. Bowdern supposedly turned to the doctor and said this was a sign that he was not in a state of grace. According to the account, the flustered doctor went out and came back half an hour later. He was greeted by roaring. In the interval he had gone to confession and cleansed himself of sin.

The physical features of the possessed person change and are said to take on the appearance of the possessing demon or spirit. In a case described by the nineteenth-century German poet and doctor, Justinus Kerner, a woman became possessed with the spirit of a local man who had recently died. 'As often as the demon took possession of her she assumed the same features which this man had had in his lifetime and which were very well marked, so that it was necessary at every attack to lead N. away from any persons who had known the deceased, because they recognised him at once in the features of the demoniac.'[5] When women are 'possessed' by male spirits there is also a change in the timbre of voice, 'He spoke to-day in a voice resembling more than ever a man's bass, and at the same time showed an insolence of look and gesture which beggars all description.'

The possessed becomes anti-religious or develops a marked fear of holy objects and, when taken into a church or confronted by the exorcist, the possessed may exhibit extreme violence and 'super-human' strength.[6] In late-nineteenth-century Germany, Father Aurelian gave the following account of the successful exorcism of a child. The parents, devout Protestants, had first turned to their local doctor, then their vicar and finally to the Capuchin prior at Wemding. All to no avail. With his son wasting away, the father had written to the Bishop of Augsburg, begging for him to arrange a Catholic exorcism. The bishop appointed Father Aurelian as the exorcist and Father Remigius as his assistant.

Since Shrove Tuesday a man called Muller and his wife noted astonishing phenomena in their eldest son M., who was ten years old. He could no longer say a prayer without getting into extraordinary rages, nor suffer near him any object which had been blessed, was guilty of the coarsest offences to his parents, and showed in his features such a transformation that they were forced to believe that something extraordinary had taken place. At first the parents sought to obtain from a doctor some remedy for this wretched state of their child, but in vain. . . . As often as the boy had to pass a church, crucifix, or monument raised in honour of the Mother of God or any other saint, he was seized thirty paces away with sudden agitation and fell unconscious to the earth.

. . . Some time before we began the exorcism, the boy boxed his parent's ears in an indescribable manner, and when we had him led into the presbytery a truly frightful scene took place. For when they would have executed our order, the possessed uttered a terrible cry. We seemed no longer to hear a human voice, but that of a savage animal and so powerful that the howlings – the word is not too strong – were heard at a distance of several hundred metres from the convent chapel, and those who heard them were overcome with fear. It may be imagined what courage we priests needed. And worse was yet to come; when his father tried to bring the boy into the presbytery he became weaker than a child beside him. The weak child flung the strong father to the earth with such violence that our hearts were in our mouths. At length, after a long struggle, he was overcome by his father, the men who were witnesses and one lay brother, and led into the presbytery. By way of precaution we had him bound hand and foot with straps, but he moved his limbs as if nothing of the kind had been done. After these preliminaries we disposed ourselves to perform the rite of exorcism, full of confidence in help from on high . . . The clamour and spitting lasted without interruption until the recitation of the litanies of the saints ... To all our questions the possessed made no reply, but he showed great contempt for us and spat upon us each time.

Finally, mention must be made of another odd association. Many cases coming to the attention of both psychiatrists and clergymen have connections with occult practices such as witchcraft, black magic, spiritualism and the use of ouija boards. Interpretations differ as to why this should be so. The priest might argue that those playing with spirits can open themselves to possession by these forces. In contrast, the doctor might contend that by entering into these 'magical' belief-systems, the patient has taken the first steps along the road to mental illness.

Traditionally, the medical profession has labelled cases of possession, 'Possession Syndrome': a cluster of minor and major psychiatric illnesses, all of which present with similar signs and symptoms. More recently, particularly in America, there has been a tendency to diagnose possession in terms of multiple personality disorder (MPD). However, the new DSM-IV manual of psychiatric diagnoses, replaces MPD with 'dissociative identity disorder' (DID). Writing to the author, Ralph Allison, an American psychiatrist with extensive experience of MPD, commented, 'I personally dislike this decision, as names are all important in this business, and changing the name is tantamount to saying that "MPD is non-existent". Those who don't like the concept of more than one personality per body find it easier to win the argument by deleting the name than by other means.' As we shall see later in this chapter, Ralph Allison has been confronted with MPD patients in whom one or more sub-personalities ('alter-personalities') claimed to be spirits.

The prosecution will not seek to enter into this debate or to outline in tedious detail the many and various mental illnesses that might seem like possession. Rather it will attempt to tease out the details of several myths about possesison which will reveal the real nature of this condition.

Our journey begins in the Norfolk home of a wealthy businessman, where the man's wife, Hilary, was writhing on the bed screaming obscenities, seemingly possessed by an evil spirit.[7] Almost out of his mind with worry, the husband telephoned the psychologist Robin Furman and his team of psychical researchers or 'ghostbusters' as they prefer to be known. In the bedroom of this suburban middle-class house, Furman found himself presented with a phenomenon as old as recorded history and it caught him off balance. His original diagnosis of hysteria became lost in the repellent and yet mesmerising theatre of a possessed woman seductively speaking in a man's voice while she pulled her night-clothes over her hips as she offered him intercourse.

> Her face seemed like a gargoyle mask. Was I imagining that a strange force coming [sic] from her eyes? ... 'Come on Hilary,' I said. 'Tell me what is really the matter.'
> 'I. AM. NOT. HILARY,' came the slow and measured reply, each word like the crack of a whip. 'I am Pazuzu. Pazuzu. Do you understand? Are you any the wiser?'
> I knew from my studies of ancient mythology that Pazuzu probably appeared about 3500 BC among the Sumerians ... a lion-eagle monster, a demon from the desert fringes of civilisation. Is there any way that Hilary could have known about Pazuzu; that he was a mythical Mesopotamian demonic entity?

Furman decided that the woman was truly possessed. How else could she have identified herself as a Sumerian demon? In fact, Pazuzu was the demon in William Peter Blatty's novel, *The Exorcist*, one of the most widely read works of fiction on possession and mentioned in Furman's own book *Ghostbusters UK* on page 122. And *The Exorcist* was truly a work of fiction.[8]

William Blatty based his novel on the case of Douglass Deen. Blatty was a student of a Jesuit tutor, Father Eugene Gallagher, a teacher at Georgetown University, who supposedly was kept informed of events by another Jesuit, Father Charles O'Hara. If we accept that a copy of Father Bowdern's diary was released to writer Thomas Allen, then much of what was written by Blatty is simply myth. The case, as described by Allen, certainly has all the ingredients of a poltergeist case. The child's bed rocked and moved away from the wall and various pieces of furniture moved around his bedroom, sometimes blocking the door and trapping the child inside. There was a secondary personality which could be interpreted as a demon and it was accompanied by a change in physiognomy, but this henchman of the 'Prince of Darkness', in fact, had very little to say for himself. The diary also mentions the sickroom becoming icy cold and the child manifesting 'superhuman' strength.

Allen also relates other claims, not in the diary, such as feats of clairvoyance/telepathy, and the child's ability to speak in a foreign language (Latin). Reports at the time mentioned more florid phenomena and in one the boy was reported to levitate!

> One night the boy brushed off his handlers and soared through the air at Father Bowdern standing some distance from the bed with the ritual in his hands. Presumably, Father was about to be attacked but the boy got no further than the book. And when his hand hit that – I assure you I saw this with my own eyes – he did not tear the book, he dissolved it. The book vapourised into confetti and fell in small pieces to the floor.

This account, from Scott Rogo's *Miracles*, was reputedly told by Father Charles O'Hara to William Blatty's tutor, Father Eugene Gallagher, and was one of the stories which so motivated Blatty to write his best-selling book. In fact, according to the diary reproduced by Thomas Allen, the child stood up in bed and *tore* the pages of the Ritual. The diary itself makes no mention of levitation, clairvoyance or the child's ability to answer questions in Latin.

The Roman Ritual warns that the possessing entity is a dangerous and astute adversary. In Blatty's book and the later Hollywood film, much was made of the possessing demon offering a very real physical, mental and spiritual threat to the two exorcists. Historical records and the five modern cases which I collected from priests and psychiatrists simply do not bear this out. It is another myth. The 'demon' often presents as an inane simple-minded personality, childish and unsophisticated. And psychiatrists would argue that this is exactly what we should expect as the 'demon' is really a fragment of an emotionally disturbed personality. Even in the florid medieval-type cases of possession, which today are extremely rare, the 'demon' rarely offers much of a fight. Many of the Protestant and Catholic priests who have experience of cases of possession agree with this view-point, including Dr Newton Malony, Professor of Mental Illness and Demonology and the J. Omar Good Visiting Professor of Evangelical Christianity at Juniata College, Pennsylvania,[9]

> In the history of the church and in modern accounts, there seem to be very few of these [cases of possession with associated paranormal phenomena], moreover, much of what the devil seems able to do in cases like this, seems to me to be very benign and inane. Simply telling you your name or having supernormal strength or a pungent odour doesn't seem to me to be much evil compared to that which we see in gangsters, in white collar crime, in greed, and in racial prejudice. If we want to use the word possession, I think some of the evil we see about us, is true possession.

Nevertheless, the clergy are very cautious when dealing with cases of possession. One Catholic priest, who serves a large town in the Midlands, described his experience of possession, which is typical of the experiences related to me by clergy who are frequently called upon to act as social workers.[10]

> I received a telephone call asking me to see a possessed boy. The child was eight years old and the eldest of two children born to an American serviceman and an English woman. The child's behaviour was disturbed and a minister of the — — Church had seen the boy and claimed that he was possessed by a devil. I took with me some holy water and the Blessed Sacrament. I entered the room where the little boy was playing with his sister and spent some time alone with the children, just talking to them. He was a delightful child. I then spoke with his parents. I told them that there was a 'presence' in the house but that they had created it [the parents were experiencing a marital breakdown] and I told them to get their act together as Catholic parents.

I remarked to a Catholic spiritual adviser that I thought it strange that while so few priests would give credence to the idea of demonic possession, many, like the above, would nevertheless take some sort of spiritual protection in the form of holy water or the Blessed Sacrament.[11] The exorcist's greatest fear is infectious possession, where the demon leaves the body of the possessed and enters the priest. I asked the adviser where he believed this strange idea had originated from. We both knew the answer and, realising that I was leading him he looked at me sharply before replying, 'Well Loudun, of course!'

The possession at Loudun must be the myth to end all myths. There were no demons at Loudun. It was simply a cold-blooded political murder. But to really understand Loudun, we must start with the possession in the Ursuline convent of Aix-en-Provence, nineteen years earlier.[12]

In 1605, at only twelve years of age, Madeleine de Demandolx de la Palud, the daughter of a wealthy and aristocratic Provencal family, entered the Ursuline convent at Aix. It was no ordinary religious community, consisting of only six nuns, all of noble birth. Within two years, Madeleine had developed the first symptoms of manic-depression. Severely depressed, she was released to her family, where she was greatly cheered by the regular visits of Father Louis Gaufridi, a family friend and the lighthearted and handsome parish priest of Accoules in Marseilles. To all accounts, Gaufridi was chaste but wiser heads cautioned against their regular liaisons.

Upon her return to the convent two years later, Madeleine confessed to intimacies with the priest. As the disease progressed into alternating periods of depression and mania, she had visions, danced and laughed, disrupted church services and told lurid stories of black sabbats. In an outbreak of hysteria, her symptoms were copied by the other nuns and one in particular, Sister Louise Capeau, who identified 6,666 devils who were possessing her and Madeleine. No doubt inflamed by sexual jealousy, Sister Capeau identified Father Gaufridi as the source of their bewitchment. He was, she told her exorcists, a black magician who had made a pact with the devil.

Various attempts at exorcism failed and the two women became the star performers in an affair whose notoriety soon spread across France. Finally, Gaufridi was led into a trap when he was ordered to exorcise the two nuns. He knew nothing of exorcism and the two nuns mocked him, claiming to remember carnal encounters during wild sabbats. The unfortunate priest was charged with witchcraft, tried by an ecclesiastical tribunal but released for lack of evidence.

His freedom was short-lived. The affair passed to the civil courts and into the hands of the notorious witch-finder, Sabastian Michaelis, the Grand Inquisitor of Avignon. In her more lucid moments during the trial, Madeleine confessed that her allegations were 'all imaginings, illusions and [had] not a word of truth in them'. It was too late. Under torture, Gaufridi admitted witchcraft but heroically refused to implicate other innocents in his 'crimes'. More dead than alive, he was strangled and his body burnt on 30 April, 1611. Madeleine survived him by sixty-one years but her florid episodes of insanity resulted in several more charges of witchcraft.

Nineteen years later, the story of the Aix-en-Provence nuns, which had been published in every country in western Europe, was to provide the blue-print for a murder. Father Urbain Grandier was not cast in the same heroic mould as Father Gaufridi. A dissolute man, he had openly made mistresses of his young penitents and was suspected of being the father of the child of Philippa Trincant, the daughter of the Loudun public prosecutor. He added one more enemy to the many in the town when he publicly lampooned the second most powerful man in France, Cardinal Richelieu, then temporarily out of favour with King Louis XIII. Grandier was charged with immorality by an ecclesiastical court on 2 June, 1630, and suspended from his duties as parish priest. Within a year this sentence had been revoked by his powerful political friend, Archbishop Sourdis of Bordeaux.

Never has fate placed so many conspirators together or provided them with such an opportunity for revenge. The Mother Superior of the Ursuline convent in Loudun, Sister Jeanne des Agnes, was related to one of Richelieu's cronies, Monsieur Jean de Laubardemont. One of her nuns, Sister Claire de Sazilly, was also related to the Cardinal. The convent's confessor, Father Mignon, was an avowed enemy of Grandier and the parents of Philippa Trincant had a powerful thirst for vengeance. The plot was quite simple: the Mother

The Sceptical Occultist

Superior and another nun practised altering their voices and looks and claimed to be possessed by evil spirits sent by Father Grandier.

As a result of the 'evidence' gathered by Father Mignon during his 'exorcisms', a charge of witchcraft was laid against the hapless priest. However, Archbishop Sourdis saw through this ruse and not only released Grandier but signed an order preventing Father Mignon from conducting further exorcisms at the convent. Urbain Grandier, over-estimating the political power of his friends, then took the offensive with a series of scurrilous pamphlets attacking Cardinal Richelieu. He would have done better to have read the account of the possessions at Aix-en-Provence.

Within weeks, Monsieur Jean de Laubardemont arrived in Loudun, using the pretence of overseeing the demolition of the town's fortified keep. In fact, Cardinal Richelieu's lieutenant was in Loudun to arrange Grandier's assassination. He did this by establishing a civil tribunal outside the Archbishop's control and then leading Grandier into the same trap as had been used at Aix, in forcing him to exorcise the nuns he had supposedly bewitched. This was fatal as the women, who had been coached in Greek and Latin, taunted Grandier with their ability to answer questions in these languages, thus apparently displaying the pre-eminent paranormal sign of 'real' possession. They also accused him of witchcraft and fornication. That was enough.

Urbain Grandier was lost and it mattered little that the Mother Superior, later struck by remorse, appeared in court with a rope around her neck, threatening to hang herself unless she was allowed to retract her evidence. Other sisters also withdrew their previous statements and even admitted details of the plot but the judges on the Cardinal's kangaroo court proved too clever for them. They argued that as the nuns had claimed to be possessed by the devil and it was known that the devil was a compulsive liar, the women's retractions were not admissible as evidence. After being so severely tortured that the marrow from his smashed bones seeped out through open wounds on his legs, Father Urbain Grandier was burnt alive on 18 August, 1634.

Demonic Possession

The nuns went through the pantomime of being publicly exorcised by the Capuchin, Father Tranquille, the Franciscan, Father Lactance, and the Jesuit, Father Surin. The exorcisms failed because although Cardinal Richelieu had granted the nuns a 'pension' for their part in his plot, the women found there was more money to be made by giving exhibitions of their 'possession' during town festivals. When the Cardinal's niece, the Duchess d'Aiguillon, reported these dangerous impostures to Richelieu, he immediately severed the pension and withdrew his protection. Now faced with the ever present threat of a charge of witchcraft against themselves, the nuns miraculously 'cured' their own possessions and withdrew into the secluded life of the convent.

There were no devils at Loudun, which makes the aftermath of this affair so incredible. Father Lactance managed to expel three 'demons' from the Mother Superior before becoming possessed himself. Within the space of a month, he lost his powers of sight, speech and memory and displayed several personalities of 'demons'. He died raving. Father Tranquille, another exorcist and one of Grandier's chief torturers, became 'possessed' and died five years later. On his death-bed he was attended by a Father Lucas and, in a powerful theatre, Lucas became possessed at the moment of Tranquille's death,

> For when Extreme Unction [sacrament for the dying] was administered to him (Father Tranquille) the demons, feeling the efficacy of this sacrament, were obliged to raise the siege; but it was not in order to go far away, inasmuch as they entered into the body of the good Father, a very excellent friar who was there present, and have always possessed him since . . . Thus at the moment of his death, in their fury and rage which they had because they could lay no further claim to him, they cried out horribly: 'He is dead!' as if to say: 'It is all over, we have no further hope of his Soul.' Thereafter, falling more fiercely than ever upon the poor friar [Father Lucas], they agitated him so strangely and terribly that although the Brethren who held him were quite numerous they could not prevent him aiming kicks at the dead man until he had been carried out of the room.

Tranquille may have been stricken by guilt but the same

cannot be said of Father Lucas and the other two Loudun exorcists who were unwitting dupes in Richelieu's plot. Father Surin, for example, was 'demonically obsessed' for the rest of his life and his letters, preserved at the Bibliothèque Nationale in Paris, reveal his belief in the reality of the possession and even Grandier's pact with the devil.

In his analysis of the possession of the Loudun exorcists, Professor Oesterreich believed that three factors were important: the exorcists had obsessive/compulsive personalities, they believed in the reality of possession and its contagious nature, and all three had been in the 'sight and company of possessed persons'.

He could be right. Three hundred years after Loudun, psychiatrists found themselves faced with many patients who believed themselves to be obsessed or possessed by demons as a result of seeing the film *The Exorcist*. In their papers, the doctors commented that no other Hollywood epic had ever produced this effect. All of the patients patently believed in the reality of possession; many admitted underlying conflicts in their lives and presented with symptoms of an obsessive/compulsive nature. Finally, the film had placed them in the 'sight and company of possessed persons' within a dramatic setting of contagious possession. Once again we see possession without demons.

Priests are damaged during exorcisms but it could be argued that they enter into these very powerful dramas perilously poised between a natural disbelief in the paranormal and a theological grounding in the reality of evil spirits. When something out of the ordinary occurs, such as objects moving by their own volition, an event witnessed by several credible parapsychologists in poltergeist cases, it is easy to jump to the conclusion that one is in the presence of embodied evil, with all that this entails.

A Catholic priest recalled how a colleague had been asked to attend an alleged case of possession in London. While he was reciting prayers over the child in the kitchen of the house, he was astonished to see a knife slowly move from the table and accelerate through the air to embed itself in a picture of the Sacred Heart. He suffered a nervous breakdown. Father

Demonic Possession

Hughes, who began the exorcism of Douglass Deen in a Georgetown hospital, was praying over the child who was apparently asleep, strapped to his bed, when somehow, the boy managed to free one of his hands. Working a bed-spring loose, the child used it as a crude knife, slashing the priest's arm so severely that it remained partially paralysed. Father Hughes took no further part in the exorcism but seemed to his colleagues 'haunted and withdrawn, as if he were forever looking inward'.

One Christian psychiatrist who believes in the reality of 'true' possession has written that the possessing entities are usually minor demons. *This is completely wrong.* In Japanese culture, the entity is a fox god ('magic fox'); in China and Laos, a serpent; in parts of Africa, a wild animal; in Vietnam, an ox or a tiger; and so on. When cultural beliefs are overlaid by Jewish, Christian and Moslem theology the entity can also take the form of a demon or a damned soul, reflecting fears of hell and damnation. Between 1954 and 1956, sixty-six men and women, all first admissions, were seen by the staff of the Hong Kong Mental Hospital. Twenty-two patients were possessed by the spirits of dead relatives; eighteen by gods of the Taoist-Buddhist Pantheon; seventeen by dead relatives and gods; two by cultural heroes (Sun Yet-sen and a legendary seer); and one each by Jesus Christ, God the Father, the Virgin Mary, an Indian Prince, and a living clairvoyant. The last two patients were possessed by fox and snake spirits respectively.

Nevertheless, alleged possession can be extremely convincing. In a famous case, described by the German psychologist Van Gennep, a man was possessed by a 'damned soul', '... Do not pray for the damned, for prayer is a torture in hell ... it is redoubling of pains ... I am speaking to you as a damned soul, do you hear? Do you understand? ... Do not follow my example.'[13] He continued to horrify his interrogators with stories of the punishments awaiting the wicked in hell. After this frantic monologue, one of the onlookers asked, 'Are your parents damned too?' To which came the reply, 'My parents are here, happily, for I can make them suffer.'

Suddenly a new personality appeared in the form of a demon who displaced the 'damned soul' and who then threatened to redouble his torments because he had 'unveiled the mysteries of hell'.

The effect of dramas such as this on the medieval mind can only be imagined! Such a powerful theatre as this might indicate the reality of true possession, yet the same sort of drama is experienced by psychiatrists treating patients with multiple personality disorder (MPD). Claiming to have experienced sadistic mental and physical cruelty in their childhood, these patients create alter-personalities to handle various aspects of everyday life which they find difficult or unpleasant. It is not uncommon for the psychiatrist treating an MPD patient to find himself faced with ten or more personalities competing for his attention, each with their own life-histories, likes and dislikes, faults and virtues. During the long period of psychotherapy required to treat MPD, the therapist attempts to fuse all the sub-personalities back into a single ego, hopefully combining all the strengths of the various alter-personalities.

Multiple personality disorder is not an uncommon illness and may represent a spectrum of severity, such that the milder cases may never present to a psychiatrist. It may explain both mediumship (but not the alleged associated ESP) and many cases of possession. Finally, alter-personalities are created with such ease that the therapist must be extremely vigilant to ensure that new personalities are not created as a result of the therapeutic process. In cases such as that described by Van Gennep, it is possible that in interrogating the 'damned soul' – simply an alter-personality which allows the patient to express his deepest terrors and conflicts in a way which avoids guilt and recriminations – the priest or doctor may induce the emergence of yet another personality (the 'demon') which seemingly adds coherence to the drama.

Clearly, much of possession is mental illness and in accepting this the case for the defence centres around the answer to several questions: Do priests see cases accompanied by the paranormal 'signs' of demonic possession? Have there been cases which were resistant to psychiatric help and yet cured by exorcism? Are there doctors outside the self-styled Christian psychiatrists who have taken on a case believing it to be mental illness but who have later become convinced that they were dealing with 'real' possession?

Such cases are very rare and my journey took me into a world sealed under layers of confidentiality. Through a series of personal contacts, I was able to speak to members of that tiny group of priests within the Catholic Church and the Churches' Council for Health and Healing who are entrusted by their diocesan bishops with handling Major Exorcisms. At every stage, assurances of confidentiality were demanded and freely given. The first case comes from a senior and highly respected minister of the Anglican Church.[14]

> In the past 15 years or more in which I have been involved in the Deliverance Ministry, I have only come across four cases where it seemed appropriate to carry out an exorcism. Three of these cases resulted in a considerable improvement whilst in one case it made no discernible difference. Two of these cases, including the one in which there was no improvement, took place at the request of psychiatrists and two others at the request of the local parish priest. I used to be the Diocesan Exorcist in the Diocese of — — and carried out three of the exorcisms while in — — . I have been in — — for seven years and have only carried out one case of exorcism.
>
> The Diocesan Bishop asked me to see a young woman. I always did so in the home of her parish priest and she would normally stay the weekend with him and his family so that she could receive protective care. She had been a member of his congregation since childhood. Her parents were also members of his congregation but had left when a number of black people began to join. They had strong racist views and were also involved in the occult. The young woman concerned had a reasonably responsible job and still lived with her parents with whom she had a love/hate relationship. They had always wanted a boy and not a girl and she was the only child. She told me that every day as a child she would be reminded that she ought to have been a boy and she would have been called Nigel. She was aware of her parents' racist views and [witch] coven membership although she could not recall being involved in the coven and made no allegations of ritual abuse. The main presenting symptom was a feeling that she had been taken over by another person who tormented her. I was told that whilst asleep

she could be observed telling the little man to go away and leave her alone. She also had outbursts of extreme violence including hitting her head against a wall whilst asleep.

The case met some of the criteria [traditional signs of possession]; there was occultism in the family, a reaction to holy things and the voice of a man whilst asleep. She attended church every week but felt unable to receive Holy Communion and often ran out of the church during a service. She would also destroy holy objects and frequently attacked her parish priest. When her priest prayed with her she would show a violent reaction and when trying to discuss her feeling of 'possession', she would continually change the subject or even disappear just before I called to see her. She believed in God but could not accept him as a loving father. She had met a psychiatrist who said that he could find no signs of psychiatric illness. She was also interviewed by a psycho-therapist who felt that she was so uncooperative that she would not be a suitable candidate for psychotherapy. There was no prior history of mental disorder or unusual physical illness.

The exorcism took place in the vicarage because she was too frightened for it to take place in the church. The parish priest and I were present and his wife was in an adjoining room. The young woman had not been told that I was coming at that particular time although she had agreed to the exorcism. Nevertheless, she was very frightened and it was felt that if she knew exactly when I was coming she would disappear. When I arrived she ran and locked herself in a bedroom and an hour later reluctantly unlocked the door. During the exorcism she reacted violently and struggled and had to be considerably restrained by her parish priest who is a large man and even he had difficulty in controlling her. She cried out, 'leave me alone, the little man will get you as well' and began to speak in the voice of the little man threatening to harm us and to harm her. The actual exorcism lasted about 15 minutes. After a considerable struggle, she collapsed and we placed her on a bed where she slept for twenty hours. When she recovered from her sleep, she felt released from the little man and was no longer afraid of holy things.

The immediate improvement was quite considerable and I visited her on a number of subsequent occasions to provide aftercare and to support her parish priest. Whilst she felt considerably better, we felt it right to carry out another exorcism although it was of a much less dramatic nature. Nevertheless, it did add to her improvement and her problems now seem permanently resolved.... My own view of exorcism is that it is not driving out spiritual entities from outside a person but exorcising deep unhealed parts of the unconscious which manifest themselves in unusual ways.

For this minister then, exorcism is an alternative psychiatric therapy, all the more powerful because it operates within the structure of the patient's beliefs. It is also obvious that the case above contains little challenge to the orthodox views held by many psychiatrists. This cannot be said of the next case which is certainly one of the few, perhaps the only, medieval-type case in Britain to have been documented in recent times.

As a young man, the Reverend Mr A. saw combat in the Second World War as an Intelligence Officer. He took part in the liberation of Europe and witnessed the horrors which awaited the British soldiers at Belsen concentration camp. He entered the Ministry in 1964 and his enthusiastic faith, military background and very sceptical approach to the paranormal made him an ideal minister to deal with alleged cases of possession.

I will answer for myself, and say at once that in 28 years as a minister, I have only performed one Major Exorcism of a person and three of places, although I have been asked time beyond count to 'do an exorcism' as though it was a matter of conjuring or catching mice. I will refer to a case where I did *not* do an exorcism. I was requested by a Diocesan to attend a large teaching hospital, where a consultant psychiatrist required help. He was an atheist and simply required an operation to be performed in the 'frame-work of the patient's belief-structure', as the psychiatrist had made no progress and was baffled. The patient claimed to be possessed by a demon, but it did not fit into my ideas of possession, nor did he react to the ancient tests for possession... Furthermore it occurrred to me that it was a poor sort of 'demon-personality/entity' which permitted its subject to ask for its expulsion. I believe that this patient was eventually exorcised by a wandering Charismatic and now accompanies him, being publicly exorcised at 'Healing Services' once a month or so.

But within the first year of the Reverend Mr A.'s ministry he was to have an experience which, he admits, he probably would not have believed had he not experienced it with his own ears and eyes.[15] It marked a watershed in his religious beliefs. Summoned by the then Bishop of Southwell, he was told, in the strictest confidence, of a case of possession which was tearing a small Nottinghamshire mining village apart. An old woman, who boasted that she was a witch, was apparently possessed by another personality who claimed to be a demon. Worse, it was reported by a local minister that she seemed suddenly endowed with the most amazing gift of clairvoyance/telepathy and was publicly airing the sexual indiscretions of her neighbours. Florid poltergeist activity accompanied the woman; tables, chairs and other objects would move about the room in her presence.

The Reverend A. chose an older man to be his assistant. He was an Anglican monk with extensive experience of the paranormal aspects of religion, gained in Swaziland and other overseas missions. The two exorcists were unknown in the village and the possessed had never travelled further than Nottingham. When they were brought into the old woman's presence, she immediately launched an attack on the Rev A.,

> On my entry, she at once called out my Christian and surnames, my army nickname and a great number of scandalous details about the lighter side of my army life: girls' names, places and what we had been doing. The monk silenced her. Ma [the old woman] sat on a chair, her daughter restraining her. No violence was offered. When peace had been restored – and my composure – the daughter told us that her mother had instituted a reign of terror amongst her family, friends and neighbours, by similar conduct over the past six weeks. Others later said it was six months. Poltergeist activity on a grand scale was also reported, but I did not actually see this.
>
> The monk then asked her a number of simple questions, which she answered. He then switched to an African tribal dialect and *she answered in the same dialect*! There is no way that I can think of to explain this! The exorcism was short and simply consisted of a command in the Name of Christ for the demon to leave and go to its own place harming no-one on the way. It was a success, the patient's powers [of clairvoyance] and the poltergeist activity ceased.
>
> No medical assistance was requested or available, as in those days no psychiatrist would have dreamed of coming. There was

Demonic Possession

no previous illness although she was described by her daughter as being a 'bloody-minded old cow'. Ma had been a high priestess of a witch coven operating in the remains of Sherwood Forest for many years. The monk and Ma are long since gone. The family remains protected. The patient was promised absolute confidentiality as were her family. This promise stands.

Here then is a case which tends to authenticate the medieval accounts of possession. The worldview that the paranormal is simply due to unsuspected laws of nature or human powers can account for the clairvoyance and poltergeist activity. Possession can be seen as a dissociative illness – an altered state of consciousness – which parapsychologists would argue unlocks the powers of telepathy and clairvoyance. Disturbed adolescents have been identified as the focus of poltergeist activity. The ability to converse in an unknown language is another matter. Experts argue that *skills* such as the ability to ride a bicycle, bake a perfect soufflé or speak a foreign language cannot be gained by mind-to-mind correspondence or clairvoyance. Skills require the essential ingredient of experience and that is why xenoglossy has always been the cardinal sign of 'real' possession. We have no documentary evidence of this woman's ability to speak in an African dialect and readers will have to come to their own decisions regarding this testimony.

When this case was written up, it was shown to a number of experts. A Catholic exorcist commented, 'Well, that was *his* experience.' An investigator who had witnessed paranormal events during two poltergeist cases asked in a sceptical tone of voice 'Do you believe this?' Another pointed out that this was only 'one case'. But how many cases do we need before we accept the *possibility* of 'real' possession; two, four, ten or even more? To believe what we experience with our own senses but to reject the experience of others is simply to experience the force of the 'lesser miracle'. But it is also a short road to solipsism or the belief that only one's self and one's own experiences have any reality or validity.

Do psychiatrists report uncanny experiences in possession cases? Certainly a number of doctors have reported medical conditions which although refractory to standard psychiatric treatment, were resolved by exorcism.

John (pseudonym) was born in 1952 to middle-aged American parents trapped in an unhappy marriage.[16] His father left when John was eight years of age. From his earliest memories John thought of himself as a girl. He rejected the games of his older brother, preferring to help his mother clean or do chores in the kitchen. At the age of four he began applying makeup and, shortly after, started cross-dressing in his sister's clothes. At Junior school his effeminate behaviour soon attracted the ridicule and scorn of his peers but this mattered little to John, who envied his mother and sister as females and hated his own masculinity.

At the age of fifteen, he read about trans-sexualism in a popular magazine and began corresponding with experts at the John Hopkins Hospital. Shortly after this, he dropped out of school and spent all of his time in the library intensively researching the subject. He learned of the effects of female hormones and was able to convince a physician that he was receiving female hormones for an endocrine disorder and needed additional prescriptions. The effects of the hormones (breast formation and the thinning of body hair) were discovered in 1969 after John was involved in a serious car accident. Still only sixteen years of age, he was referred to a psychiatrist. The discovery of John's trans-sexualism caused a rift with his family and he joined the Navy, in response to the demands of his mother and her friends to 'make a man of himself'. Immediately discharged after a psychiatric examination, he was referred to a team of psychologists and psychiatrists to begin preparations for the surgical operation which would give him all the secondary attributes of a woman.

He fulfilled all of the necessary criteria for this irreversible procedure: he had a steady job as manager of a fast food restaurant, he had normal male chromosomes and there was no evidence of mental illness or defective judgement. With help from his doctors, he began cross-living as a female in the winter of 1972. The influence of the female hormones was such that, even wearing a bikini, he could pass for a woman and he had progressed to a bra size 36B. Assuming the name of 'Judy', he dealt with all the legal aspects of his new identity and, in view of his excellent adjustment, he was referred to a medical centre in a nearby state for the final operation. In the summer of 1972, 'Judy' sent her doctors a postcard announcing that she had arrived at the clinic.

In late autumn, Dr David Barlow was sitting at his desk when a research assistant carrying a half-eaten lunch of fried chicken, rushed into his office shouting, 'Judy is back at the restaurant, but she's not Judy anymore, she's John!' Several months later John was invited back for another interview with his doctors. He entered the office wearing a three-piece business suit and polished shoes, his hair was short, his fingernails clipped and his speech and body language were consistently masculine. The only evidence of his former femininity was a lack of facial hair. When questioned about this amazing transformation, he enthusiastically related the following story.

John had promised the woman who owned the fast food restaurant where he worked that he would see a physician who practised in the same city before checking in to the female identity clinic. John had developed a close relationship with this woman who had a fundamentalist protestant faith which was quite foreign to John. The doctor, who was also a protestant fundamentalist, gave John a full medical examination and said that he would be able to live quite well as a woman but that the real problem was possession by evil spirits. John agreed to an exorcism which amounted to exhortations and prayers, while the physician laid his hands on John's head and shoulders. During this session, which lasted for two to three hours, John reported fainting several times as the doctor exorcised twenty-two demons, calling them by name as they left the patient's body. At the end of the exorcism, John reported feeling waves of God's love pouring over him. For the first time in his life, John felt like a man, and attempting to hide his breasts, he went to a barber's shop and had his hair cut short.

In a letter to John's physicians, the doctor who performed the exorcism confirmed the patient's story. The case presented John's psychologists and psychiatrists with an embarrassing conundrum. Leaving aside the demons and viewing the exorcism as psychotherapy did little to solve this mystery. John had no belief in possession and psychotherapy simply does not work in trans-sexualism. In their clinical report, the doctors concluded,

> Although most psychotherapists would not deny the role suggestion, instructions and persuasion [play] with many psychological disorders, what is important in the case is that no psychotherapeutic procedure of any kind, with whatever element of suggestion or persuasion, has been effective for trans-sexualism. ... What cannot be denied, however, is that a patient who was very clearly a trans-sexual, by the most conservative criteria, assumed a long-lasting masculine gender identity in a remarkably short period of time following an exorcism.

This is about as far as many psychiatrists are ever likely to go in admitting that a religious exorcism may be dealing with an alternative reality. This case appears to deny us the traditional escape of claiming that exorcism heals the patient's unconscious and only works because it operates with the 'structure of the patient's beliefs'. Anticipating the incredulity and hostility of their colleagues, Dr Barlow's team took the unusual step of prefacing the 'Conclusions' section of their paper with a quote from Lewis Carroll's *Through the Looking Glass*,

> 'I can't believe that,' said Alice.
> 'Can't you?' the Queen said in a pitying tone. 'Try again, draw a long breath, and shut your eyes.'

There is one psychiatrist who would want to go a lot further. Ralph Allison is a doctor who has specialised in the bizarre world of multiple personality disorder and who believes that he has been confronted with spirits and devils masquerading as alter-personalities. Working within shadowlands of psychiatry, Allison has provided us with a unique modern record of a conversation with a 'damned soul'.[17]

Elise was twenty-four years of age when she was first seen by Ralph Allison and she initially presented with sixteen alter-personalities governed by a hierarchy of five 'Inner Self Helpers'. All served a specific purpose in Elise's life and, true to the pattern in MPD, the girl would continually create new alters to handle relatively minor life problems such as deciding what to have for dinner or whether to go shopping or watch a film. The appearance of a new male alter calling itself 'Dennis' did not surprise her psychiatrist greatly as male alters are common in female patients who believe that their parents wanted a son instead of a daughter. In order to win their fathers' affections, these women will create a male alter to become the 'son' their fathers have always desired. But Dennis was neither a 'surrogate son' nor a typical alter-personality. He claimed to be a disembodied spirit inhabiting Elise's body because he was sexually aroused by 'Shannon' – a female alter which Elise created to handle the death of her baby, two years previously. Dennis appeared to serve no obvious purpose within Elise's hierarchy of alters and, most unusually, Allison was unable to pin-point the time of his 'birth' which is usually referenced to a specific life problem or trauma.

Allison remarked that he was 'completely taken aback by this story'. He had never encountered one alter-personality falling in love with another and indeed doubted that it was possible, even within the strange world of multiple personality disorder. Allison reasoned that Elise had never shown any lesbian tendencies, nor did she require a 'man' to handle any of the traumas in her life. Elise's Inner Self Helpers also claimed that Dennis was not an alter-personality but a spirit who would not be removed by 'fusion': the psychotherapeutic process used to integrate the alters into a single coherent personality.

Allison, unable to believe that he was actually confronted with a spirit, now felt that his only approach to banishing Dennis lay through the use of logic. In Ralph Allison's experience of MPD, logic had proved a powerful tool. In another case, a female patient assumed a male alter-personality while shopping in a department store but found herself in a fix when she wanted to use the toilet. After arguing with shop assistants, 'he' pushed 'his' way into the men's toilet and, stepping up to the urinal, discovered to 'his' horror that 'his' penis was missing. This instant castration unlocked the horrifying revelation that 'he' was really a woman and the male sub-personality receded into the mind for a long period. When it finally reappeared it was easily eliminated. Allison decided to use the same approach with Dennis but found himself pitched from psychiatry into a situation more familiar to the exorcist.

Allison asked Dennis how he expected to enjoy sex with Shannon, hoping that his logic would upset him. In a deep male voice, Dennis merely replied that whenever Shannon was in charge of Elise's body, he would enter the man she was dating and in that way enjoy the sensation. When Dennis finally disappeared, he was replaced by Shannon, who confirmed what he had said and reported that he would make his presence felt by pinching her after intercourse. She complained that usually none of the men she dated ever pinched her and it only happened when Dennis was in possession of their bodies. 'It was his "calling card" and she hated him for it.'

Allison decided to tape another interview with Dennis. 'I wanted proof so that I could report this startling information to others, and I wanted to be able to listen to the conversation again, to try to come to grips privately with what I'd inadvertently discovered.'

> Our conversation was general at first. Then I asked him how he had originally become acquainted with Shannon.
>
> 'I saw her out and I thought, Far out, hey, that's what I want!' he told me.
>
> 'Where were you at the time?' I asked.
>
> 'Out and about, doing my thing.'
>
> 'In somebody else or just floating between people?' I didn't really know what to ask or even what I meant by the question. Since he claimed to be a spirit, I assumed it was possible for him to be away from the body.
>
> 'I was in somebody else.'
>
> 'Why didn't you stay in that somebody else?'
>
> 'Because she [Shannon] didn't like him.'

Dennis then explained that he had wanted Shannon to develop a long-term relationship with a male, whom he could use as a 'permanent home', complaining that she was 'too picky'. He spoke about his love for Shannon and the fact that none of the other alter-personalities known to date men interested him in the slightest, despite the fact that they were all creations of the same mind.

Eventually I asked Dennis if he had ever had his own body. 'A long time ago,' he said with a touch of sadness.

'What did you do?'
'I was a stockbroker, till somebody shot me.'
'Where were you living?'
'Down south somewhere – Louisiana.'
'How old were you when you were shot?'
'I was about seventy.'
'Why were you shot?'
'Cause somebody pointed a gun at me and it went off!'
'I understand that, but I was wondering...'
'I was being robbed!'
'Oh okay. Were you a successful stockbroker?'

Dennis indicated that he had had only moderate success. He did enjoy the gambling aspect of the field, however.

'When were you shot... what year?'
'Nineteen forty-something. I don't remember.'
'... Name?'
'Julius.'
'Julius what?'
'That you will never know.'
'We have a lot of people buried in the cemetery out there,' I added. 'I always wondered what happens to their spirits when they go into the ground.'
'I'm not one of them.'
'I know you're not.'
'It's cold down there, and I decided, you know it's really weird, watching your own funeral. Why are we talking about this? Let's talk about Shannon.'

Dennis went on to relate the different people whom he had possessed since his death and his descriptions were marked by a cold, almost psychopathic, indifference to other human beings. He told Allison that he was 'assigned to each body' but that he never knew who or what assigned him.

Allison then talked about Dennis to Elise's major Inner Self Helper and was told that Dennis had entered Elise's body when she and a group of teenage friends had experimented with satanic black magic practices. Shortly after this, there was a most unusual occurrence. Under hypnosis, Elise was questioned by Ralph Allison about the satanic ritual as it provided a point of origin for 'Dennis'. Still under hypnosis, Elise was asked to listen to the taped interview with Dennis. Suddenly, Elise's eyes opened and a new personality appeared. Calling herself 'Michelle' she claimed to be 'against God' and taunted the psychiatrist with the promise that she would not leave Elise's body without a fight.

The situation was eventually resolved in time-honoured, hair-raising fashion. One evening Elise, in a ward of a California hospital, began to switch personalities every thirty seconds. The nurses were frightened and called Ralph Allison at home. When he arrived at the hospital, Allison and a nurse took Elise to a grassy knoll in the hospital grounds where she could writhe around without hurting herself. Suddenly she slumped to the ground and began screaming, 'Get out of my body! Get out! Get out!' A different voice from within Elise replied, 'I am not going to leave!' Then Elise screamed, 'If there is a God, help me!' Seconds later she became unconscious. She became hysterical again on the way back to the ward and let 'Sandi', an alter-personality, take over. Sandi reported seeing three dark blue spheres leaving Elise's mind. In the morning the major Inner Self Helper reported that Dennis, Michelle and one other spirit, whom Allison had never met, had all been expelled.

The 'Shannon' alter-personality, and object of Dennis's desire, later claimed to be the soul of Elise's baby and was removed in a similar cathartic event. Her last words were, 'I'll be dying in a few hours. I'll belong to another child, beyond Elise, in another time. I have given up my battle. I don't know why. She will have no dreams about me and will barely remember the child ... Her belief in God is becoming stronger.'

We have come full circle. At the beginning of this chapter we saw cases of possession through the eyes of medieval priests and we ended with the same strange phenomena seen from the perspective of a modern psychiatrist. I have too much respect for Ralph Allison and too much sympathy for the dilemma in which he found himself, to want to double-guess his expertise. But two points should be noted. Allison's case has a strong resemblance to that reported by the psychologist Van Gennep. In one case the second personality is a 'demon', in the other it is 'Michelle' who is 'against God'. Are they entities or alter-personalities created in response to the exorcist's/psychiatrist's interrogation of the patient? 'Dennis' also makes the classical mistake of describing his funeral from the point of view of an 'invisible man', rather than a disembodied intelligence. Many would argue that life without a body could only be a dream state and telepathy the only available contact with the living and the dead. But the philosophers could be wrong.

While researching this book, I was provided with a number of introductions to psychiatrists by way of medical associations such as the Royal College of Psychiatry in London. Many chose not to answer my enquiries. One replied in a terse note that even to ask these questions was, in itself, an indication of delusion. With this in mind, I will leave the last word to the respected academic, Anita Kohsen Gregory. It stands for all of the material which has been covered in this book.

Invited to write an introduction to a recent edition of Professor Oesterreich's standard text *Possession*, she recalled the story told by Jacob Fromer, a Russian Jew who watched the exorcism of a child possessed by a 'damned soul'. An enlightened man, Fromer believed he was observing a form of religious madness but left the house unable to credit his senses.

Under the Rabbi's interrogation, in a harsh male voice the 'entity' identified itself as 'Chaim ben Sarah'. Between insults and physical assaults on the exorcist, it claimed to have been the soul of a Jew who, after a life of study, had become alienated from his religion and turned to Christianity. Finally he had become an alcoholic and had drowned himself. After death, he had been evicted from heaven and then hell and was left to roam the earth. First he inhabited a pig. After it was slaughtered, he had taken possession of a horse and finally the girl Esther. At the climax of the exorcism, the child collapsed and, with a loud bang, a hole the size of a pea appeared in one of the windows of the room. Relating this story in his later autobiography, Fromer wrote, 'Now, that I write down my reminiscences I can, if I want to, describe all these people as fools. Who forbids it? I am sitting alone in my room. I have pen and paper and can think and write as I please.' Anita Gregory concluded her introduction with these words,

> Having studied these matters over a number of years, I feel rather like Jacob Fromer. It would be simple for me and acceptable to others if I were to say that all of these people were dupes, frauds, lunatics and psychopaths, and to suggest that this constituted some sort of explanation. Who forbids it? I am sitting in my study and have pen and paper and can write what I please. So I shall conclude by writing that the phenomena described by Oesterreich are very much in need of an explanation.

Summary of the Evidence

The prevailing medical view of possession is that it is a collection of major and minor psychiatric illnesses. Where a secondary personality is present, it may be imaginary or a real alter-personality arising from multiple personality disorder. It is claimed that the life-histories of the 'entities' are often vague and superficial because they are merely a creation of the sick person's mind and simply reflect their ability to construct these fantasies. Most psychiatrists would hold that the associated paranormal phenomena are simply the product of superstition and delusion. Caught up in the powerful drama of possession, people merely see what they expect to see.

The 'supernature' worldview argues that in some rare cases of possession there really are paranormal phenomena. The disturbed person is in an altered state of consciousness, which has been shown to unlock the 'gifts' of extra-sensory perception and spontaneous psychokinesis (poltergeist activity). This view holds that these rare cases of possession are just Psi phenomena and multiple personality disorder. There are real paranormal events but no spirits or demons.

Some theologians and psychiatrists consider that there are 'real' cases of demonic and spirit possession. A few argue that the key to unlocking possession involves seeing it as a 'both-and' rather than an 'either-or' situation. That is to say that possession can be both mental illness and spirit possession, each contributing to the other. The paranormal phenomena

Demonic Possession

may be real and can be a product of a disturbed mind or an attribute of spirit. It might be argued that extra-sensory perception (telepathy) and psychokinesis are the only ways in which any spirit can interact with the physical world. In cases of possession they are combined with xenoglossy, threats, and obscenities because these represent the entire 'box of tricks' at the disposal of a possessing entity. In other words, possession can be a manifestation of a reality beyond that described by science.

10

Explaining the Inexplicable

It is, of course, one thing to attempt to demonstrate the reality of paranormal phenomena and quite another to explain them in terms of science. Many and various explanations of the paranormal have been proposed, but nearly all these trade on the uncertainty in quantum mechanics or they appeal to metaphysical entities in Man's unconscious. Books have been devoted to this subject but none have offered any coherent or complete explanation of phenomena such as telepathy and ESP. However, their authors would all agree on one thing: everyone is waiting for a revolution in the scientific worldview. I suspect that if we ever come to understand the paranormal at all, it will require several such 'paradigm-shifts'.

Let us return to Barrie Colvin's case of 'Susan', her mother and the rapping entity 'Eric'.[1] Firstly, there was no compelling evidence that 'Eric' was a discarnate entity. The evidence suggested that 'Eric' was wholly dependent upon 'Susan' and had no reality as an historical person. There were underlying conflicts in the household and all of the evidence points to 'Eric' being the dramatic vehicle for the child's emotional problems, partly expressed as psychokinesis in the form of rappings. In addition, Susan's mother appeared to contribute to the phenomena and, like many poltergeist cases, there were associations with telepathy. To what extent can we explain this in terms of science or quasi-scientific hypotheses?

Ehrenwald's hypothesis provides an account of how telepathy comes about and its role in mother-child relationships. Other psychiatrists argued that telepathy may act as a compensation for a 'defect in the channels of conscious communication' (physical or mental impairment) or as a 'release' phenomenon, where conflicts and feelings escape repression

Explaining the Inexplicable

in the person's unconscious. Berthold Schwartz added that the actual events occurred at the intersection of the parent's and child's emotional needs.

Similarly, psychiatrists have reported patients who appeared to be the focus of poltergeist activity. Dr Joel Whitton, who was allowed to observe the 'Philip' experiments, believed that psychokinesis might also have its origins in the strange, frightening, helpless world of infancy.[2] During later emotional conflicts, patients regress to a more primitive level of functioning to escape overwhelming anxiety. Whitton believed that spontaneous psychokinesis was symptomatic of the ego's defences against anxiety and that poltergeist activity should be grouped with other symptom neuroses such as the conversion reactions of hysterical blindness or hysterical deafness. In conversion reactions, emotional conflicts become translated into physical illness.

Still we have the problem of explaining why so many poltergeist cases are centred on adolescents, often young girls, like 'Susan' and the children described by Bender and Roll. Barrie Colvin has suggested that an anxiety/hormone imbalance may provide the necessary physiological setting for the release of spontaneous psychokinesis.[3]

The main events in the 'Eric' case took place just prior to 'Susan' starting to menstruate. This is not an isolated observation. In an ongoing case which also centres around a young girl, it soon became clear to the child and her mother, and indeed to the investigators, that the disturbances were peaking and following a monthly cycle. The girl and her mother, avid fans of astrology, ascribed this to the 'influence of the Moon'. The more obvious explanation was that it was influenced by the girl's menstrual cycle. When, in the 1940s, Harry Price investigated the case of Eleanore Zugun, he noted in his report, 'With the first sign of the menses, Eleanore's phenomena completely stopped.' Again, A. R. G. Owen, whose wife Iris was a member of the 'Philip' group, recorded a 28-day cycle of events at the famous poltergeist case at Sauchie in Scotland which also focused on a young girl, Virginia Campbell.

The essence of Colvin's hypothesis is that some pubescent

girls experience anxiety due to the physiological changes in their bodies and the psychological stresses of growing up. Some of the young girls associated with poltergeist activity have shown symptoms of anxiety-related illnesses such as St Vitus's dance and Sydenham's chorea – frequently seen in children at the age of puberty. Colvin points to the association between anxiety and the non-release of gonadotrophin hormones; and between high oestrogen levels and anxiety-linked illnesses such as chorea. Anxiety can result in the gonadotrophins not being released by the pituitary gland which in turn results in the absence of menstrual periods, high oestrogen levels and anxiety – some of which are translated into recurrent spontaneous psychokinesis. This hypothesis provides an explanation for those poltergeists centring around pubescent girls but one would have to propose other physiological mechanisms for those cases apparently focusing on boys and adults.

So far, these hypotheses have said nothing about the physical nature of the telepathic impulse or the psychokinetic force. In parapsychology's heyday of the 1960s, telepathy was an attractive and seemingly accessible phenomenon for physicists and engineers who had become interested in the results coming out of the university labs. Mathematical treatises were published which showed that telepathy was possible; many envisaged it as a new form of energy which worked in much the same way as radio waves.

A perusal of spontaneous cases reported to the various societies should have warned these investigators that it could not be quite that simple. For instance, the strength of electromagnetic radiation declines with distance (the inverse square law), requiring a large power-output in cases where, say, telepathy is reported between individuals on opposite sides of the world.

Then there is the problem of specificity. How was it that a new form of 'radio waves' were correctly addressed to the target and not other members of the family or indeed other good 'receivers' such as 'psychics'? There is also the problem discussed in chapter four, where several people see an apparition and all see the figure from their own unique perspective. This

Explaining the Inexplicable

is not so puzzling when we consider that, for a telepathic message to be 'received', it has to be processed by a brain – and, in the case of apparitions, projected on to a person's visual field.

Yet another problem arises with the other ESP phenomena such as clairvoyance and precognition. While we can conceive of communication between two minds, how can we explain how the human mind acquires knowledge that is not in other minds or learns of events which have yet to occur? It was for this reason that many held that telepathy was the only form of ESP. Pure clairvoyance remained a puzzle but precognition might still be explained in terms of telepathy, if it was assumed that the agent responsible for sending the information was an observer at some future event. Precognition, then, might be telepathy from the future.

Neither telepathy nor psychokinesis yielded to conventional physics. Neither did it seem that known types of energies could account for many of the aspects of telepathy or poltergeist cases. This has led to the belief that ESP and psychokinesis may hint at a deeper structure to the universe. Faced with the strange micro-world of quantum mechanics, physicists have certainly contemplated such ideas. Werner Heisenberg, reflecting on the role of measurement and the observer in quantum mechanics, finally decided that the structure of the universe consisted of two levels: the world of actuality – the reality experienced by ourselves and experimental physicists – and the reality from which it is constructed: the deeper reality of potential ('potentia').

A similar idea has been proposed by the mathematician and mystic, Michael Whiteman, to explain ESP and psychokinesis.[4] Whiteman believed that 'paranormal' events occur in the sub-structural or potential universe, transcending the constraints of the actual physical universe. He envisaged telepathy as the mutual resonance of the 'thought image spheres' of the agent and the recipient. Physical distance is not 'actualised' at the level of potentia and is therefore not a consideration. He believed clairvoyance to be the interaction between the 'impersonal potentialities of a physical event' and the 'thought image potentials' of an individual, which would leave an impression in the individual's mind of that physical event. He considered precognition to result from a similar interaction between a person's 'thought image sphere' and the 'potentiality spheres of physical manifestation'. Again, time is not an element in this interaction because physical time is manifested in the actual world and not in the deeper reality of potentia. Finally, psychokinesis would be a sort of 'reverse clairvoyant interaction' between an individual's 'thought image sphere' and the 'potentiality sphere' of some physical manifestation that is resonating with it.

The physicist, David Bohm, has developed similar ideas based on the notion of enfolded, or *implicate*, order in which the 'whole of the universe is in some way enfolded in everything and that each thing is enfolded in the whole ... The external relationships are then displayed in the unfolded or *explicate* order in which each thing is seen as separate and extended and related only externally to other things.'[5] Bohm too believes that his ideas shed light on the strange world of ESP and psychokinesis.

> Indeed, especially at the level of wavefunctions of higher orders, one might say that contact can depend more on similarity or 'resonance' of meanings than location in space. On this basis, psychokinesis could arise if the mental processes of one or more people were focused on meanings that were in harmony with those guiding the basic processes of the material systems in which this psychokinesis was to be brought about ... Telepathy and transmissions of thoughts and dreams can always be looked at as particular forms of psychokinesis, which act directly from brain to brain to convey thoughts or dream images.

It is interesting that both Whiteman's and Bohm's ideas link telepathy with psychokinesis. However it would be foolish to suggest that they provide anything approaching complete explanations for psychokinesis and ESP. What we have, in sum, is a range of unconnected explanations which offer an account of these phenomena at different levels.

Is there any evidence that the strange worlds of quantum mechanics and paranormal phenomena may overlap? One of the enigmatic aspects of quantum mechanics is that particles such as electrons appear to enjoy particle/wave duality, manifesting themselves as either a particle or a wave depending on the design of the experiment. As quantum objects, they are described only by a wavelike quantity which specifies the probability of an attribute taking one or more of its potential values when actually measured. At the moment of measurement, all uncertainty disappears as only one of the possible values of the attribute is singled out by the measuring device. But what is it about the act of measurement which brings about the so-called collapse of the state vector? Some physicists have argued that only human consciousness can bring about the collapse or that, in some way, the human observer helps to create reality.

The parapsychologist, Helmut Schmidt, had been conducting PK tests based on sequences of random binary numbers.[6] Electrons emitted by the decay of Strontium-90 triggered a Geiger counter and the momentary position of a binary high frequency counter at the time an electron was registered determined whether a $+1$ or a -1 was generated. The numbers of electrical pulses produced on the $+1$ output and the -1 output were recorded by two electromechanical reset counters, and the complete sequence of generated numbers was recorded on paper punch tape. A sequence of four million numbers generated over different days produced a series of $+1$s and -1s entirely consistent with randomness.

Under experimental conditions, the $+1$ or -1 numbers were recorded by a visually stimulating circle of nine lights. One light was illuminated at a time; each time $+1$ or -1 was generated, the light jumped one step in the clockwise or counter-clockwise direction, respectively. During experiments, subjects with a proven ability in other PK-tests, such as influencing the fall of a dice, were asked to 'will' the light on the display panel to advance in an overall direction (usually clockwise). Some of Schmidt's subjects produced statistically significant deviations from randomness. The deviations were either positive (more $+1$s) or negative (more -1s).

Schmidt then asked if these results were in accordance with the 'quantum collapse model'. Could his subjects influence series of numbers after they had been generated, provided that nobody had listened to them in the meantime?

Blocks of 201 binary numbers were generated and recorded on to six 'primary' tapes at a rate of twenty numbers per second, each block separated by 20-second intervals. The +1s and −1s were registered as clicks in the right and left channels of a stereo cassette recorder. The first three primary tapes were then copied on to one-channel tapes, such that each +1 or −1 appeared on these secondary tapes as a weak (+1) or loud (−1) click. Nobody was present during the generation and recording and the primary tapes were not examined until after the experiment.

The secondary tapes were then given to the subjects, who were told to listen to them at their leisure in the comfort of their own homes and thus probably under the conditions most conducive to PK. The subject was asked to ignore the loud clicks and to 'will' an increased number of weak clicks.

Only after the subjects had reported listening to their secondary tapes, were the +1s and −1s on the corresponding *primary tapes* electronically counted. In a pilot run with a Mr Lalsingh Harribance as the subject, blocks of numbers with more +1s (weak clicks) exceeded the blocks of numbers with more −1s (loud clicks) by 236 to 189 respectively. Schmidt also obtained statistically significant results with other subjects. Later, Schmidt showed that only the *first* attempt to influence the number of clicks had any effect, all in accordance with the laws of quantum mechanics.

> The result suggests that the first PK effort has a stronger, or even the only, effect on the outcome, as if the first observation of the scores would lock in the result, blocking all further PK effects. Taking the quantum collapse model seriously, one would say that the first observation collapses the wave function, forcing nature into a fully determined state that leaves no room for [additional] PK effects.

What of the more extreme events, such as those reported by witnesses in the Cardiff poltergeist disturbances? The conservation laws tell us that objects cannot simply pop in and out of existence; while that part of Einstein's special theory of relativity dealing with the equivalence of mass and energy, indicates the phenomenal release of energy that would result from the dematerialisation of just one of the coins which

Explaining the Inexplicable

appeared to fall from the workshop ceiling. Consequently, when objects appear to materialise out of thin air, or disappear from a closed space by passing through a physical barrier, it is clear that something else must be happening.

The answer may lie with the old concept of higher space. If space has one more physical dimension than the three of which we are aware, objects would enjoy a fourfold freedom of movement. Consequently, objects apparently passing through physical barriers might really be traversing higher space. In the early years of this century, the famous German physicist, Ernst Mach, discussed higher space in purely mathematical terms. Mach could find no scientific evidence for the concept but decided that the sudden disappearance and reappearance of objects would be the best evidence for higher dimensions of space.

Cardiff presents us with a very strange case. The disturbances appeared to focus on no one individual in particular. Paul was at the centre of many of these events but certainly not all. For example, Paul was on holiday and Michael was the only one present when Fontana conducted one of his reciprocal stone-throwing experiments. The British and Canadian sitter-group experiments suggest that poltergeist activity which manifests as an entity can arise from the group psyche. Psychiatrist Joel Whitton believed that regression was an important factor in the 'Philip' experiments.

> In the Philip experiment regression was attained by consciously attempting to be child-like – by singing children's songs and deliberately behaving like children. In this regressed condition, thinking takes on a magical quality. As opposed to the adult who states that moving or levitating tables by thought is against the laws of physics and therefore impossible, the child simply states, 'If I want it to happen, it will.'

However, Whitton believed that, even in the regressed condition, each individual's ego will not accept the fact that the self has the power to move objects at a distance – or in poltergeist cases that the disturbances result from emotional conflicts – and consequently the phenomena are projected out on to an imaginary external entity. In the Canadian experiments, the group's deliberate focus was 'Philip'; in Colvin's case, 'Eric' and in the Cardiff case, 'Pete'.

The men in the Cardiff workshop treated the phenomena in a light-hearted, almost childish manner. They were not afraid of the disturbances; they played games with 'Pete' and challenged 'him' to perform tasks. And correspondingly 'Pete' performed the sort of pranks associated with schoolboys. After two years of living with an invisible 'schoolboy', and believing that the disturbances *were* caused by a discarnate entity, is it strange that one of the men should finally conjure an apparition of a child? The figure had no face, legs or hands but Paul clearly saw the short trousers and Cub's cap. Were these just symbols which identified the figure as a 'small boy'? From his description, the figure was also diminutive, prompting comparisons with the 'Lilliputianism' described in hypnogogic hallucinations, apparitions of the Virgin Mary and alleged encounters with aliens.

In the light of the sitter-group experiments, we can account for some of the extreme phenomena reported at Cardiff. Batcheldor's group reported objects, such as stones and matches appearing as if by magic and the 'Philip' group reported the movement of a table at an apartment on the other side of the city. Still these experiments fall far short of providing a complete explanation for what happened at Cardiff. I leave it to the reader to decide whether they are best explained by the presence of a discarnate entity.

If there are such entities, if there are ghosts, it must be said that we find it very difficult to separate them from subjective hallucinations. Even when the context of the apparition seems to provide additional evidence that it is more than an hallucination, such as the Chaffin Will case, other less marvellous explanations can always be found. And yet, some anecdotes seem to argue for the figure being independent of the observers.

We face the same problems with collectively perceived apparitions. There is always the possibility that one of the people in the room has created an hallucination, which is then shared with the others by way of telepathy. And yet, some cases seem to argue for the apparition being independent of the observers.

By now, the reader will have drawn his own conclusions

about the possibility of telepathy. It remains for the author to point out that for centuries people have known that there was something 'strange' about ghosts; that they could only be seen by some people or under special conditions. A ghost story related by an unknown Irish author in the ninth century tells of two foster-brothers who pondered on the eternal question of what happens to us after death.[7] 'It is a sad journey on which our dear ones and friends go from us, that they never come back again with news for us of the land to which they go. Let us make a plan, that whoever of us dies first should come back with news of the other. Let it be done truly.'

The terms of the compact were that whoever died first would appear to the other within one month. Not long after the compact was made, one of the brothers died. The other waited, but no apparition appeared. At first he prayed for the soul of his brother to appear but as time progressed he fell to cursing God and the Trinity.

Then the living brother suffered a near fatal accident and experienced an out-of-the-body experience. Leaving his body, his soul went to the church, where he saw the spirit of his departed brother.

'Well now', the soul said, 'you have been a long time in coming; yours was a bad promise.' 'Do not reproach me,' said the other, 'I have come many a time, and would be beside your pillow pleading with you and you did not hear; for the dense heavy body does not hear the light ethereal tenuous soul.' 'I hear it now,' it said. 'No,' said the other, 'it is your soul only that is here. It is from your own body that you are escaping. . . . Go and find your body before it is put in the grave.'

Even if this story was better authenticated, it does not provide evidence for a ghost because psychologists would classify the out-of-the-body experience as another kind of hallucination. And yet, it is clear that people have reported these experiences for many centuries. Are 'ghosts' just hallucinations derived from archetypes and shared mythology? Or do we truly survive death? A final answer requires us to embark on that 'sad journey'. As a Dominican philosopher once remarked to the author, if there is nothing after death, we will not be worrying about it, but if something of us does survive, there will be cause for much rejoicing.

The behaviour of our second class of apparition, the haunting ghost, also suggests an independence of observers. However, in this case the recurrent apparition is place-centred. Hauntings and some apparitions hint at retrocognition, or the experience of seeing the past, but we must face the embarrassing fact that many haunting ghosts *cannot* be identified with an historical person.

The evidence suggests that at least some of the Marian apparitions are simply subjective hallucinations. We see reflected in the apparition's messages both cryptic references to the early family life of the seer and fears which are troubling the seer's community. On 30 May, 1950, Mary Ann Van Hoof's apparition told her, 'You took punishment for others to protect them. You received no love which you longed for in your home. You always worked hard and were honest to your family. Yes, you committed sins, your surroundings were more to blame than you.'

The messages of Mary Ann's apparition were also concerned in part with the 'Brown Bear' (Russia), Soviet mini-submarines penetrating the St Lawrence Seaway and a Zionist conspiracy to rule the world in the form of the 'Learned Elders of Zion': a conspiracy theory based on a novel written in the thirties and much publicised in the 1940s by Nazi Party propaganda.

Reporting the findings of a commission established to investigate Mary Ann's apparitions, Father Claude Heithaus, speaking at Marquette University on 14 July, 1955, said that Mary Ann and her mother, Elizabeth Bieber, had lived in fear of Mary Ann's abusive father. As a child Mary Ann had been repeatedly beaten by her father, and her dislike of him approached hatred.[8] Mary Ann's view of America was of a vulnerable nation threatened by a hostile, dangerous and unpredictable neighbour. Many psychologists would argue that childhood trauma leads to a paranoid view of the world, in which events are interpreted as part of a conspiracy, all of which can later become projected on to an hallucination of a religious figure.

Explaining the Inexplicable

The apparitions of other seers can be interpreted in the same light. America in the late 1970s was concerned with the second OPEC oil embargoes of 1978–79, which resulted in price rises and further limitations of supply. Then early on Sunday morning, 4 November, 1979, America suffered her greatest humiliation since the withdrawal of American troops from Vietnam, when some 500 Iranian revolutionary guards and students seized the American Embassy in Teheran and imprisoned the occupants. On Thursday 24 April, 1980, another humiliation was suffered when an attempt to rescue the hostages using commandos ground to a halt in the desert of southern Iran. The hostages were finally released after 444 days in captivity. In the aftermath of this crisis, on February 28, 1982, Eileen George, a resident of Worcester, Massachusetts, and the mother of eight children, alleged that God the Father had graced her with a vision of the Anti-Christ who was to bring about the apocalypse.[9]

> The war is not going to come till later, because we are going to be fighting about oil. Then the Antichrist is going to arise from the Mohammedan race, a Moslem. He is going to have a turban. The people will call it 'the eye of Satan.' ... My Father said he is already planning it. They are building up arms ... He is connected with the Russians, the communists. He will be very intelligent and well equipped for nuclear war ... This Moslem is going to fire rockets at us ...

Many would argue that Mrs George's vision of the apocalypse simply mirrored fears prevalent in America at that time. In this vision of the apocalypse, we see reflections of the anti-Western stance of the Ayatollah Khomeini's revolutionary government in Iran, the OPEC oil crisis and ongoing preoccupations with the Cold War, all intermingling in a conspiracy theory.

Other Marian apparitions are more complex. At La Salette, Lourdes, Fatima, Garabandal and Medjugorje the seers were poorly-educated children from simple rural communities. They are part of a tradition which, in Catholic countries such as Spain and Italy, can be traced back to the fifteenth century. La Salette, the first secular apparition of modern times, introduced the tradition of secrets. Twelve years later at

Lourdes, serial apparitions were introduced, and the resulting tradition was later refined at Fatima by the addition of visions of angels and miracles. At Garabandal, visions of angels and alleged public miracles became the most outstanding features of the apparition.

Pointing to this pattern, psychologists argue that this results from the seers modelling their hallucinations on previous apparitions of the Virgin Mary. But is such perfect imitation really within the capabilities of these village children? And what of the two seers at La Salette? Did they have the knowledge to model their experiences on the Marian tradition of the fifteenth century? If this is wholly imitation, what was it that was watched and photographed above the Coptic church at Zeitoun? Surely we should consider the possibility that there is an independent and external entity which is refining its performance at each successive apparition.

In these complex cases, the 'hallucination' controls the situation, manipulating not only the seers but the community and church authorities. It is the vision which sets the time-frame, often predicting the date of the final apparition. The lady is often collectively perceived and her appearances are associated with paranormal phenomena; while the testimony of witnesses credits the seers with the gift of prophecy. Against this we have our justified unwillingness to associate secret messages, flawed prophecies, cryptic messages and the often strange appearance and behaviour of the apparition with a supernatural Intelligence.

Some writers and parapsychologists have attempted to solve this riddle by invoking 'thought forms' or artificial entities created by psychic energy. Some Christians believe that prayer can create thought forms, such that a deeply devout mother who prays for angels to protect her young child can literally will non-physical beings, independent of both the mother and the child, into existence. This has been the position of Scott Rogo, while Michael Talbot preferred to see the Virgin of Zeitoun as a 'psychic hologram'.[10] They would argue that the apparition's messages and prophecies of an impending apocalypse are simply a reflection of the community's 'collective unconscious' disturbed by perceived external

Explaining the Inexplicable

threats. Consequently, we find the vision's messages perplexing because we are attempting to decipher our own riddles.

Unfortunately, this explanation begs too many questions. For example, why do these 'psychic holograms' appear to some people and not to others? Why do we see a progression of increasingly complex apparitions from La Salette to Medjugorje? Why are these experiences associated with children from simple rural communities? Why do they almost exclusively centre on the Virgin Mary and why are the lady's warnings always depicted in terms of the Revelations of St John the Divine?

Even if we dismiss all of the Marian tradition as hallucinatory and we reject the many photographs of the Virgin of Zeitoun as fakes, we are still left with the testimony of the many thousands of people who witnessed this public apparition, among them Cynthia Nelson who was honest about her desire to rationalise the figure in terms of an illusion. Can we, then, on the basis of the evidence, construct a case for some of the Marian apparitions representing the real presence of a spiritual entity? I believe that we can, but I fear that the resulting analysis will please neither the devoutly religious or those wishing to seek an explanation for these phenomena purely in terms of the scientific worldview.

The evidence from some of the apparitions can be interpreted as representing an interface between God and Man. The interface is manifested not as the historical Mary but rather as a religious figure – the Virgin Mary. Its appearance is friendly and tailored to its audience. To some children in fifteenth century Spain it appeared simply as a child. The Virgin has also appeared as a young woman or has resembled the familiar religious icons of the Virgin Mary. Angels and Archangels at Fatima and Garabandal appeared not at the head of a heavenly army but as young boys. The apparition speaks as a mother would speak to her child. It is the apparition's message which matters and not its assumed identity and for this reason it is reluctant to identify itself and allows the seers to impose their own identification. At Fatima the apparition was initially described by Lucia as a 'lovely lady brighter than the sun' (the woman in Revelations) but on 13 October it also appeared as 'Our Lady of Sorrows' and 'Our Lady of the Rosary': two purely devotional forms of the Virgin Mary. These are the 'masks of God'.

The serial apparitions, secrets, messages and miracles are all part of a drama which turns an essentially private experience into a public spectacle, ensuring that the apparition site becomes a focus of devotion and a source of spiritual energy.[11] In this way its messages are broadcast to the widest possible audience, despite local religious and political expediencies. It becomes a grass-roots phenomenon which bypasses the church hierarchy.

Nevertheless, there is another essential component of the interface: the seer. The drama is all the more powerful and convincing because the seers are often simple children. Children from a devout rural community have a simple faith and may be more likely to carry the message without much elaboration or interpretation. And yet some interpretation and elaboration must take place. Lucia de Santos wrote three *Memoirs* covering her experiences. These were written between eighteen and twenty-four years after the events at Fatima and included pages of monologue representing the apparition's messages and secrets. Is it possible that, after all this time, these were word-perfect? Did twelve-year-old Ines Martinez simply misunderstand the apparition's promises relating to the time that her hand would be released from its paralytic contortion? Is it the human aspect of the interface which results in the flawed prophecies?

Because we have difficulty in accepting the authenticity of these apparitions, we analyse these brief encounters in fine detail, consequently finding it impossible to reconcile all of the narrative with divine omniscience. But does any of this detract from the apparition's message? Would the apparition at La Salette have had a wider following if the Virgin had noted that one of the very frightened children spoke French imperfectly? Much of the Virgin's message was concerned with a decline in religious faith. The apparition's concerns about men blaspheming in the fields and boys not going to Mass may appear trifling to us but were readily understood and remembered by the children and surely just as easily understood by the townsfolk.

Explaining the Inexplicable

Many of the apparitions' secrets and messages have centred around future chastisements and Mary's interventions on Man's behalf. More recently, they have concerned an end-time and a final apocalyptic war. The seers have warned that these will be accompanied by public miracles and signs at Garabandal and Medjugorje. At Medjugorje the Virgin told the seers that this was to be the last Marian apparition, while 'Conchita' Gonzalez-Gonzalez was told by her apparition that 'after Pope John [Pope John XXIII], there will be three more popes, one will reign only a short time, and then it will be the end of times'.[12] Within a relatively short time history will test, and possibly falsify, these statements. We shall then be left to ponder why the subjective hallucinations of village children consistently mirrored the writings of an early Christian mystic, John the Divine.

We tend to associate the idea of reincarnation with Eastern mystical writings. Professor Ian Stevenson's research strips away the mysticism. Stevenson has found no evidence for retributive Karma – simply reincarnation. Nowhere in his papers does Stevenson find it necessary to underpin his ideas with a supernatural reality. It is not even necessary to invoke the idea of a soul surviving bodily death, as the Treravada Buddhists hold the doctrine of *anatta* or 'no soul', where at death it is the person's last mental processes which in some way activate a new body.

Some of the most hardened sceptics, whom I interviewed during this project, claimed, despite their personal beliefs, to be impressed by Stevenson's evidence. I introduced the 'Trojan Horse' of falsification to underscore what I believe to be inconsistencies in the evidence. Falsification in science is rarely that simple, but I think that more attention should be paid to the reincarnation-type cases which appear moulded by cultural beliefs or those individual cases where the evidence suggests that the child, and the person whom the child claimed to have been in a previous life, were both alive at one and the same time.

Possession and demonic possession are very strange concepts to the modern mind. Nevertheless, cases of possession which appear to be more than mental illness are still reported by priests and doctors. We have the alter-personalities in MPD patients which claim to be spirits, rare cases of exorcism accompanied by the traditional 'signs' of 'real' possession and intractable medical conditions which were abruptly terminated by exorcism.

Modern psychiatry tends to dismiss such accounts as fantasies but psychiatry, as a proto-science like parapsychology, has no monopoly on the truth. Advances in psychiatry have not been arrived at by theory and experiment but by serendipity. Psychiatry's standards of normality are drawn from the culture in which psychiatrists find themselves. Spirit possession is deemed a normal religious manifestation in Haiti but would probably be diagnosed as schizophrenia or possession-syndrome in London or New York.

Psychiatry's reliance on cultural norms has led to more than one iniquity being perpetrated in the name of science. Until quite recently, British and American psychiatrists condemned unmarried mothers to long periods of confinement in mental institutions. In America, in the thirties and forties, people unfortunate enough to be epileptic, simple or just plain poor, were forcibly sterilised, while patients showing 'antisocial' tendencies were reduced to a vegetative state by lobotomy. In the former Soviet Union, dissidents, and those attempting to escape to the West, were confined in mental hospitals and treated with psychotropic drugs by doctors who believed that any rejection of Soviet society was in itself self-evident proof of a severe personality disorder or schizophrenia.

Not surprisingly, there is not even a uniform agreement on psychiatric diagnoses. In a famous American investigation, a team of psychiatrists, psychologists and other volunteers had themselves admitted to psychiatric hospitals on the basis of very minimal symptoms.[13] This ruse was never exposed during medical consultations. Even when one volunteer, a graduate psychologist, had his wife bring in his textbooks and even held therapy groups for the patients, his real identity and purpose were never discovered by the staff. Ironically, it was the patients who frequently saw through the ruse, confronting the investigators with the charge that they were 'college professors, checking up on them'. When *On Being Sane in Insane*

Places was finally published in a top American science journal, it was reported that unfortunate individuals with real symptoms were being turned away from hospitals on the suspicion that they were members of the investigation team. When psychiatrists make statements condemning parapsychology and the occult, they are preaching from a self-erected pedestal built on sand.

Like Jacob Fromer and Anita Gregory, I am alone in my room and I can write as I please. So I will conclude by writing that I believe that the paranormal topics discussed in this book present us with real and intriguing problems. However, their ultimate solution will require us to suspend our beliefs and pay more attention to the 'gems of fact'.

Appendix
Useful Contact Addresses

The following people and organisations can provide access to professional investigators and advice for members of the public on the subjects covered in this book.

Telepathy in children:	Dr Terry White, c/o The Society for Psychical Research, 49 Marloes Road, London, W8 6LA.
Poltergeist Phenomena:	The Honorary Spontaneous Cases Liaison Officer, The Society for Psychical Research, 49 Marloes Road, London, W8 6LA.
	Dr Barrie Colvin, Poltergeist Research Institute, P.O. Box 118, East Winch, King's Lynn, Norfolk, PE32 1ND.
	Cheltenham Psychic Research Group, 22 Cleeveland Street, St Peters, Cheltenham, Gloucestershire, GL51 9HN.
Apparitions and hauntings:	The Honorary Spontaneous Cases Liaison Officer, The Society for Psychical Research, 49 Marloes Road, London, W8 6LA.
	Cheltenham Psychic Research Group, 22 Cleeveland Street, St Peters, Cheltenham, Gloucestershire, GL51 9HN.
Reincarnation:	Professor Ian Stevenson MD, Division of Personality Studies, Box 152, Health Sciences Center, University of Virginia, Charlottesville, Virginia 22908, USA.

Appendix Useful Contact Addresses

Possession: Christian Exorcism Study Group, The Churches' Council for Health and Healing, St Marylebone Parish Church, Marylebone Road, London, NW1 5LT.
Dr Terry White, c/o The Society for Psychical Research, 49 Marloes Road, London, W8 6LA.

Chapter Sources

Chapter One: Of Philosophers and the Evidence for Miracles

1. David Hume's essay, *Of Miracles*, is Section X of his *An Enquiry Concerning Human Understanding*.
2. Coincidence and miracles: Blackmore, Susan, Psychic Illusions, *Edinburgh International Science Festival Parapsychology Conference 18 April, 1993*, abstract printed in the *Psi Researcher*, No 10, Summer, 1993.
3. Antony Flew's interpretation of Hume's essay: Flew, Antony, The Problem of Evidencing the Improbable and the Impossible in *Exploring the Paranormal: Perspectives on Belief and Experience* Zollschan, G. K., Schumaker, J. F., and Walsh G. F., (eds), Prism Press, Dorset, 1989.
4. Distinguishing knowledge from belief: Hamlyn, C. W., *The Theory of Knowledge*, Macmillan, London, 1970.
5. The Glasgow miracle: Hickey, Des, and Smith, Gus., *Miracle*, Hodder & Stoughton, London, 1978.
6. Stephan Ossowiecki: Barrington, Mary Rose, Stephan Ossowiecki, *Psi Researcher*, No 10, Summer 1993.
7. John Beloff's investigation into the Ossowiecki experiments: Beloff, John, *The Relentless Questions: Reflections on the Paranormal*, McFarland & Co, Inc, Jefferson, North Carolina, 1990.
8. The letter (part) Hume wrote to the Reverend George Campbell is to be found in the 'Introduction' to Hume, David, *A Treatise of Human Nature*, Penguin, Harmondsworth, 1969.
9. The modern Catholic Church and miracles: interview with Monsignor M.

Chapter Sources

10. The moving statue in Malta: Thurston, Herbert, *Beauraing and Other Apparitions: An Account of Some Borderland Cases in the Psychology of Mysticism*, Burns, Oates and Washbourne Ltd, Great Britain, 1934.
11. Annual miracles: Rogo, Scott D., *Miracles*, Aquarian Press, London, 1983.
12. The Census Question: Sidgwick, H., Johnson, A., Myers, F. W. H., Podmore, F., and Sidgwick, E., Report of the Census of Hallucinations, *Proceedings of the Society for Psychical Research*, 10, 25–422, 1894.
13. Apparitions and telepathy: Sidgwick, E. M., (ed), *Phantasms of the Living*, Arno Press, New York, 1923/1975.
14. The problem of fraud and the Census Question: Tyrrell, G. N. M., *Apparitions*, Society for Psychical Research, London, 1943/1973.
15. Recent studies using the Census Question: Palmer, John, A Community Mail Survey of Psychic Experiences, *Journal of the American Society for Psychical Research*, 73, 221–51, 1979.
16. The Oxford survey of apparitions: Green, Celia, and McCreery, Charles, *Apparitions*, Hamish Hamilton, London, 1975.
17. Interpretation of Rees's data and apparitions as hallucinations: McCreery, Charles, interview and McCreery, Charles, *Hallucinations of the Sane*, D.Phil thesis, Oxford University.
18. Post-bereavement hallucinations: Rees, Dewi, W., The Hallucinations of Widowhood, *British Medical Journal*, 4, 37–41, 1971.
19. LSD-induced post-bereavement apparition: Masters, R. E. L., and Houston, Jean, *The Varieties of Psychedelic Experience*, Turnstone Books, London, 1973.
20. The Freiburg study: Sannwald, Gerhard, On the Psychology of Spontaneous Paranormal Phenomena, *International Journal of Parapsychology*, 5, 274–90, 1963.
21. Psi and Australian Aborigines: Hausfeld, Russell, private communication.
22. The medical evidence for telepathy: Ehrenwald, Jan, The Telepathy Hypothesis and Schizophrenia, *Journal*

of the American Academy of Psychoanalysis, 2, 159–69, 1974 and Ehrenwald, Jan, Mother-Child Symbiosis: Cradle of ESP, *Psychoanalytical Review*, 58, 455–66, 1971.

23. Telepathy in children: Rhine, L. E., *The Hidden Channels of the Mind*, William Sloane Associates, New York, 1961; Burlingham, D., Child Analysis and the Mother, *Psychoanalytic Quarterly*, 4, 1935; Schwarz, B. E., Telepathic Events in a Child Between One and Three and a Half Years of Age, *International Journal of Parapsychology*, 3–4, 5–52, 1961: and FitzHerbert, J., The Role of Extrasensory Perception in Early Childhood, *Journal of Medical Science*, 106, 1960.

24. Telepathy in severely handicapped children: Recordon, E. E., Stratton, F. J. M., and Peters, R. A., Some Trials in a Case of Alleged Telepathy, *Journal of the American Society for Psychical Research*, 44, 390–99, 1968; Drake, Raleigh M., An Unusual Case of Extra-Sensory Perception, *Journal of Parapsychology*, 2, 184–98, 1938; Ehrenwald, J., Hirnpathologische Bemerkungen zu einem Falle von "Paranormalen" Erscheinungen bei einem Kinde (Ferdinand von Neureiter), *Zeitschrift fur die gesamte Neurologie und Psychiatrie*, Nr 132, 1931; and Bender, Hans, The Case of Ilga K.;Report of a Phenomenon of Unusual Perception, *Journal of Parapsychology*, 2, 5–22, 1938.

25. ESP, Australian Aborigines and the Lizzie Williams experiments: Rose L., Psi Patterns amongst Australian Aborigines, *Journal of the American Society for Psychical Research*, 45, 71–6, 1951; Rose L., and Rose, R., Psi Experiments with Australian Aborigines, *Journal of Parapsychology*, 15, 122–131, 1951; Rose, R., Psi and Australian Aborigines, *Journal of the American Society for Psychical Research*, 46, 17–28, 1952; and Rose, R., *Living Magic*, Rand McNally, New York, 1956.

Chapter Two: Telepathy

1. Mrs Y.'s Case: interview with author.
2. Lake Coniston case: Gurney, E., Myers, F. W. H., and Podmore, F., *Phantasms of the Living*, 1, 188.

3. The case of 'Bo': Drake, Raleigh, M., An Unusual Case of Extra-Sensory Perception, *Journal of Parapsychology*, 2, 184–98, 1938.

4. The case of Ilga K.: Ehrenwald, Jan, *Telepathy and Medical Psychology*, George Allen & Unwin Ltd, London, 1947; and Bender, Hans, The Case of Ilga K.; Report of a Phenomenon of Unusual Perception, *Journal of Parapsychology*, 2, 5–22, 1938.

5. The 'Cambridge Boy': Recordon, E. G., Stratton, F. J. M., and Peters, R. A., Some Trials in a Case of Alleged Telepathy, *Journal of the Society for Psychical Research*, 44, 390–99, 1968.

6. The medical evidence for telepathy: Ehrenwald, Jan, Psychopathological Aspects of Telepathy, *Journal of the Society for Psychical Research*, Part 163, 1940; Ehrenwald, Jan, *Telepathy and Medical Psychology*, George Allen & Unwin Ltd, London, 1947; Ehrenwald, Jan, *New Dimensions of Deep Analysis: A Study of Telepathy in Interpersonal Relationships*, George Allen & Unwin Ltd, London, 1954; Ehrenwald, Jan, Human Personality and the Nature of Psi Phenomena, *Journal of the American Society of Psychical Research*, 62, 366–80, 1968; Ehrenwald, Jan, Mother-Child Symbiosis: The Cradle of ESP, *Psychoanalytical Review*, 58, 455–66, 1971; Ehrenwald, Jan, The Telepathy Hypothesis and Schizophrenia, *Journal of the American Academy of Psychoanalysis*, 2, 159–69, 1974; Burlingham, D., Child Analysis and the Mother, *Psychoanalytic Quarterly*, 4, 1935; Schwarz, B. E., Telepathic Events in a Child Between One and Three and a Half Years of Age, *International Journal of Parapsychology*, 3–4, 5–52, 1961; and FitzHerbert, J., The Role of Extrasensory Perception in Early Childhood, *Journal of Medical Science*, 106, 1960.

Chapter Three: Psychokinesis and Poltergeists

1. French police investigations into poltergeists: Tizane, Emile, *Sur la Piste de l'Homme Inconnu. Les Phenomenes de Hantise et Possession*, Paris, 1951.

2. History of poltergeists: see Owen, A. R. G., *Can We Explain the Poltergeist?*, Garrett Publications, New York, 1964.
3. Poltergeist activity associated with possession: see Oesterreich, T. K., *Possession Demoniacal and Other*, Kegan Paul, Trench, Trubner & Co Ltd, London, 1930.
4. Poltergeists as discarnate entities: see Stevenson, Ian, Are Poltergeists Living or Are They Dead?, *Journal of the American Society for Psychical Research*, 66, 233–52, 1972 and Gauld, Alan and Cornell, A. C., *Poltergeists*, Routledge & Kegan Paul, London, 1979.
5. Paranormal phenomena in poltergeists: interview with Barrie G. Colvin.
6. 'Poltergeists' with a normal explanation: Cornell, A. C., The Intelligence behind Poltergeists; and Gauld, A., What have we learnt about Poltergeists, *SPR Study Day No. 23, Poltergeists*, 25 April, 1992.
7. The German poltergeist cases: Bender, Hans, New Developments in Poltergeist Research, *Proceedings of the Parapsychological Association*, No 6, 1969.
8. Person-centred poltergeist cases in America: Roll, W. G., Poltergeist Phenomena and Interpersonal Relations: *Journal of the American Society for Psychical Research*, 64, 130–45, 1973.
9. The 'Eric' Case: interview with Barrie G. Colvin and The Character of Percussive and Related Sounds in Recurrent, Spontaneous Psychokinesis (RSPK), *International Conference*, City University, 14 April, 1977.
10. The Cardiff poltergeist: Fontana, David, A Responsive Poltergeist: A Case From South Wales, *Journal of the Society for Psychical Research*, 57, 385–402, 1991; and Fontana, David, The Responsive South Wales Poltergeist: A Follow-Up Report, *Journal of the Society for Psychical Research*, 58, 225–31, 1992.
11. Batcheldor's sitter-experiments: Batcheldor, Kenneth J., Report on a Case of Table Levitation and Associated Phenomena, *Journal of the Society for Psychical Research*, 43, 339–56, 1966; and Batcheldor, Kenneth J., Contributions to the Theory of PK Induction from Sitter-Group Work,

Chapter Sources

Journal of the American Society for Psychical Research, 78, 105–21, 1984.
12. The 'Philip' experiments: Owen, Iris M., with Sparrow, M., *Conjuring Up Philip: An Adventure in Psychokinesis*, Fitzhenry & Whiteside, Toronto, Canada, 1976; and Owen, Iris M., 'Philip's Story Continued', *New Horizons*, April 1975.
13. Failure to translate to the laboratory: Isaacs, Julian, The Batcheldor Approach: Some Strengths and Weaknesses, *Journal of the American Society for Psychical Research*, 78, 123–31, 1984.

Chapter Four: Ghosts

1. Jack Wilson's 'little grey man': Siegal, Ronald K., *Fire in the Brain: Clinical Tales of Hallucination*, Dutton, New York, 1992.
2. Officer in the Indian Army: Gurney, E., Myers, F. W. H., and Podmore, F., *Phantasms of the Living*.
3. 'Mass Hallucination': Price, H. H., Preface to Tyrrell, G. N. M., *Apparitions*, Society for Psychical Research, London, 1943, 1973.
4. Mrs Percival of Cape Town: Bennett, Ernest, *Apparitions and Haunted Houses*, Faber and Faber, London, 1939.
5. Agnes McCaskill's ghostly knight: *Journal of the Society for Psychical Research*, 6, 135.
6. Mr Z.'s haunting: Bennett, Ernest, *Apparitions and Haunted Houses* Faber and Faber, London, 1939.
7. Ruth: Schatzman, Morton, *The Story of Ruth*, Duckworth & Co Ltd, London, 1980.
8. Analysis of collective apparitions: Tyrrell, G. N. M., *Apparitions*, Society for Psychical Research, London, 1943, 1973.
9. Mrs Clerke's brother: Gurney, E., Myers, F. W. H., and Podmore, F., *Phantasms of the Living*.
10. Reverend Jupp's apparition: Sidgwick, E., Notes on the Evidence, Collected by the Society for Phantasms of the Dead, *Proceedings of the Society for Psychical Research*, III, 69–150, 1885.

11. Father's apparition seen by nurse: Jaffe, Aniela, *Apparitions and Precognition*, University Books, New York, 1963.
12. Apparition of mother over dying child (H.G.): G. 275 Collective Apparition, *Journal of the Society for Psychical Research*, XI, 185–7, 1904.
13. Mother's apparition in Malta: Gurney, Edmund, and Myers, F. W. H., On Apparitions Occurring Soon After Death, *Proceedings of the Society for Psychical Research*, V, 403–85, 1888–1889.
14. Lukianowicz, N., Hallucinations à Troix, *Archives of General Psychiatry*, 1, 322–37, 1959. For Hilary Evans's comments see: Evans, Hilary, Ghosts: Fact or Fantasy?, SPR lecture 11.2.93. Lecture cassette available from SPR, 49 Marloes Road, London, W8 6LA.
15. Reverend Father C. (Catholic priest): Bennett, Ernest, *Apparitions and Haunted Houses*, Faber and Faber, London, 1939.
16. Chaffin Will Case: Case of the Will of James L. Chaffin, *Proceedings of the Society for Psychical Research*, XXXVI, 517–24, 1928.

Chapter Five: Hauntings

1. The Morton Ghost: Morton, R. C., Record of a Haunted House, *Proceedings of the Society for Psychical Research*, VIII, 311–32, 1892.
2. The underground stream hypothesis: Lambert, G. W., The Cheltenham Ghost: A Reinterpretation, *Journal of the Society for Psychical Research*, 39, 267–77, 1958.
3. Recent sightings: MacKenzie, Andrew, Continuation of the 'Record of a Haunted House', *Journal of the Society for Psychical Research*, 55, 25–32, 1988.
4. The apparition of the music teacher: Murphy, Gardner, and Klemme, Herbert, Unfinished Business, *Journal of the American Society for Psychical Research*, 60, 306–20, 1966.

Chapter Six: The Marian Apparitions

1. The apparition seen by Ines Martinez: Christian, William

Chapter Sources

A., *Apparitions in Late Medieval and Renaissance Spain*, Princeton University Press, New Jersey, 1981.

2. 'Our Lady of Guadalupe': Rogo, Scott D., *Miracles*, The Aquarian Press, London, 1983, 1991.

3. Marian apparitions as hallucinations: in Zimdars-Swartz, S. L., *Encountering Mary: From La Salette to Medjugorje*, Princeton University Press, New Jersey, USA, 1991; Carroll, Michael P., Visions of the Virgin Mary: The Effect of Family Structures on Marian Apparitions, *Journal for the Scientific Study of Religion*, 22, 205–21, 1983; Carroll, Michael P., The Virgin Mary at La Salette and Lourdes: Whom Did the Children See?, *Journal for the Scientific Study of Religion*, 24, 56–74, 1985 and Carroll, Michael P., *The Cult of the Virgin Mary: Psychological Origins*, Princeton University Press, 1986.

4. Thurston's interpretation of various apparitions: Thurston, Herbert, *Beauraing and Other Apparitions: An Account of Some Borderland Cases in the Psychology of Mysticism*, Oates and Washbourne Ltd, Great Britain, 1934; and Thurston, Herbert, *The Physical Phenomena of Mysticism*, Henry Regnery Company, Chicago, 1952.

5. The apparition at Fatima: see Zimdars-Swartz, S. L., *Encountering Mary: From La Salette to Medjugorje*, Princeton University Press, New Jersey, USA, 1991.

6. The apparition at Garabandal: Pelletier, Joseph, *Our Lady comes to Garabandal*, Assumption Publications, Worcester, Mass., 1971; and Zimdars-Swartz, S. L., *Encountering Mary: From La Salette to Medjugorje*, Princeton University Press, New Jersey, USA, 1991; Sanchez-Ventura y Pascual, F., *The Apparitions of Garabandal*, San Miguel Publishing Co, Detroit, Michigan, 1966; and Perez, R., and Orhelein, A., (eds), *Garabandal: The Village Speaks*, The Workers of Our Lady of Mount Carmel, Lindenhurst, NY, 1971.

7. The apparition at Zeitoun: Nelson, Cynthia, The Virgin of Zeitoun, *World View*, 16, 5–11, 1973; Rogo, Scott D., *Miracles*, Aquarian Press, London, 1983; and Palmer, Jerome, *Our Lady Returns to Egypt*, Culligan Publications, San Bernardino, California, 1969.

Chapter Seven: Miraculous Cures

1. The surgeon's letter: in Nelson, Cynthia, The Virgin of Zeitoun, *World View*, 16, 5–11, 1973.
2. Professor West's analysis of the miracles at Lourdes: in West, D. J., *Eleven Lourdes Miracles*, Duckworth & Co, London, 1957.
3. Discrepancies in medical diagnoses: Decision Making: Professional Judgement, Course D 300, Open University.
4. Stephen Black's work: in Black, Stephen, *Mind and Body*, William Kimber, London, 1969; and Mason, A. A., and Black, S., Allergic Skin Responses Abolished under Treatment of Asthma and Hayfever by Hypnosis, *Lancet*, i, 1129–35, 1958.
5. The Glasgow Miracle: see Hickey, Des, and Smith, Gus., *Miracle*, Hodder & Stoughton, London, 1978.
6. Coley's toxins: Coley, William B., A Report of Recent Cases of Inoperable Sarcoma Successfully Treated with Mixed Toxins of Erysipelas and Bacillus Prodigiosus, *Surgery, Gynecology and Obstetrics*, 13, 174–90, 1911; and Coley-Nauts, Helen, Swift, Walker E., and Coley, Bradley L., The Treatment of Malignant Tumors by Bacterial Toxins as Developed by the Late William B. Coley, M.D., Reviewed in the Light of Modern Research, *Cancer Research*, 6, 205–16, 1946.

Chapter Eight: Returning from the Abyss? Reincarnation

1. The case of Ma Tin Aung Myo: in Stevenson, Ian, The Southeast Asian Interpretation of Gender Dysphoria: An Illustrative Case Report, *Journal of Nervous and Mental Disease*, 165, 201–8, 1977.
2. An Analysis of 'solved' and 'unsolved' cases: Cook, Emily, Williams, Pasricha, Satwant, Samararatne, Godwin, Maung, U, Win, and Stevenson, Ian, A Review and Analysis of "Unsolved" Cases of the Reincarnation Type: I. Introduction and Illustrative Case Reports, *Journal of the American Society for Psychical Research*, 77, 45–62, 1983; and Cook, Emily, Williams, Pasricha, Satwant, Samararatne, Godwin, Maung, U, Win, and Stevenson, Ian, A

Review and Analysis of "Unsolved" Cases of the Reincarnation Type: II. Comparison of Features of Solved and Unsolved Cases, *Journal of the American Society for Psychical Research*, 77, 115–35, 1983.

3. Phobias in reincarnation-type cases: Stevenson, Ian, Phobias in Children Who Claim to Remember Previous Lives, *Journal of Scientific Exploration*, 4, 243–54, 1990.

4. The case of Reena Kulshreshtha: Mills, Antonia, A Replication Study: Three Cases of Children in Northern India Who Are Said to Remember a Previous Life, *Journal of Scientific Exploration*, 3, 133–84, 1989.

5. The importance of source amnesia: see Stevenson, Ian, Cryptomnesia and Parapsychology, *Journal of the Society for Psychical Research*, 52, 1–31, 1983.

6. Ian Wilson's refutation of regression cases: see Wilson, Ian, *Mind Out of Time*, Victor Gollancz Ltd, London, 1981.

7. The Hindu/Moslem cases: Mills, Antonia, Moslem Cases of the Reincarnation Type in Northern India: A Test of the Hypothesis of Imposed Identification Part 1: Analysis of 26 Cases, *Journal of Scientific Exploration*, 4, 171–88, 1990.

8. Congenital circumcision as a rare disorder: James, Theodore, Aplasia of the Male Prepuce with Evidence of Hereditary Transmission, *Journal of Anatomy*, 85, 370–72, 1951; and James, Theodore, A Causerie on Circumcision, Congenital and Acquired, *South African Medical Journal*, 45, 151–54, 1971.

9. American cases: see Stevenson, Ian, American Children Who Claim to Remember Previous Lives, *Journal of Nervous and Mental Disease*, 171, 742–8, 1983.

10. The religious beliefs of the Gitksan and Beaver Indians: Mills, Antonia, A Preliminary Investigation of Cases of Reincarnation Among the Beaver and Gitksan Indians, *Anthropologica*, XXX, 23–59, 1988; and Mills, Antonia, A Comparison of Wet'suwet'en Cases of the Reincarnation Type with Gitksan and Beaver, *Journal of Anthropological Research*, 44, 385–415, 1988.

11. Jung on Soul Splitting: see Jaffe, Aniela, *Apparitions and Precognition*, University Books, New York, 1963.

The Sceptical Occultist

12. The 'Titu' case: see Mills, Antonia, A Replication Study: Three Cases of Children in Northern India Who Are Said to Remember a Previous Life, *Journal of Scientific Exploration*, 3, 133–84, 1989.
13. Saving anomalous cases from falsification: author's correspondence with Ian Stevenson.
14. The 'Sharada' case: see Stevenson, Ian, A Preliminary Report of an Unusual Case of the Reincarnation Type with Xenoglossy, *Journal of the American Society for Psychical Research*, 74, 331–48, 1980; and Akolkar, V. V., The Search for Sharada, *Journal of the American Society for Psychical Research*, 86, 209–47, 1992.

Chapter Nine: Demonic Possession

1. The confrontation between Christian fundamentalism and occult groups: see Parker, John, *At the Heart of Darkness: Witchcraft, Black Magic and Satanism Today*, Sidgwick & Jackson, London, 1993.
2. St Norbert's exorcism: Von Gorres, Joseph, *Die christliche Mystik* reproduced in part in Oesterreich, T. K., *Possession Demoniacal and Other*, Kegan Paul, Trench, Trubner & Co Ltd, London, 1930.
3. Dialogues of Lucian: Lucian, The Lover of Lying, *Dialogue 16*. Complete works, C. Jacobitz, Teubner series.
4. The Lutheran boy's exorcism: see Allen, Thomas, *Possessed*, Doubleday (Transworld), New York, London, Ontario, Sydney, 1993.
5. New physiognomy and change in voice: in Kerner, Justinus, *Nachricht von dem Vorkommen des Besessenseins*, Stuttgart and Augsburg, 1836; reproduced in part in Oesterreich, T. K., *Possession Demoniacal and Other*, Kegan Paul, Trubner & Co Ltd, London, 1930.
6. The exorcism conducted by Father Aurelian and Father Remigius showing a fear of religion and super-human strength: *Am Ausgang des neunzehnten Jahrhunderts*, Barmen, 1892; reproduced in part in Oesterreich, T. K., *Possession Demoniacal and Other*, Kegan Paul, Trubner & Co Ltd, London, 1930.

Chapter Sources

7. The case of Hilary: Furman, Robin, and Martingale, Moira, *Ghostbusters UK: A Casebook of Hauntings and Exorcisms*, Robert Hale, London, 1991.
8. William Blatty's novel: Blatty, Wiliam Peter, *The Exorcist*, Anthony Blond, London, reprinted 1985.
9. Dr Newton Malony's view of possession: correspondence with author.
10. The Catholic priest's investigation of the American serviceman's child: interview with author.
11. Catholic spiritual adviser's view of possession: interview with author.
12. The possessions at Aix-en-Provence and Loudun: Huxley, Aldous, *The Devils of Loudun*, Harper and Brothers, New York, 1953; Robbins, Rossell Hope, *The Encyclopedia of Witchcraft and Demonology*, Spring Books, London, 1959; Surin, Jean Joseph, *Histoire abregee de la possession des Ursalines de Loudun et des peines du pere Surin*, Paris, 1928; Oesterreich, T. K., *Possession Demoniacal and Other*, Kegan Paul, Trench, Trubner & Co Ltd, London, 1930.
13. Van Gennep's case: Van Gennep, *Archives de Psychologie, 10*, 92, 1911; reproduced in Oesterreich, T. K., *Possession Demoniacal and Other*, Kegan Paul, Trench, Trubner & Co Ltd, London, 1930.
14. The case of the 'little man': correspondence with author.
15. The case related by the Reverend Mr A.: correspondence and interview with author.
16. The trans-sexual case: Barlow, David H., Abel, Gene G., and Blanchard, Edward B., Gender Identity Change in a Transsexual: An Exorcism, *Archives of Sexual Behaviour, 6*, 387–95, 1977.
17. The case of Elise and the conversation with 'Dennis': Allison, Ralph B., with Ted Schwarz, *Minds in Many Pieces*, Rawson, Wade Publishers Inc, New York, 1980.

Chapter Ten: Explaining the Inexplicable

1. The 'Eric' poltergeist: interview with Barrie G. Colvin and The Character of Percussive and Related Sounds in Recurrent, Spontaneous Psychokinesis (RSPK), *International Conference*, City University, 14 April, 1977.

2. Joel Whitton's analysis of PK: in Owen, Iris M., with Sparrow, M., *Conjuring Up Philip: An Adventure in Psychokinesis*, Fitzhenry & Whiteside, Toronto, Canada, 1976.
3. Colvin's anxiety/hormonal imbalance hypothesis: in Related Sounds in Recurrent, Spontaneous Psychokinesis (RSPK), *International Conference*, City University, 14 April, 1977.
4. Michael Whiteman's philosophy: Poynton, John, 'Whiteman's Philosophy of Space and Time', SPR lecture 16.9.93. Lecture cassette available from SPR, 49 Marloes Rd, London W8 6LA.
5. David Bohm's philosophy: see Bohm, David J., A New Theory of the Relationship of Mind and Matter, *Journal of the American Society for Psychical Research*, 80, 113–35, 1986.
6. Helmut Schmidt's experiments: Schmidt, Helmut, Precognition of a Quantum Process, *Journal of Parapsychology*, 33, 99–108, 1969; Schmidt, Helmut, A PK Test with Electronic Equipment, *Journal of Parapsychology*, 34, 175–81, 1970; Schmidt, Helmut, PK Effect on Pre-Recorded Targets, *Journal of the American Society for Psychical Research*, 70, 267–91, 1966; and Schmidt, Helmut, Addition Effect for PK on Prerecorded Targets, *Journal of Parapsychology*, 49, 229–43, 1985.
7. Ninth century ghost story: Jackson, Kenneth, Hurlstone, No 229. A Ghost Story, in *A Celtic Miscellany*, Penguin, Harmondsworth, Middlesex, 1971.
8. Mary Ann Hoof's apparitions of the Virgin Mary: in Zimdars-Swartz, S. L., *Encountering Mary: From La Salette to Medjugorje*, Princeton University Press, New Jersey, USA, 1991.
9. Eileen George's apparition of the Virgin Mary: in Flynn, Ted, and Flynn, Maureen, *The Thunder of Justice*, MaxKol Communications, Inc, VA 20165, USA, 1993.
10. Marian apparitions as thought forms and holograms: see Rogo, Scott D., *Miracles*, The Aquarian Press, London, 1983, 1991; and Talbot, Michael, *The Holographic Universe*, Grafton Books, London, 1991.
11. The Marian apparitions as dramas: see Zimdars-Swartz,

S. L., *Encountering Mary: From La Salette to Medjugorje*, Princeton University Press, New Jersey, USA, 1991.
12. Apocalyptic warnings in the Marian apparitions: see Flynn, Ted, and Flynn, Maureen, *The Thunder of Justice*, MaxKol Communications, Inc, VA 20165, USA, 1993.
13. The American evaluation of psychiatric diagnoses: Rosenhan, D. L., On Being Sane in Insane Places, *Science, 179*, 250–58, 1973.

Selected Bibliography

Anon, Case of the Will of James L. Chaffin, *Proceedings of the Society for Psychical Research*, XXXVI, 517–24, 1928.

Anon, Cases: G. 275 Collective Apparition, *Journal of the Society for Psychical Research*, XI, 185–7, 1904.

Anon, Cases Received by the Literary Committee, *Journal of the Society for Psychical Research*, VI, 179–87, 1893–1894.

Akolkar, V. V., The Search for Sharada, *Journal of the American Society for Psychical Research*, 86, 209–47, 1992.

Allen, Thomas, *Possessed*, Doubleday (Transworld), New York, London, Ontario, Sydney, 1993.

Allison, Lydia W., Note on Securing Survival, *Journal of the American Society for Psychical Research*, 39, 210–15, 1945.

Allison, Ralph B., with Ted Schwarz, *Minds in Many Pieces*, Rawson, Wade Publishers Inc, New York, 1980.

Allison, Ralph B., The Possession Syndrome on Trial, *American Journal of Forensic Psychiatry*, 6, 46–56, 1985.

Anderson, R. A., A History of Witchcraft: A Review with Some Psychiatric Comments, *American Journal of Psychiatry*, 126, 1727–35, 1970.

Anderson, Rodger J., Commentary on the Akolkar and Stevenson Reports, *Journal of the American Society for Psychical Research*, 86, 249–56, 1992.

Appleyard, Bryan, *Understanding the Present*, Pan Books, London, 1992.

Van Asperen de Boer, S. R., Barkema, P. R., and Kappers, J., Is it Possible to Induce ESP with Psilocybine? An Exploratory Investigation, *International Journal of Neuropsychiatry*, 5, 447–73, 1966.

Aug, R. C., and Ables, B. S., Hallucinations in Nonpsychotic Children, *Child Psychiatry and Human Development*, 1, 152–67, 1971.

Selected Bibliography

Balducci, Corrado, Parapsychology and Diabolic Possession, *International Journal of Parapsychology*, 5, 193–207, 1963.

Barlow, David H., Abel, Gene G., and Blanchard, Edward B., Gender Identity Change in a Transsexual: An Exorcism, *Archives of Sexual Behaviour*, 6, 387–95, 1977.

Barrington, Mary Rose, Stephan Ossowiecki, *Psi Researcher*, No 10, Summer 1993.

Batcheldor, Kenneth J., Report on a Case of Table Levitation and Associated Phenomena, *Journal of the Society for Psychical Research*, 43, 339–56, 1966.

Batcheldor, Kenneth J., Contributions to the Theory of PK Induction from Sitter-Group Work, *Journal of the American Society for Psychical Research*, 78, 105–21, 1984.

Beloff, John, Extreme Phenomena and the Problem of Credibility in *Exploring the Paranormal: Perspectives on Belief and Experience*, (Zollschan, G. K., Schumaker, J. F., and Walsh, G. F., eds), Prism Press, Dorset, 1989.

Beloff, John, *The Relentless Question: Reflections on the Paranormal*, McFarland & Co, Inc, Jefferson, North Carolina, 1990.

Bender, Hans, New Developments in Poltergeist Research, *Proceedings of the Parapsychological Association*, No 6. 1969.

Bender, Hans, The Case of Ilga K.: Report of a Phenomenon of Unusual Perception, *Journal of Parapsychology*, 2, 5–22, 1938.

Bennett, Ernest, *Apparitions and Haunted Houses*, Faber and Faber, London, 1939.

Berwick, Peter R., Hypnosis, Exorcism and Healing: A Case Report, *American Journal of Clinical Hypnosis*, 20, 146–8, 1977.

Black, Stephen, *Mind and Body*, William Kimber, London, 1969.

Blackmore, Susan, Psi in Science, *Journal of the Society for Psychical Research*, 57, 404–11, 1991.

Blackmore, Susan, Do We Need a New Psychical Research, *Journal of the Society for Psychical Research*, 55, 49–58, 1988.

Blatty, William Peter, *The Exorcist*, Anthony Blond, London, reprinted 1985.

Bohm, David J., A New Theory of the Relationship of Mind

and Matter, *Journal of the American Society for Psychical Research*, 80, 113–35, 1986.

Bozzuto, James C., Cinematic Neurosis Following 'The Exorcist': Report of Four Cases, *Journal of Nervous and Mental Disease*, 161, 43–8, 1975.

Branden, Victoria, *Understanding Ghosts*, Victor Gollancz, London, 1980.

Brandon, Ruth, *The Spiritualists: The Passion for the Occult in the Nineteenth and Twentieth Centuries:* Weidenfeld & Nicolson, London, 1983.

Braude, Stephen E., *First Person Plural: Multiple Personality and the Philosophy of Mind*, Routledge, London, USA and Canada, 1991.

Brennan, J. H., *Experimental Magic*, The Aquarian Press, Wellingborough, 1972.

Broughton, Richard, *Parapsychology: The Controversial Science*, Ballantine Books, New York, 1991.

Burlingham, Dorothy, Child Analysis and the Mother, *Psychoanalytic Quarterly*, 4, 69–92, 1935.

Campbell, Joseph, *The Hero With a Thousand Faces*, Paladin (HarperCollins publishers), Great Britain, 1988.

Carroll, Michael P., Visions of the Virgin Mary: The Effect of Family Structures on Marian Apparitions, *Journal for the Scientific Study of Religion*, 22, 205–21, 1983.

Carroll, Michael P., The Virgin Mary at La Salette and Lourdes: Whom Did the Children See?, *Journal for the Scientific Study of Religion*, 24, 56–74, 1985.

Carroll, Michael P., *The Cult of the Virgin Mary: Psychological Origins*, Princeton University Press, 1986.

Casti, John L., *Paradigms Lost*, Scribners, London & Sydney, 1989.

Casti, John L., *Searching for Certainty*, Scribners, London & Sydney, 1992.

Cavendish, Richard, *The Black Arts*, Routledge & Kegan Paul, London, 1967.

Chadha, N. K., and Stevenson, Ian, Two Correlates of Violent Death in Cases of the Reincarnation Type, *Journal of the Society for Psychical Research*, 55, 71–9, 1988.

Challman, A., Letter to the Editor: Exorcism, *Journal of the American Medical Association*, 229, 140, 1974.

Selected Bibliography

Chalmers, A. F., *What is this thing called Science?*, University of Queensland Press, St Lucia, Queensland, 1976.

Christian, William A., *Apparitions in Late Medieval and Renaissance Spain*, Princeton University Press, New Jersey, 1981.

Clark, Kitson G., *The Critical Historian*, Heinemann, London, 1967.

Coley, William B., A Report of Recent Cases of Inoperable Sarcoma Successfully Treated with Mixed Toxins of Erysipelas and Bacillus Prodigiosus, *Surgery, Gynecology and Obstetrics*, 13, 174–90, 1911.

Coley-Nauts, Helen, Swift, Walker E., and Coley, Bradley L., The Treatment of Malignant Tumours by Bacterial Toxins as Developed by the Late William B. Coley, M.D., Reviewed in the Light of Modern Research, *Cancer Research*, 6, 205–16, 1946.

Conway, David, *Magic: An Occult Primer*, The Aquarian Press, Wellingborough, Northamptonshire, 1988.

Cook, Emily, Williams, Pasricha, Satwant, Samararatne, Godwin, Maung, U, Win, and Stevenson, Ian, A Review and Analysis of "Unsolved" Cases of the Reincarnation Type: I. Introduction and Illustrative Case Reports, *Journal of the American Society for Psychical Research*, 77, 45–62, 1983.

Cook, Emily, Williams, Pasricha, Satwant, Samararatne, Godwin, Maung, U, Win, and Stevenson, Ian, A Review and Analysis of "Unsolved" Cases of the Reincarnation Type: II. Comparison of Features of Solved and Unsolved Cases, *Journal of the American Society for Psychical Research*, 77, 115–35, 1983.

Cooper, Henry, The Presence of Evil in Men and Places, *Practitioner*, 212, 367–9, 1974.

Coren, H. Z., and Saldinger, J. S., Visual Hallucinations in Children: A Report of Two Cases, *Psychoanalytic Study of the Child*, 22, 331–56, 1967.

Cornwell, John, *Powers of Light and Powers of Darkness*, Viking, London, 1991.

Davies, Paul, *Other Worlds*, Abacus, London, 1982.

Davies, Paul and Gribbin, John, *The Matter Myth*, Viking, London, 1991.

Dean, S. R., Metapsychiatry: The Interface Between Psychiatry and Mysticism, *American Journal of Psychiatry*, *130*, 1036–38, 1973.

Downs, John Dahmer, Sharon K., and Battle, Allen O., Multiple Personality Disorder in India, *American Journal of Psychiatry*, *147*, 1260, 1990.

Drake, Raleigh M., An Unusual Case of Extra-Sensory Perception, *Journal of Parapsychology*, *2*, 184–98, 1938.

Edge, H. L., Morris, Robert L., Palmer, John and Rush, Joseph H., *Foundations of Parapsychology*, Routledge & Kegan Paul, London and New York, 1986.

Ehrenwald, Jan, Psychopathological Aspects of Telepathy, *Journal of the Society for Psychical Research*, Part 163, 1940.

Ehrenwald, Jan, *Telepathy and Medical Psychology*, George Allen & Unwin Ltd, London, 1947.

Ehrenwald, Jan, *New Dimensions of Deep Analysis: A Study of Telepathy in Interpersonal Relationships*, George Allen & Unwin Ltd, London, 1954.

Ehrenwald, Jan, Human Personality and the Nature of Psi Phenomena, *Journal of the American Society for Psychical Research*, *62*, 366–80, 1968.

Ehrenwald, Jan, Mother-Child Symbiosis: The Cradle of ESP, *Psychoanalytical Review*, *58*, 455–66, 1971.

Ehrenwald, Jan, The Telepathy Hypothesis and Schizophrenia, *Journal of the American Academy of Psychoanalysis*, *2*, 159–69, 1974.

Ehrenwald, Jan, Possession and Exorcism: Delusion Shared and Compounded, *Journal of the American Academy of Psychoanalysis*, *3*, 105–19, 1975.

Eisenbud, Jules, Two Camera and Television Experiments with Ted Serios, *Journal of the American Society for Psychical Research*, *64*, 309–20, 1970.

Ellison, Arthur, *The Reality of the Paranormal*, Harrap, London, 1988.

Evans, Hilary, *Visions, Apparitions and Alien Visitors*, Aquarian Press, Great Britain, 1984.

FitzHerbert, Joan, The Role of Extra-Sensory Perception in Early Childhood, *Journal of Medical Science*, *106*, 1560–67, 1960.

Selected Bibliography

FitzHerbert, Joan, The Perception of Apparitions, *International Journal of Parapsychology*, 5, 75–89, 1963.

Flew, Antony, Is There a Case for Disembodied Survival? *Journal of the American Society for Psychical Research*, 66, 129–44, 1972.

Flew, Antony, The Problem of Evidencing the Improbable, and the Impossible in *Exploring the Paranormal: Perspectives on Belief and Experiences* (Zollschan, G. K., Schumaker, J. F., & Walsh, G. K., eds), Prism Press, Dorset, 1989.

Flynn, Ted, and Flynn, Maureen, *The Thunder of Justice*, MaxKol Communications, Inc, VA 20165, USA, 1993.

Fontana, David, A Responsive Poltergeist: A Case From South Wales, *Journal of the Society for Psychical Research*, 57, 385–402, 1991.

Fontana, David, The Responsive South Wales Poltergeist: A Follow-Up Report, *Journal of the Society for Psychical Research*, 58, 225–31, 1992.

Furman, Robin, and Martingale, Moira, *Ghostbusters UK: A Casebook of Hauntings and Exorcisms*, Robert Hale, London, 1991.

Gallup, G. H., and Newport, F., Belief in Paranormal Phenomena among Adult Americans, *Skeptical Inquirer*, 15, 137–46, 1991.

Galvin, J. A. V., and Ludwig, A. M., A Case of Witchcraft, *Journal of Nervous and Mental Diseases*, 133, 161–8, 1961.

Gauld, Alan, A Series of 'Drop In' Communicators, *Proceedings of the Society for Psychical Research*, 55, 273–340, 1971.

Gauld, Alan and Cornell, A. C., *Poltergeists*, Routledge & Kegan Paul, London, 1979.

Green, Celia and McCreery, Charles, *Apparitions*, Hamish Hamilton, London, 1975.

Green, Celia, Waking Dreams and Other Metachoric Experiences, *Psychiatry Journal of the University of Ottawa*, 15, 123–8, 1990.

Greeson, R. R., Letter to the Editor: Exorcism, *Journal of the American Medical Association*, 228, 828, 1974.

Gurney, Edmund, and Myers, F. W. H., On Apparitions Occurring Soon After Death, *Proceedings of the Society for Psychical Research*, V, 403–85, 1888–89.

Hall, Rupert, A., *The Scientific Revolution: The Formation of the Modern Scientific Attitude*, Longmans, London, 1954.

Hamlyn, D. W., *The Theory of Knowledge*, Macmillan, Great Britain and the USA, 1970.

Haraldsson, E,. Subject Selection in a Machine Precognition Test, *Journal of Parapsychology*, 34, 182–91, 1970.

Harner, Michael J., Common Themes in South American Indian *Yage* Experiences in *Hallucinogens and Shamanism* (Harner, Michael J,. ed), Oxford University Press, London, Oxford and New York, 1973.

Harner, Michael J., The Role of Hallucinogenic Plants in European Witchcraft, in *Hallucinogens and Shamanism* (Harner, Michael J,. ed), Oxford University Press, London, Oxford and New York, 1973.

Harner, Michael J., The Sound of Rushing Water in *Hallucinogens and Shamanism* (Harner, Michael J,. ed), Oxford University Press, London, Oxford and New York, 1973.

Harre, Rom, (ed), *The Problems of Scientific Revolution: The Herbert Spencer Lectures 1973*, Clarendon Press, Oxford, 1975.

Harrison, Peter, and Harrison, Mary, *The Children that Time Forgot*, Kenneth Mason Publications Ltd, Great Britain, 1991.

Hart, Hornell, and Hart, Ella B., Visions and Apparitions Collectively and Reciprocally Perceived, *Proceedings of the Society for Psychical Research*, 41, 205–49, 1932–33.

Hart, Hornell, Six Theories About Apparitions, *Proceedings of the Society for Psychical Research*, 50, 153–81, 1956.

Hickey, Des, and Smith, Gus, *Miracle: The Cure of a Glasgow Man from Cancer that led to a Canonisation in Rome*, Hodder & Stoughton, London, 1978.

Honorton, Charles, Significant Factors in Hypnotically-Induced Clairvoyant Dreams, *Journal of the American Society for Psychical Research*, 66, 86–102, 1972.

Honorton, Charles, Reported Frequency of Dream Recall and ESP, *Journal of the American Society for Psychical Research*, 60, 369–74, 1966.

Hume, David, *An Enquiry Concerning Human Understanding and Dialogues Concerning Natural Religion*, in *The Empiricists:*

Selected Bibliography

Locke, Berkeley and Hume, Anchor Books, Garden City, New York, 1974.

Hume, David, *A Treatise of Human Nature* in *Hume: A Treatise of Human Nature* (Mossner, Ernest C., ed), Penguin Books, Harmondsworth, England, 1969.

Hutch, Richard A., Uncanny experiences in psychoanalytic perspective in *Exploring the Paranormal: Perspectives on Belief and Experience* (Zollschan, G. K., Schumaker, J. F., and Walsh, G. F., eds), Prism Press, Dorset, 1989.

Inglis, Brian, *Coincidence*, Hutchinson, London, 1990.

Inglis, Brian, *Science and Parascience: A History of the Paranormal: 1914–1939*, Hodder & Stoughton, London, 1984.

Irwin, H. J., Coding Preferences and the Form of Spontaneous Extrasensory Experiences, *Journal of Parapsychology*, 43, 205–20, 1979.

Irwin, Harvey J., On Paranormal Disbelief: The Psychology of the Sceptic, in *Exploring the Paranormal: Perspectives on Belief and Experience* (Zollschan, G. K., Schumaker, J. F., and Walsh, G. F., eds), Prism Press, Dorset, 1989.

Isaacs, Julian, The Batcheldor Approach: Some Strengths and Weaknesses, *Journal of the American Society for Psychical Research*, 78, 123–31, 1984.

Jaffe, Aniela, *Apparitions and Precognition*, University Books, New York, 1963.

James, Theodore, Aplasia of the Male Prepuce with Evidence of Hereditary Transmission, *Journal of Anatomy*, 85, 370–72, 1951;

James, Theodore, A Causerie on Circumcision, Congenital and Acquired, *South African Medical Journal*, 45, 151–54, 1971.

Jee, Adityan, Raju, G. S. P., and Khandelwal, S. K., Current Status of Multiple Personality Disorder in India, *American Journal of Psychiatry*, 146, 1607–10, 1989.

Jee, Adityan, Dr Adityan Jee Replies, *American Journal of Psychiatry*, 147, 1260–61, 1990.

Kensinger, K. M., *Banisteriopsis* Usage Among the Peruvian Cashinahua, in *Hallucinogens and Shamanism* (Harner, Michael J., ed), Oxford University Press, London, Oxford and New York, 1973.

Khun, T. S., *The Copernican Revolution*, Harvard University Press, Cambridge, USA, 1957/1985.

Khun, T. S., *The Structure of Scientific Revolution*, University of Chicago Press, 1962/1970.

Kiev, Ari, Spirit Possession in Haiti, *American Journal of Psychiatry, 118*, 133–8, 1961.

Kloppenburg, Bonaventure, The Dimensions of Evocative Witchcraft under Theological Investigation, *International Journal of Parapsychology, 5*, 213–23, 1963.

Kogan, I. M., Is Telepathy Possible, *Telecommunications and Radio Engineering, 21*, 75–81, 1966.

Krippner, Stanley, Some Touchstones for Parapsychological Research in *Exploring the Paranormal: Perspectives on Belief and Experience* (Zollschan, G. K., Schumaker, J. F., and Walsh G. F., eds), Prism Press, Dorset, 1989.

Kurtz, Paul, (ed), *A Skeptics Handbook of Parapsychology*, Prometheus Books, New York, 1985.

Lambert, G. W., The Cheltenham Ghost: A Reinterpretation, *Journal of the Society for Psychical Research, 39*, 267–77, 1958.

Lakatos, Imre, and Musgrave, Alan, (eds), *Criticism and the Growth of Knowledge*, Cambridge University Press, 1970.

Larkin, C,. Demonic Influence and Psychopathology, in *Baker Encyclopedia of Psychology*, Benner, D. G., (ed), Baker Book House, Grand Rapids, Michigan, 1985.

Leininger, Madeleine, Witchcraft Practices and Psychocultural Therapy with Urban U.S. Families, *Human Organisation, 32*, 73–83, 1979.

Leon, Carlos A., 'El Duende' and Other Incubi: Suggestive Interactions Between Culture, the Devil, and the Brain, *Archives of General Psychiatry, 32*, 155–62.

LeShan, Lawrence, *The Medium, The Mystic and the Physicist: Toward a General Theory of the Paranormal*, Turnstone Books, London, 1974.

Lister, John, By the London Post – The Dangers of Exorcism, *New England Journal of Medicine, 292*, 1391–3, 1975.

Ludwig, Arnold M., Witchcraft Today, *Diseases of the Nervous System, 26*, 288–91, 1965.

Selected Bibliography

Lukianowicz, N., Hallucinations à Troix, *Archives of General Psychiatry*, *1*, 322–37, 1959.

Mackarness, Richard, Occultism and Psychiatry, *Practitioner*, *212*, 363–6, 1974.

MacKenzie, Andrew, *A Gallery of Ghosts*, Arthur Barker Ltd, London, 1972.

MacKenzie, Andrew, Continuation of the 'Record of a Haunted House', *Journal of the Society for Psychical Research*, *55*, 25–32, 1988.

Maniam, T., Exorcism and Psychiatric Illness: Two Case Reports, *Medical Journal of Malaysia*, *42*, 317–19, 1987.

Maple, Eric, *The Realm of Ghosts*, Robert Hale Ltd, London, 1964.

Mason, A. A., and Black, S., Allergic Skin Responses Abolished under Treatment of Asthma and Hayfever by Hypnosis, *Lancet*, i, 1129–35, 1958.

Masters, R. E. L., and Houston, Jean, *The Varieties of Psychedelic Experience*, Turnstone Books, London, 1973.

Matlock, James G., Cats Paw: Margery and the Rhines, 1926, *Journal of Parapsychology*, *51*, 229–47, 1987.

May, Rollo, *Love and Will*, Souvenir Press, London, 1969.

McAll, R. K., Demonosis or the Possession Syndrome, *International Journal of the Society of Psychiatry*, *17*, 150–58, 1971.

McClure, Kevin, *The Evidence for Visions of the Virgin Mary*, The Aquarian Press, Northamptonshire, England, 1983.

McConnell, R. A., (ed), *Parapsychology and Self-Deception in Science*, Biological Sciences Department, University of Pittsburgh, 1982.

McCready, W. C., and Greeley, A. M., *The Ultimate Values of the American Population*, Sage, Beverly Hills, California, 1976.

Meerloo, Joost A. M., Four Hundred Years of 'Witchcraft', 'Projection' and 'Delusion', *American Journal of Psychiatry*, *120*, 83–86, 1963.

Mills, Antonia, A Preliminary Investigation of Cases of Reincarnation Among the Beaver and Gitksan Indians, *Anthropologica*, *XXX*, 23–59, 1988.

Mills, Antonia, A Comparison of Wet'suwet'en Cases of the

Reincarnation Type with Gitksan and Beaver, *Journal of Anthropological Research*, 44, 385–415, 1988.

Mills, Antonia, A Replication Study: Three Cases of Children in Northern India Who Are Said to Remember a Previous Life, *Journal of Scientific Exploration*, 3, 133–84, 1989.

Mills, Antonia, Moslem Cases of the Reincarnation Type in Northern India: A Test of the Hypothesis of Imposed Identification Part 1: Analysis of 26 Cases, *Journal of Scientific Exploration*, 4, 171–88, 1990.

Mitchell, Edgar D., An ESP Test From Apollo 14, *Journal of Parapsychology*, 35, 89–107, 1971.

Morton, R. C., Record of a Haunted House, *Proceedings of the Society for Psychical Research*, VIII, 311–32, 1892.

Motoyama, Hiroshi, *Karma & Reincarnation*, Judy Piatkus Ltd, London, 1992.

Murphy, Gardner, Field Theory and Survival, *Journal of the American Society for Psychical Research*, 39, 181–209, 1945.

Murphy, Gardner, and Klemme, Herbert, Unfinished Business, *Journal of the American Society for Psychical Research*, 60, 306–20, 1966.

Murray, H. A., The Personality and Career of Satan, *Social Issues*, 18, 36–54, 1962.

Myers, F. W. H., On Recognised Apparitions Occurring More Than a Year After Death, *Proceedings of the Society for Psychical Research*, VI, 13–65, 1889.

Naegeli-Osjord, Hans, *Possession & Exorcism*, Colin Smythe Ltd, Bucks, England, 1988.

Naranjo, Claudio, Psychological Aspects of the *Yage* Experience in an Experimental Setting, in *Hallucinogens and Shamanism* (Harner, Michael J., ed), Oxford University Press, London, Oxford and New York, 1973.

Nelson, Cynthia, The Virgin of Zeitoun, *World View*, 16, 5–11, 1973.

Nicola, John, *Demonic Possession and Exorcism*, Tan Books, Rockford, Illinois, 1974.

Obeyesekere, Gananath, The Idiom of Demonic Possession: A Case Study, *Social Science and Medicine*, 4, 97–111, 1970.

Oesterreich, T. K., *Possession Demoniacal and Other*, Kegan Paul, Trench, Trubner & Co Ltd, London, 1930.

Selected Bibliography

Orme, J. E., Precognition and Time, *Journal of the Society for Psychical Research*, *47*, 351–65, 1974.

Oteri, Laura, (ed), *Quantum Physics and Parapsychology: Proceedings of an International Conference Held in Geneva, Switzerland, August 26–27, 1974*, Parapsychology Foundation, Inc, New York, 1975.

Owen, A. R. G., *Can We Explain the Poltergeist?*, Garrett Publications, New York, 1964.

Owen, Iris M., with Sparrow, M., *Conjuring Up Philip: An Adventure in Psychokinesis*, Fitzhenry & Whiteside, Toronto, Canada, 1976.

Palmer, John, A Community Mail Survey of Psychic Experiences, *Journal of the American Society for Psychical Research*, *73*, 221–51, 1979.

Parker, Adrian, *States of Mind: ESP and Altered States of Consciousness*, Malaby Press, London, 1975.

Parker, A., A Sceptical Evaluation of a Skeptics Handbook, *Journal of the Society for Psychical Research*, *55*, 90–98, 1988.

Parker, John, *At the Heart of Darkness: Witchcraft, Black Magic and Satanism Today*, Sidgwick & Jackson, London, 1993.

Pasricha, Satwant, and Stevenson, Ian, Indian Cases of the Reincarnation Type Two Generations Apart, *Journal of the Society for Psychical Research*, *54*, 239–46, 1987.

Paulos, John Allen, *Beyond Numeracy*, Viking, London, 1991.

Peck, Scott M., *People of the Lie: The Hope for Healing Human Evil*, Century Hutchinson, London, 1988.

Perry, Michael, *Psychic Studies: A Christian's View*, The Aquarian Press, Northants, 1984.

Perry, Michael, (ed), *Deliverance: Psychic Disturbances and Occult Involvement*, The Christian Exorcism Study Group, SPCK, London, 1987.

Perovsky-Petrovo-Solovovo, Count, A Phantasm of the Dead Conveying Information Unknown to the Percipient, *Journal of the Society for Psychical Research*, *26*, 95–9, 1930.

Powers, Jonathan, *Philosophy and the New Physics*, Methuen, London and New York, 1982.

Prasad, J., and Stevenson, Ian, A Survey of Spontaneous Psychical Experiences in School Children of Uttar Pradesh, India, *International Journal of Parapsychology*, *10*, 241-61, 1968.

Pratt, J. G., and Ransom, Champe, Extrasensory Perception or Extraordinary Sensory Perception? A Recent Series of Experiments with Paval Stepanek, *Journal of the American Society for Psychical Research*, 66, 63–85, 1970.

Pratt, J. G., A Decade of Research with a Selected ESP Subject: An Overview and Reappraisal of the Work with Paval Stepanek, *Proceedings of the American Society for Psychical Research*, 30, 1–78, 1973.

Puthoff, Harold E., and Targ, Russell, A Perceptual Channel for Information Transfer over Kilometer Distances: Historical Perspective and Recent Research, *Proceedings of the Institute of Electronics and Electrical Engineering*, 64, 329–54, 1976.

Putnam, Frank W., *Diagnosis and Treatment of Multiple Personality Disorder*, The Guildford Press, New York and London, 1989.

Recordon, E. G., Stratton, F. J. M., and Peters, R. A., Some Trials in a Case of Alleged Telepathy, *Journal of the Society for Psychical Research*, 44, 390–99, 1968.

Rees, Dewi W., The Hallucinations of Widowhood, *British Medical Journal*, 4, 37–41, 1971.

Reichbart, Richard, Magic and Psi: Speculations on Their Relationship, *Journal of the American Society for Psychical Research*, 72, 1978.

Rhine, Louisa E., Frequency of Types of Experience in Spontaneous Precognition, *Journal of Parapsychology*, 18, 93–123, 1954.

Rhine, L. E., Research Methods with Spontaneous Cases, *Handbook of Parapsychology* (Wolman, B. B., ed), Van Nostrand Reinhold Co, New York and London, 1977.

Robbins, Rossell Hope, *The Encyclopedia of Witchcraft and Demonology*, Spring Books, London, 1959.

Roberts, W. W., Normal and Abnormal Depersonalization, *Journal of Mental Science*, 106, 478–93, 1960.

Rogo, Scott D., *Miracles*, The Aquarian Press, London, 1983, 1991.

Roll, W. G., The Newark Disturbances, *Journal of the American Society for Psychical Research*, 63, 123–74, 1969.

Selected Bibliography

Roll, W. G., Poltergeist Phenomena and Interpersonal Relations, *Journal of the American Society for Psychical Research*, *64*, 130–45, 1973.

Rosenhan, D. L., On Being Sane in Insane Places, *Science*, *179*, 250–58, 1973.

Ross, Colin, A., and Joshi, Shaun, Paranormal Experiences in the General Population, *Journal of Mental and Nervous Disorders*, *180*, 357–61, 1992.

Sannwald, Gerhard, On the Psychology of Spontaneous Paranormal Phenomena, *International Journal of Parapsychology*, *5*, 274–90, 1963.

Schatzman, Morton, *The Story of Ruth*, Duckworth & Co Ltd, London, 1980.

Schendel, E., and Kourang, R. C., Cacodemonomania and Exorcism in Children, *Journal of Clinical Psychiatry*, *41*, 119–23, 1980.

Schmidt, Helmut, Precognition of a Quantum Process, *Journal of Parapsychology*, *33*, 99–108, 1969.

Schmidt, Helmut, A PK Test with Electronic Equipment, *Journal of Parapsychology*, *34*, 175–81, 1970.

Schmidt, Helmut, PK Effect on Pre-Recorded Targets, *Journal of the American Society for Psychical Research*, *70*, 267–91, 1976.

Schmidt, Helmut, Addition Effect for PK on Prerecorded Targets, *Journal of Parapschology*, *49*, 229–43, 1985.

Schonbar, R. A., Some Manifest Characteristics of Recallers and Nonrecallers, *Journal of Consulting Psychology*, *23*, 414–18, 1959.

Schwarz, Berthold E., Telepathic Events in a Child Between 1 and 3½ Years of Age, *International Journal for Parapsychology*, *3/4*, 5–52, 1961.

Shapin, B., and Coly, Lisette, (eds), *The Repeatability Problem in Parapsychology: Proceedings of an International Conference Held in San Antonio, Texas, October 28–29, 1983*, Parapsychology Foundation, Inc, New York, 1985.

Sidgwick, E., Notes on the Evidence, Collected by the Society for Phantasms of the Dead, *Proceedings of the Society for Psychical Research*, *III*, 69–150, 1885.

Sidgwick, H., Sidgwick, E., Johnson, A., Report on the Census of Hallucinations, *Proceedings of the Society for Psychical Research*, 10, 25–422, 1894.

Siegal, Ronald K., *Fire in the Brain: Clinical Tales of Hallucination*, Dutton, New York, 1992.

Siegal, Ronald K., and West, Louis Joylon, (eds), *Hallucinations: Behaviour, Experience and Theory*, John Wiley and Sons, USA and Canada, 1975.

Sprigge, T. L. S., *Theories of Existence*, Penguin, Harmondsworth, 1984.

Stevenson, Ian, *Children Who Remember Past Lives: A Question of Reincarnation*, University Press of Virginia, Charlottesville, 1974.

Stevenson, Ian, Are Poltergeists Living or Are They Dead?, *Journal of the American Society for Psychical Research*, 66, 233–52, 1972.

Stevenson, Ian, A Communicator of the 'Drop In' Type in France: The Case of Robert Marie, *Journal of the American Society for Psychical Research*, 67, 47–76, 1973.

Stevenson, Ian, *Twenty Cases Suggestive of Reincarnation*, University Press of Virginia, Charlottesville, 1974.

Stevenson, Ian, *Cases of the Reincarnation Type. Vol I. Ten Cases in India*, University Press of Virginia, Charlottesville, 1975.

Stevenson, Ian, *Cases of the Reincarnation Type. Vol II. Ten Cases in Sri Lanka*, University Press of Virginia, Charlottesville, 1977.

Stevenson, Ian, The Southeast Asian Interpretation of Gender Dysphoria: An Illustrative Case Report, *Journal of Nervous and Mental Disease*, 165, 201–8, 1977.

Stevenson, Ian, The Explanatory Value of the Idea of Reincarnation, *Journal of Nervous and Mental Disease*, 164, 305–26, 1977.

Stevenson, Ian, *Cases of the Reincarnation Type. Vol III. Twelve Cases in Lebanon and Turkey*, University Press of Virginia, Charlottesville, 1980.

Stevenson, Ian, and Pasricha, Satwant, A Preliminary Report on an Unusual Case of the Reincarnation Type with Xenoglossy, *Journal of the American Society for Psychical Research*, 74, 331–48, 1980.

Selected Bibliography

Stevenson, Ian, The Contribution of Apparitions to the Evidence for Survival, *Journal of the American Society for Psychical Research*, 76, 341–58, 1982.

Stevenson, Ian, American Children Who Claim to Remember Previous Lives, *Journal of Nervous and Mental Disease*, 171, 742–8, 1983.

Stevenson, Ian, Cryptomnesia and Parapsychology, *Journal of the Society for Psychical Research*, 52, 1–31, 1983.

Stevenson, Ian, *Cases of the Reincarnation Type. Vol IV. Twelve Cases in Thailand and Burma*, University Press of Virginia, Charlottesville, 1983.

Stevenson, Ian, Phobias in Children Who Claim to Remember Previous Lives, *Journal of Scientific Exploration*, 4, 243–54, 1990.

Talbot, Michael, *The Holographic Universe*, Grafton Books, London, 1991.

Tarazi, Linda, An Unusual Case of Hypnotic Regression with Some Unexplained Contents, *Journal of the American Society for Psychical Research*, 84, 309–44, 1990.

Tart, Charles T., Frequency of Dream Recall and Some Personality Measures, *Journal of Consulting Psychology*, 26, 467–70, 1962.

Tart, Charles T., A Second Psychophysiological Study of Out-of-the-Body Experiences in a Gifted Subject by Charles T. Tart. *International Journal of Parapsychology*, 9, 251–8, 1967.

Tart, Charles T., A Psychological Study of Out-of-the-Body Experiences in a Selected Subject, *Journal of the American Society for Psychical Research*, 62, 3–37, 1968.

Tart, Charles T., (ed), *Altered States of Consciousness*, John Wiley & Sons Inc., New York and London, 1969.

Taylor, J. G., Is There Any Scientific Explanation of the Paranormal, *Nature*, 279, 631-3, 1979.

Taylor, J. G., *Science and the Supernatural*, Temple Smith, London, 1980.

Thurston, Herbert, *Beauraing and Other Apparitions: An Account of Some Borderland Cases in the Psychology of Mysticism*, Oates and Washbourne Ltd, Great Britain, 1934.

Thurston, Herbert, *The Physical Phenomena of Mysticism*, Henry Regnery Company, Chicago, 1952.

Tietze, Thomas R., 'The Margery' Affair, *Journal of the American Society for Psychical Research*, 79, 339–79, 1985.

Trevor-Roper, H. R., *The European Witch-Craze of the Sixteenth and Seventeenth Centuries*, Penguin Books, Harmondsworth, 1967.

Tyrrell, G. N. M., *Apparitions*, Society for Psychical Research, London, 1943, 1973.

Vilenskaya, L., Clarification of Factors which Facilitate Production of Parapsychological Abilities, *International Journal of Paraphysics*, 12, 110, 1978.

Weiss, Gerald, Shamanism and Priesthood in Light of the Campa *Ayahuasca* Ceremony, *Hallucinogens and Shamanism* (Harner, Michael J., ed), Oxford University Press, London, Oxford and New York, 1973.

West, D. J., The Trial of Mrs Duncan, *Proceedings of the Society for Psychical Research*, 48, 32–64, 1948.

West, D. J., *Eleven Lourdes Miracles*, Duckworth & Co, London, 1957.

White, John, *The Masks of Melancholy*, Inter-Varsity Press, Leicester, England, 1982.

Wilson, Ian, *Mind Out of Time*, Victor Gollancz Ltd, 1981, London.

Wolf, Margret S., Witchcraft and Mass Hysteria in Terms of Current Psychological Theories, *Journal of Psychiatric Nursing*, 14, 23–8, 1976.

Wolman, B. B., (ed), *Handbook of Parapsychology*, Van Nostrand Reinhold Co, New York and London, 1977.

Yap, P. M., The Possession Syndrome: A Comparison of Hong Kong and French Findings, *Journal of Mental Science*, 106, 14–37, 1960.

Zimdars-Swartz, S. L., *Encountering Mary: From La Salette to Medjugorje*, Princeton University Press, New Jersey, USA, 1991.

Zorab, George, Cases of the Chaffin Will Type and the Problem of Survival, *Journal of the Society for Psychical Research*, 41, 407–17, 1962.